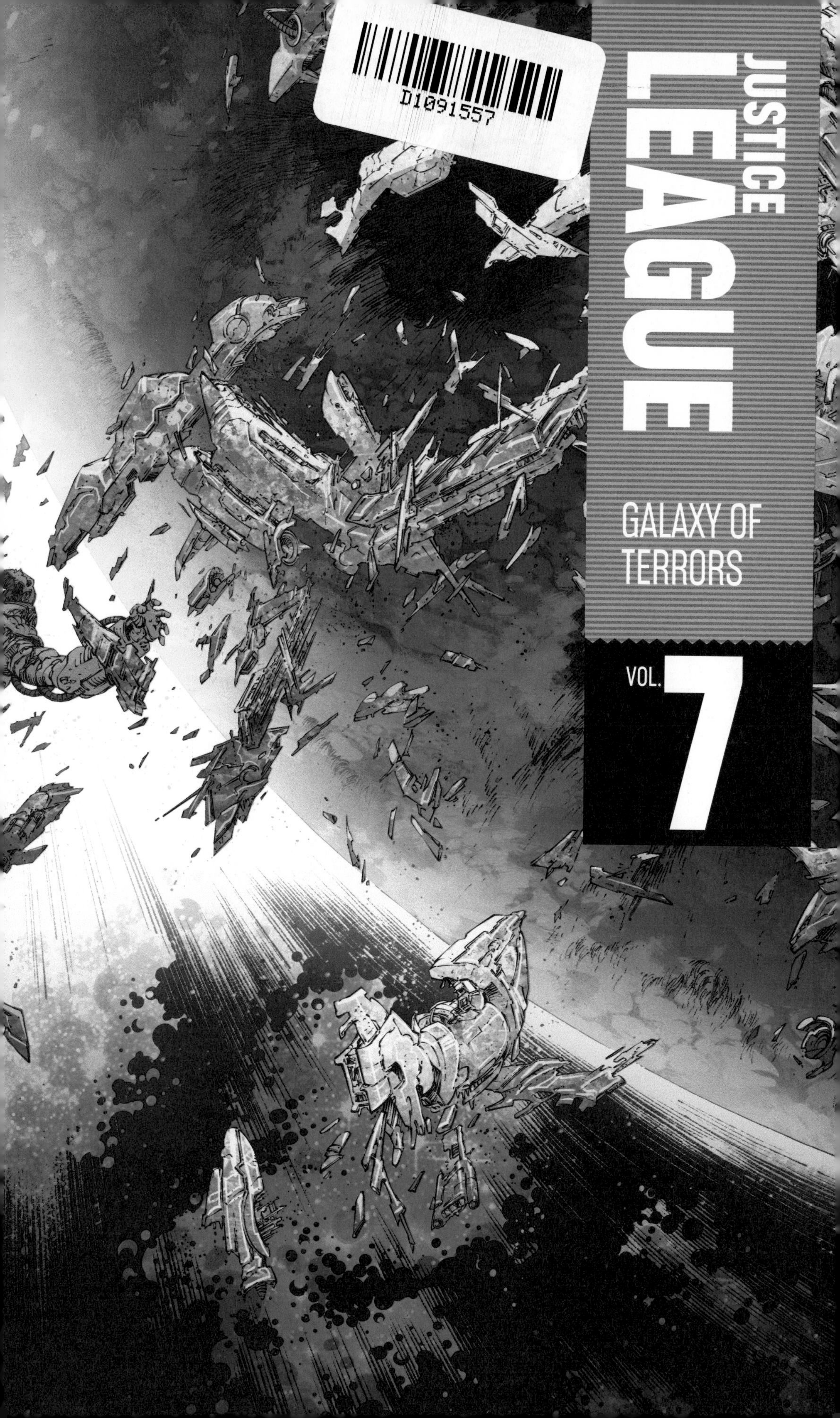
JUSTICE LEAGUE
GALAXY OF TERRORS
VOL. 7

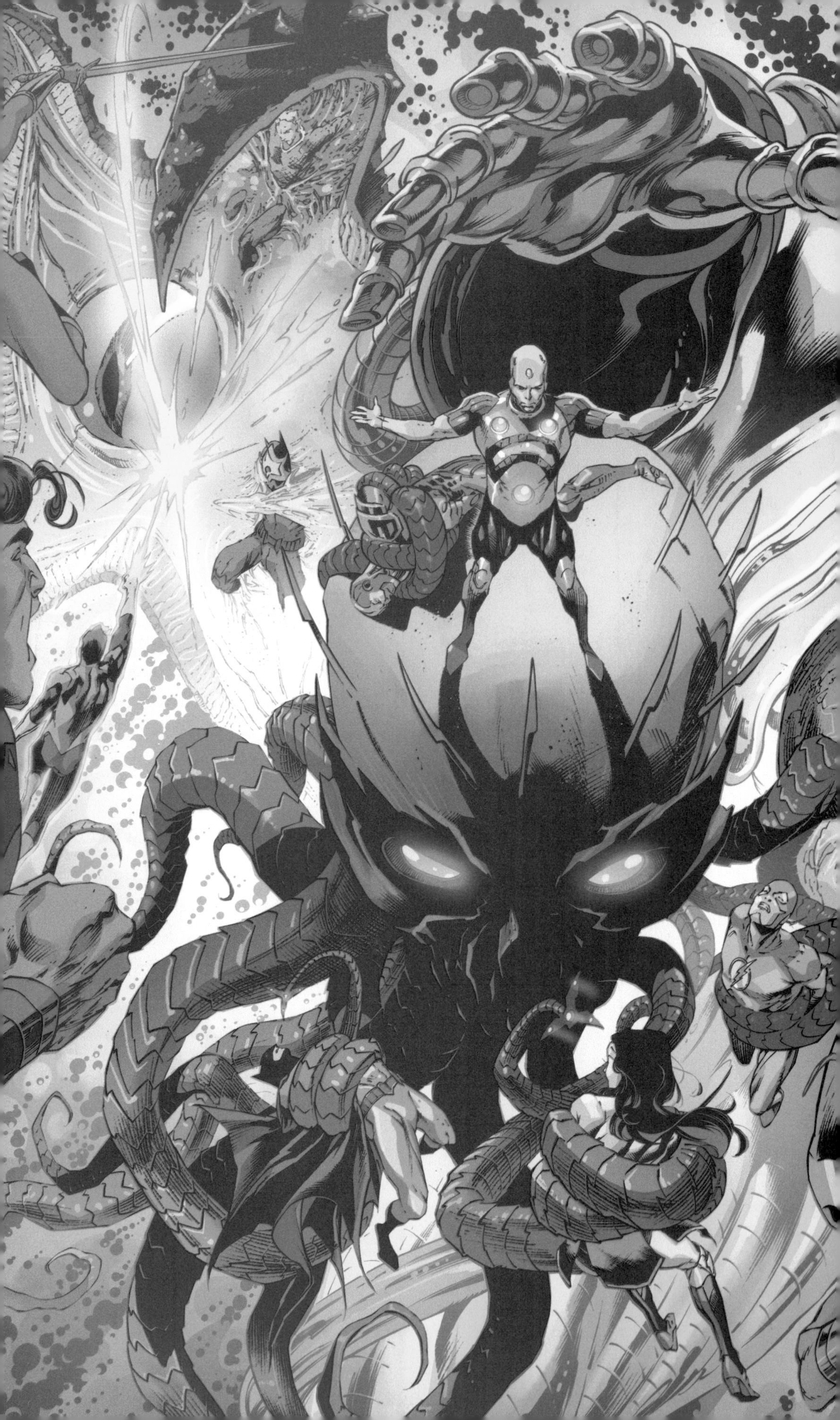

JUSTICE
LEAGUE
GALAXY OF TERRORS

writers
SIMON SPURRIER
JEFF LOVENESS

pencillers
AARON LOPRESTI
ROBSON ROCHA

inkers
MATT RYAN
DANIEL HENRIQUES

colorists
DAVID BARON
ROMULO FAJARDO JR.

letterer
TOM NAPOLITANO

collection cover artist
NICK DERINGTON

SUPERMAN created by JERRY SIEGEL and JOE SHUSTER.
By special arrangement with the Jerry Siegel family.

VOL. **7**

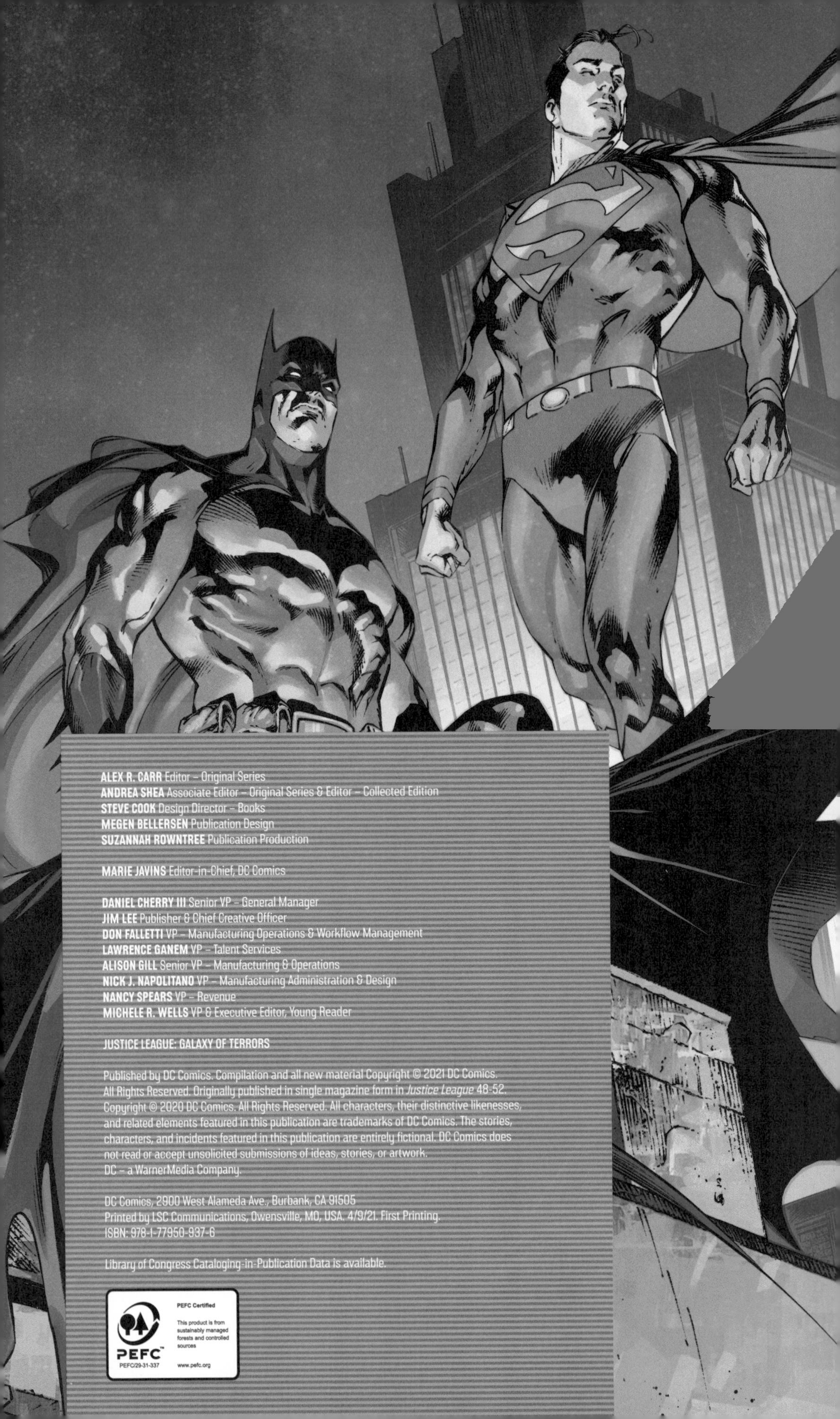

ALEX R. CARR Editor – Original Series
ANDREA SHEA Associate Editor – Original Series & Editor – Collected Edition
STEVE COOK Design Director – Books
MEGEN BELLERSEN Publication Design
SUZANNAH ROWNTREE Publication Production

MARIE JAVINS Editor-in-Chief, DC Comics

DANIEL CHERRY III Senior VP – General Manager
JIM LEE Publisher & Chief Creative Officer
DON FALLETTI VP – Manufacturing Operations & Workflow Management
LAWRENCE GANEM VP – Talent Services
ALISON GILL Senior VP – Manufacturing & Operations
NICK J. NAPOLITANO VP – Manufacturing Administration & Design
NANCY SPEARS VP – Revenue
MICHELE R. WELLS VP & Executive Editor, Young Reader

JUSTICE LEAGUE: GALAXY OF TERRORS

DC Comics, 2900 West Alameda Ave., Burbank, CA 91505
Printed by LSC Communications, Owensville, MO, USA. 4/9/21. First Printing.
ISBN: 978-1-77950-937-6

Library of Congress Cataloging-in-Publication Data is available.

PEFC Certified
This product is from sustainably managed forests and controlled sources
PEFC™
PEFC/29-31-337
www.pefc.org

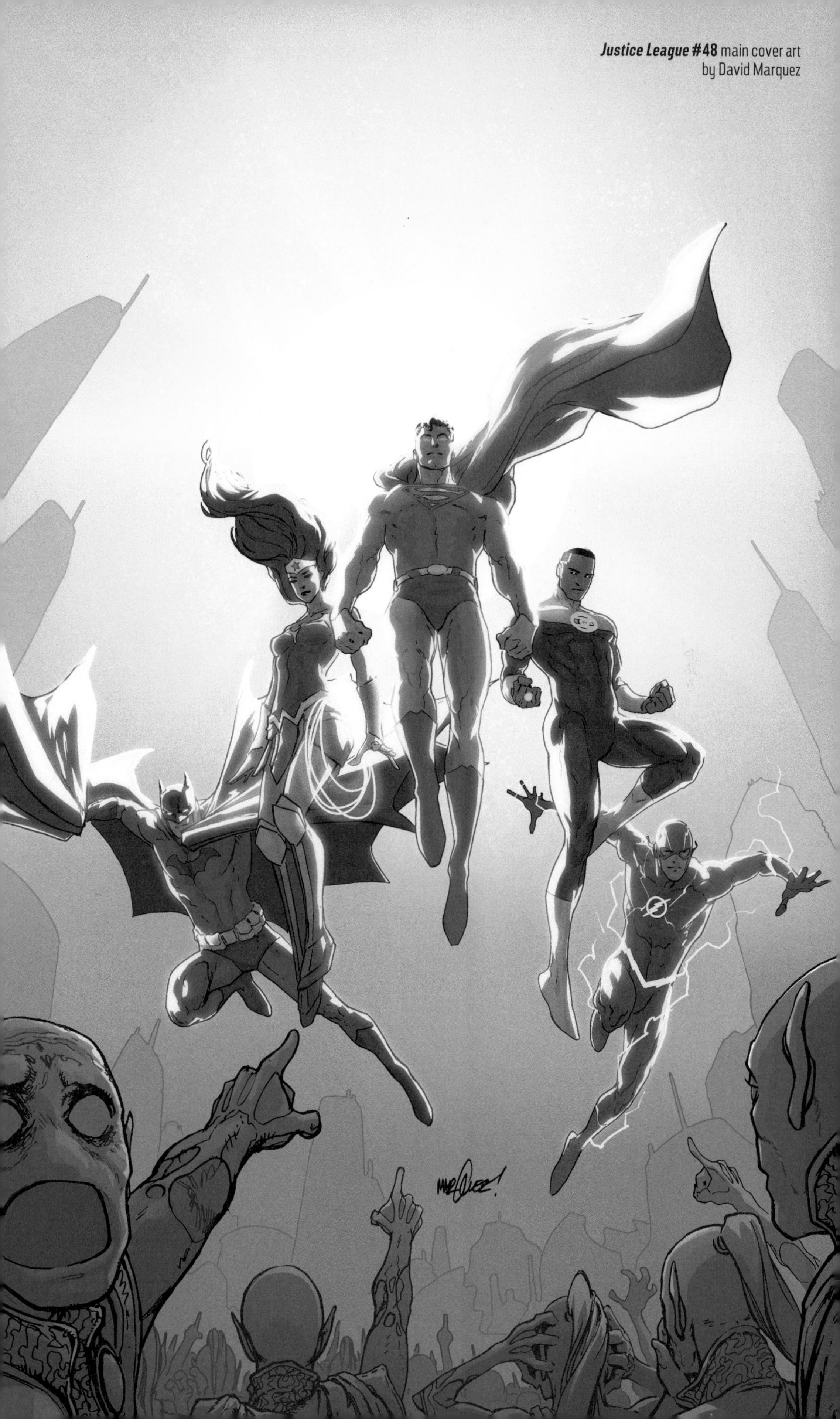

***Justice League* #48** main cover art
by David Marquez

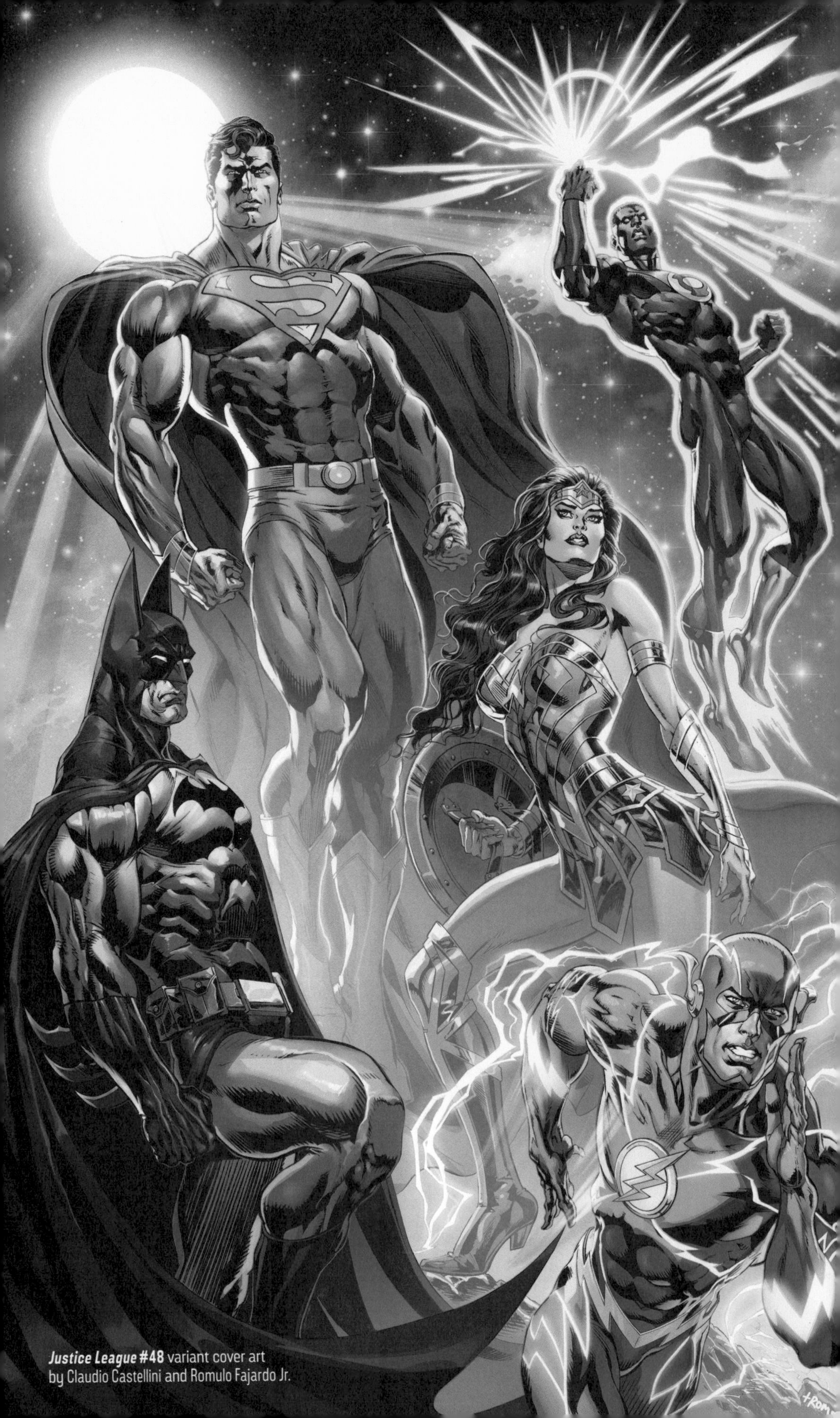

***Justice League* #48** variant cover art
by Claudio Castellini and Romulo Fajardo Jr.

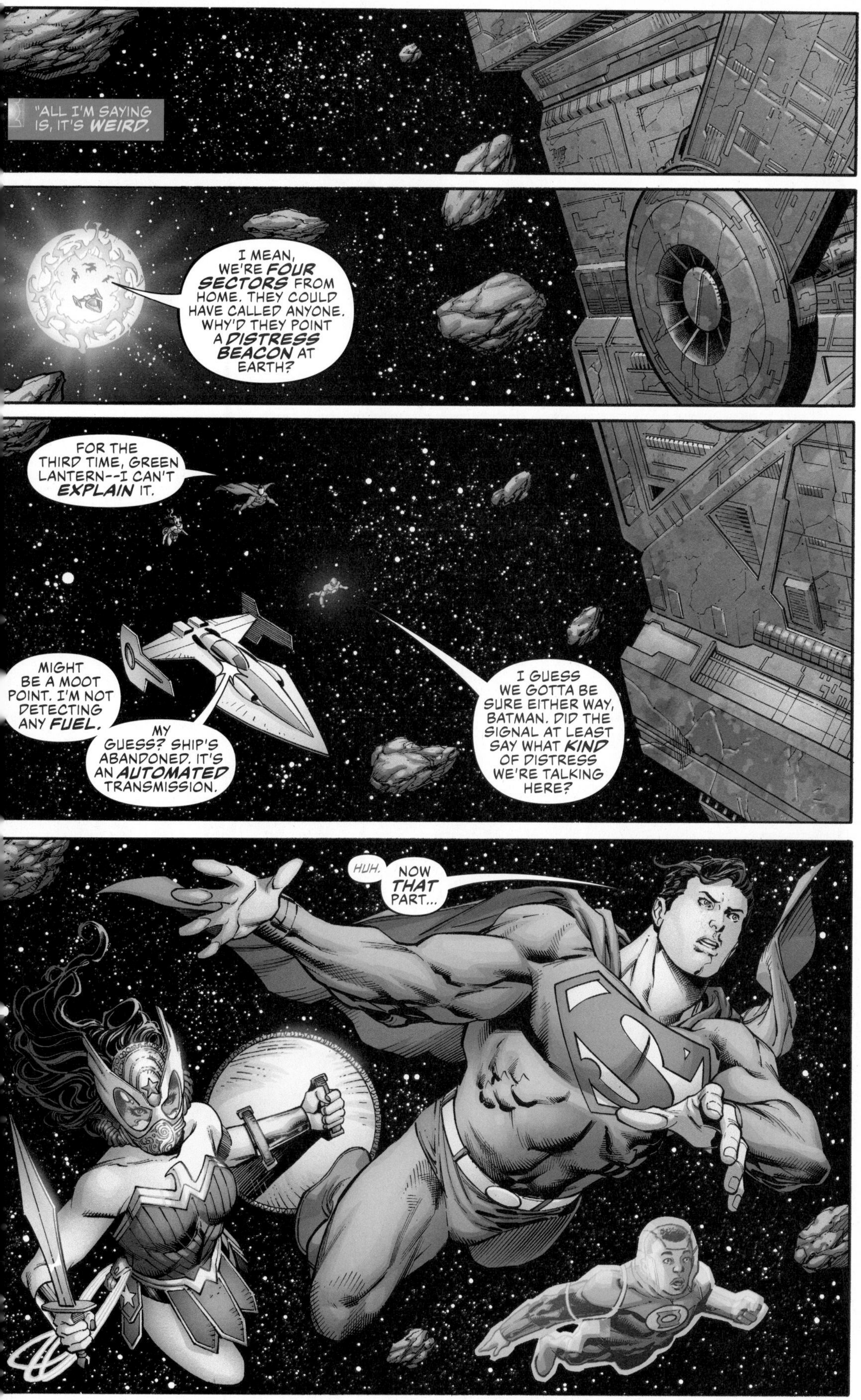
"ALL I'M SAYING IS, IT'S WEIRD.
I MEAN, WE'RE FOUR SECTORS FROM HOME. THEY COULD HAVE CALLED ANYONE. WHY'D THEY POINT A DISTRESS BEACON AT EARTH?
FOR THE THIRD TIME, GREEN LANTERN--I CAN'T EXPLAIN IT.
MIGHT BE A MOOT POINT. I'M NOT DETECTING ANY FUEL.
MY GUESS? SHIP'S ABANDONED. IT'S AN AUTOMATED TRANSMISSION.
I GUESS WE GOTTA BE SURE EITHER WAY, BATMAN. DID THE SIGNAL AT LEAST SAY WHAT KIND OF DISTRESS WE'RE TALKING HERE?
HUH.
NOW THAT PART...

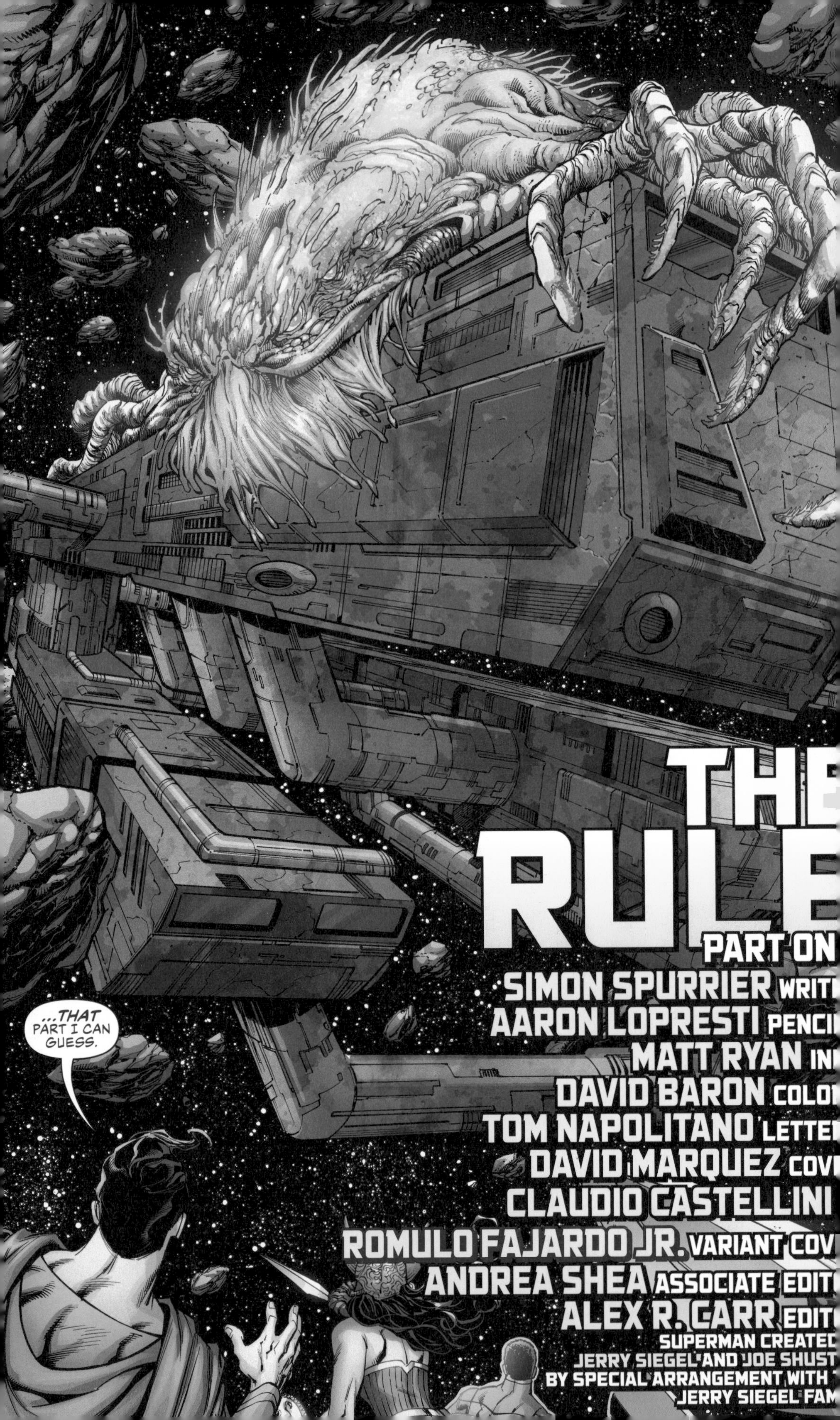
...THAT PART I CAN GUESS.
THE RULE
PART ON
SIMON SPURRIER WRIT
AARON LOPRESTI PENCI
MATT RYAN IN
DAVID BARON COLO
TOM NAPOLITANO LETTE
DAVID MARQUEZ COV
CLAUDIO CASTELLINI
ROMULO FAJARDO JR. VARIANT COV
ANDREA SHEA ASSOCIATE EDIT
ALEX R. CARR EDIT
SUPERMAN CREATED
JERRY SIEGEL AND JOE SHUST
BY SPECIAL ARRANGEMENT WITH
JERRY SIEGEL FAM

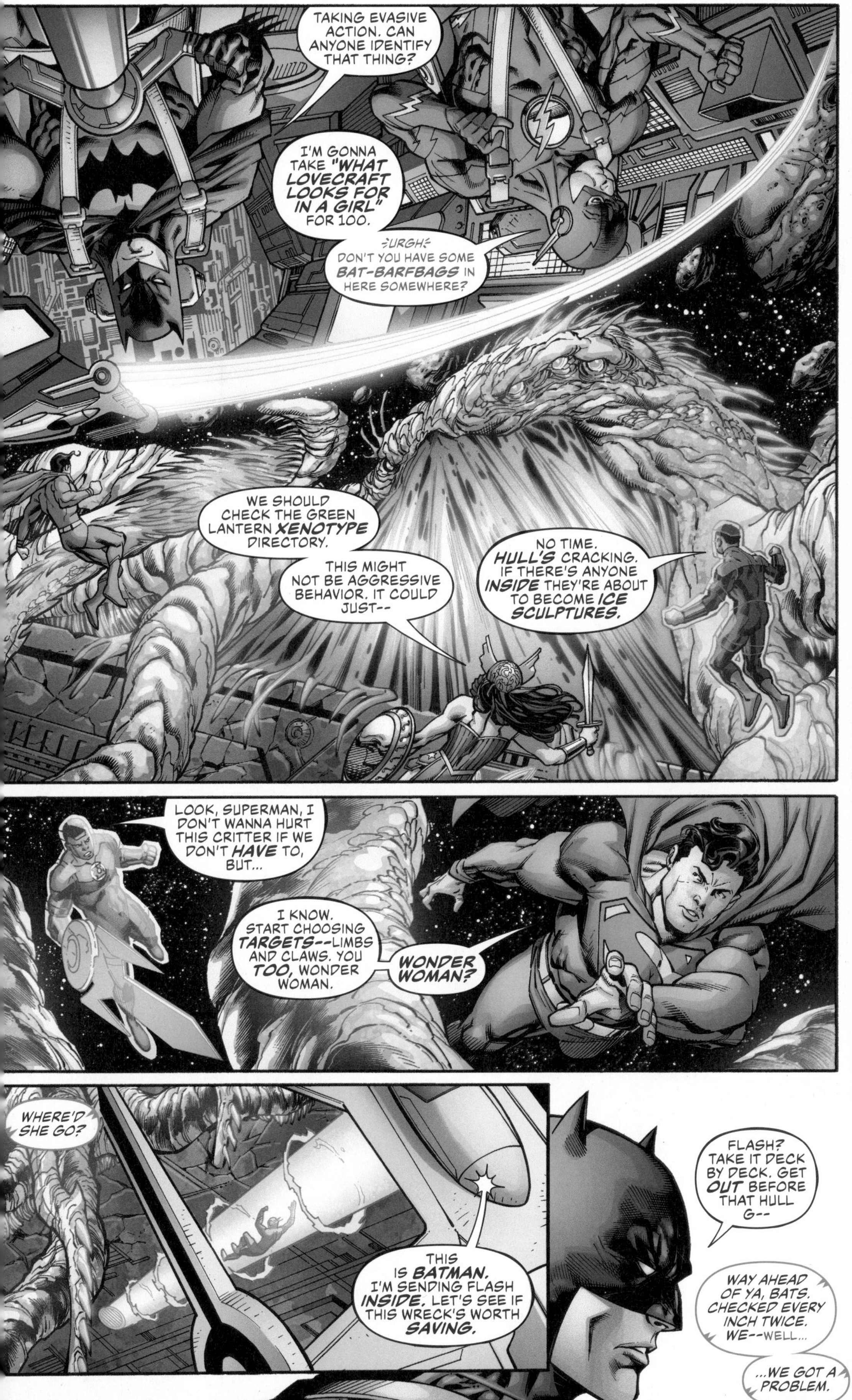
TAKING EVASIVE ACTION. CAN ANYONE IDENTIFY THAT THING?
I'M GONNA TAKE "WHAT LOVECRAFT LOOKS FOR IN A GIRL" FOR 100.
URGH
DON'T YOU HAVE SOME BAT-BARFBAGS IN HERE SOMEWHERE?
WE SHOULD CHECK THE GREEN LANTERN XENOTYPE DIRECTORY.
THIS MIGHT NOT BE AGGRESSIVE BEHAVIOR. IT COULD JUST--
NO TIME. HULL'S CRACKING. IF THERE'S ANYONE INSIDE THEY'RE ABOUT TO BECOME ICE SCULPTURES.
LOOK, SUPERMAN, I DON'T WANNA HURT THIS CRITTER IF WE DON'T HAVE TO, BUT...
I KNOW. START CHOOSING TARGETS--LIMBS AND CLAWS. YOU TOO, WONDER WOMAN.
WONDER WOMAN?
WHERE'D SHE GO?
THIS IS BATMAN. I'M SENDING FLASH INSIDE. LET'S SEE IF THIS WRECK'S WORTH SAVING.
FLASH? TAKE IT DECK BY DECK. GET OUT BEFORE THAT HULL G--
WAY AHEAD OF YA, BATS. CHECKED EVERY INCH TWICE. WE--WELL...
...WE GOT A PROBLEM.

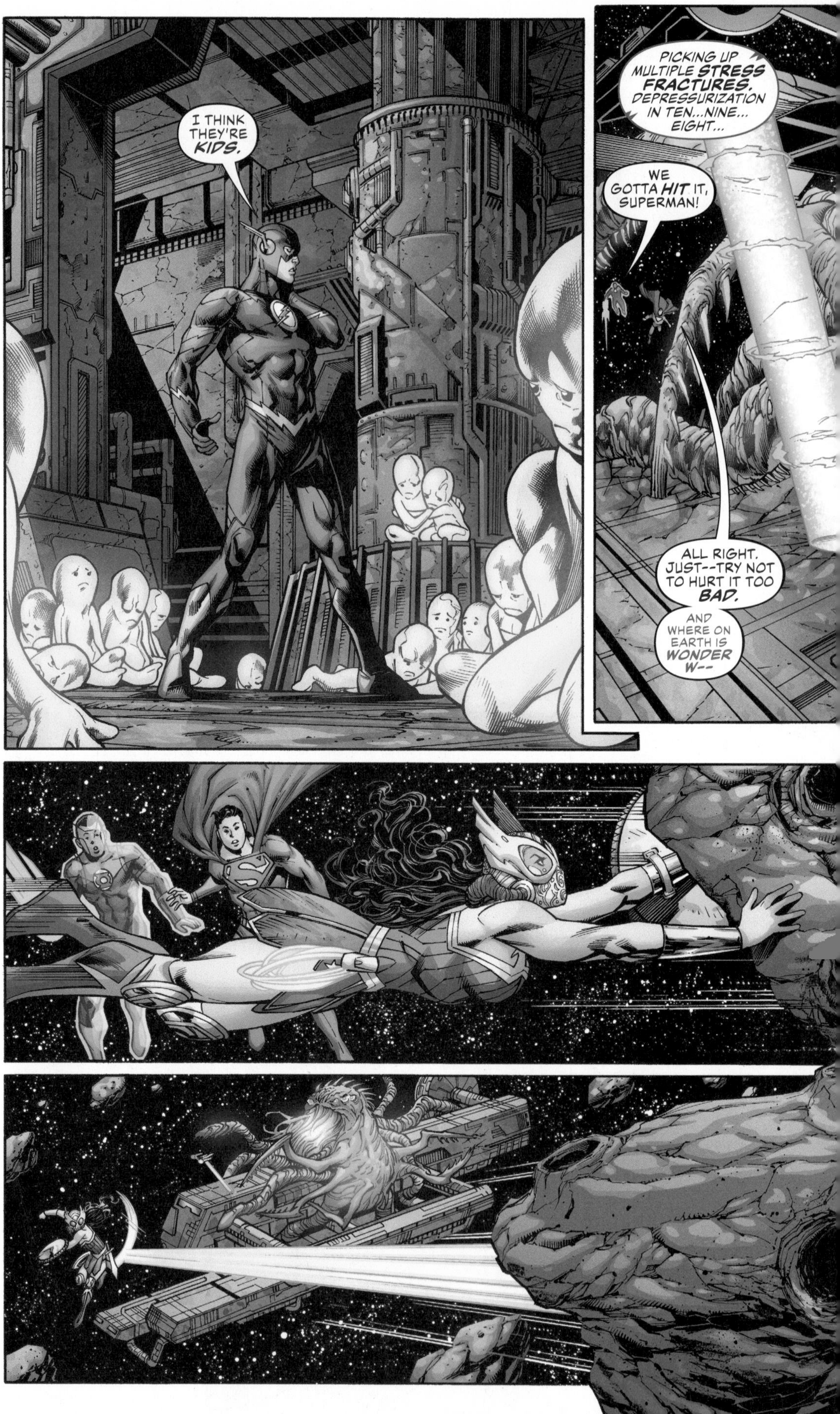
I THINK THEY'RE KIDS.
PICKING UP MULTIPLE STRESS FRACTURES. DEPRESSURIZATION IN TEN...NINE... EIGHT...
WE GOTTA HIT IT, SUPERMAN!
ALL RIGHT. JUST--TRY NOT TO HURT IT TOO BAD.
AND WHERE ON EARTH IS WONDER W--

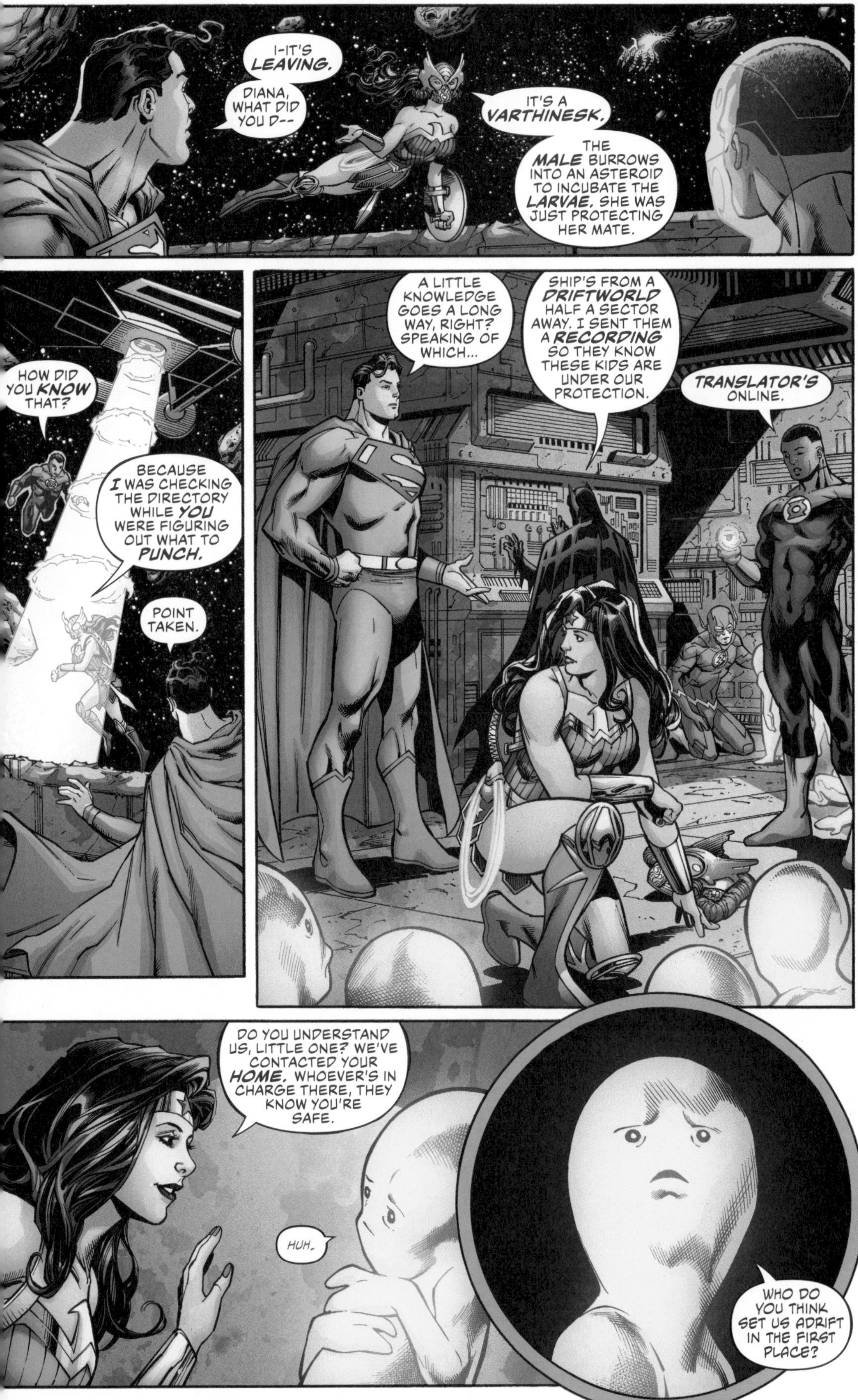
I-IT'S LEAVING.
DIANA, WHAT DID YOU D--
IT'S A VARTHINESK.
THE MALE BURROWS INTO AN ASTEROID TO INCUBATE THE LARVAE. SHE WAS JUST PROTECTING HER MATE.
HOW DID YOU KNOW THAT?
BECAUSE I WAS CHECKING THE DIRECTORY WHILE YOU WERE FIGURING OUT WHAT TO PUNCH.
POINT TAKEN.
A LITTLE KNOWLEDGE GOES A LONG WAY, RIGHT? SPEAKING OF WHICH...
SHIP'S FROM A DRIFTWORLD HALF A SECTOR AWAY. I SENT THEM A RECORDING SO THEY KNOW THESE KIDS ARE UNDER OUR PROTECTION.
TRANSLATOR'S ONLINE.
DO YOU UNDERSTAND US, LITTLE ONE? WE'VE CONTACTED YOUR HOME. WHOEVER'S IN CHARGE THERE, THEY KNOW YOU'RE SAFE.
HUH.
WHO DO YOU THINK SET US ADRIFT IN THE FIRST PLACE?

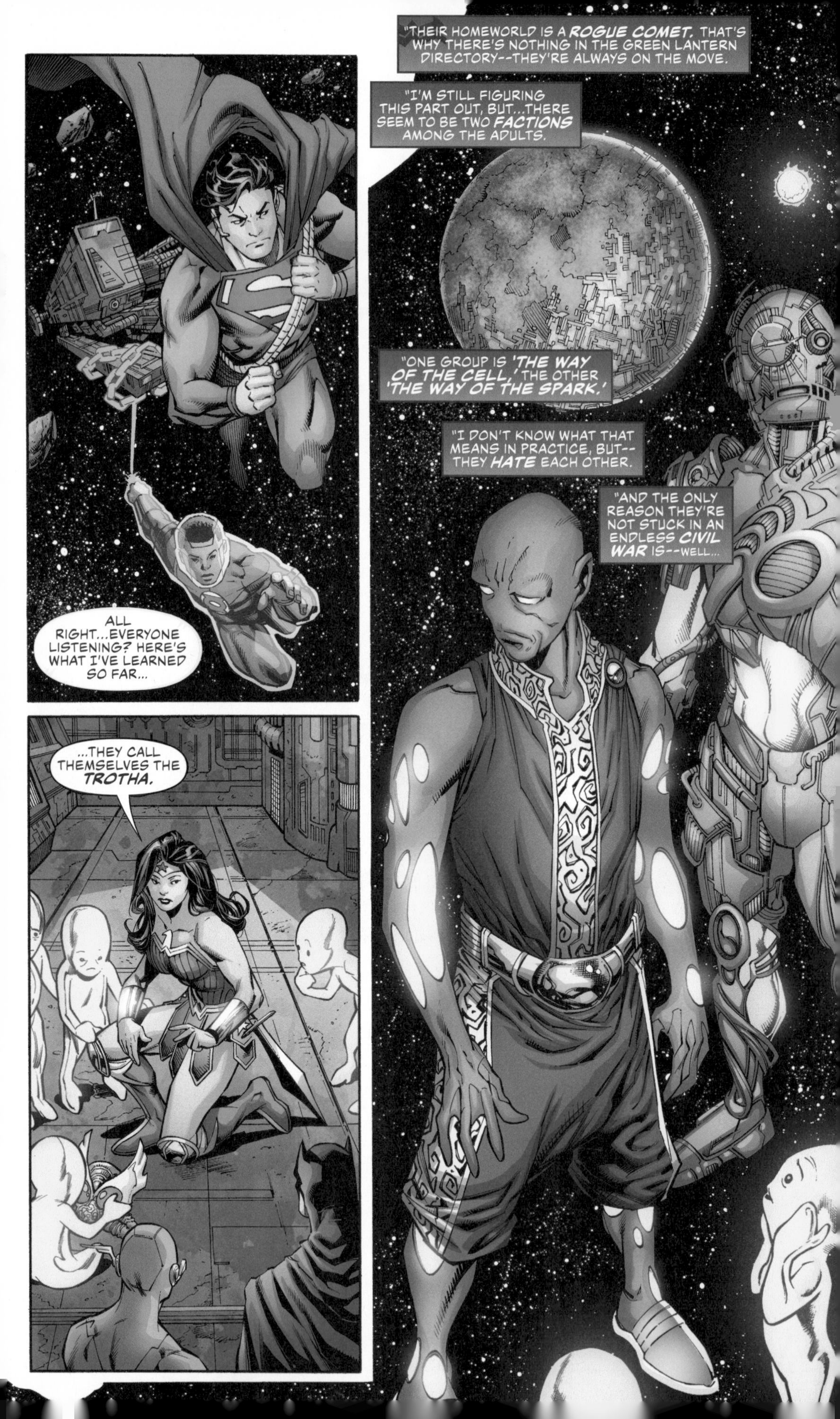

ALL RIGHT...EVERYONE LISTENING? HERE'S WHAT I'VE LEARNED SO FAR...
...THEY CALL THEMSELVES THE TROTHA.
"THEIR HOMEWORLD IS A ROGUE COMET. THAT'S WHY THERE'S NOTHING IN THE GREEN LANTERN DIRECTORY--THEY'RE ALWAYS ON THE MOVE.
"I'M STILL FIGURING THIS PART OUT, BUT...THERE SEEM TO BE TWO FACTIONS AMONG THE ADULTS.
"ONE GROUP IS 'THE WAY OF THE CELL,' THE OTHER 'THE WAY OF THE SPARK.'
"I DON'T KNOW WHAT THAT MEANS IN PRACTICE, BUT--THEY HATE EACH OTHER.
"AND THE ONLY REASON THEY'RE NOT STUCK IN AN ENDLESS CIVIL WAR IS--WELL...

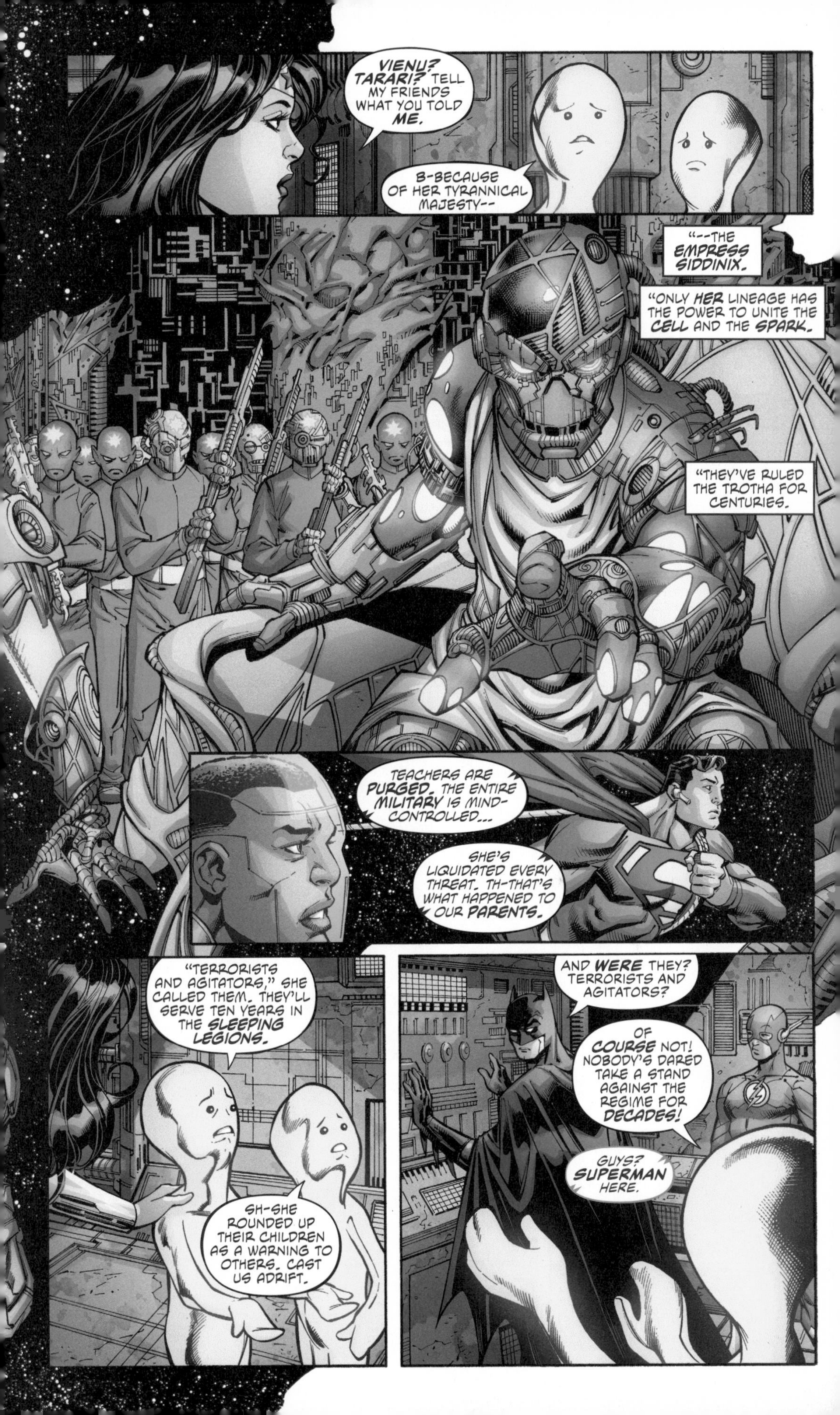
VIENU? TARARI? TELL MY FRIENDS WHAT YOU TOLD ME.
B-BECAUSE OF HER TYRANNICAL MAJESTY--
"--THE EMPRESS SIDDINIX.
"ONLY HER LINEAGE HAS THE POWER TO UNITE THE CELL AND THE SPARK.
"THEY'VE RULED THE TROTHA FOR CENTURIES.
TEACHERS ARE PURGED. THE ENTIRE MILITARY IS MIND-CONTROLLED...
SHE'S LIQUIDATED EVERY THREAT. TH-THAT'S WHAT HAPPENED TO OUR PARENTS.
"TERRORISTS AND AGITATORS," SHE CALLED THEM. THEY'LL SERVE TEN YEARS IN THE SLEEPING LEGIONS.
SH-SHE ROUNDED UP THEIR CHILDREN AS A WARNING TO OTHERS. CAST US ADRIFT.
AND WERE THEY? TERRORISTS AND AGITATORS?
OF COURSE NOT! NOBODY'S DARED TAKE A STAND AGAINST THE REGIME FOR DECADES!
GUYS? SUPERMAN HERE.

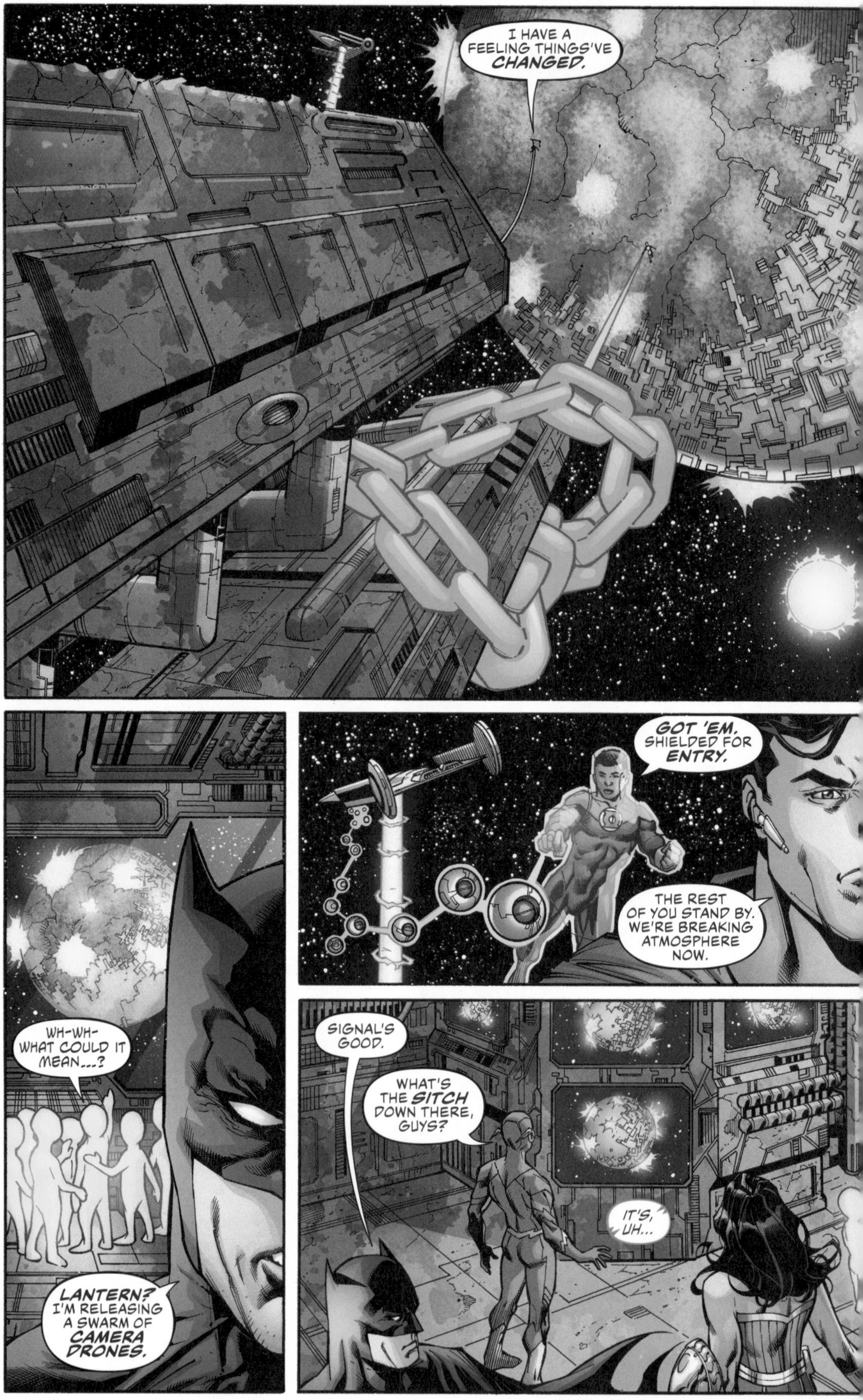

I HAVE A FEELING THINGS'VE CHANGED.
WH-WH- WHAT COULD IT MEAN...?
LANTERN? I'M RELEASING A SWARM OF CAMERA DRONES.
GOT 'EM. SHIELDED FOR ENTRY.
THE REST OF YOU STAND BY. WE'RE BREAKING ATMOSPHERE NOW.
SIGNAL'S GOOD.
WHAT'S THE SITCH DOWN THERE, GUYS?
IT'S, UH...

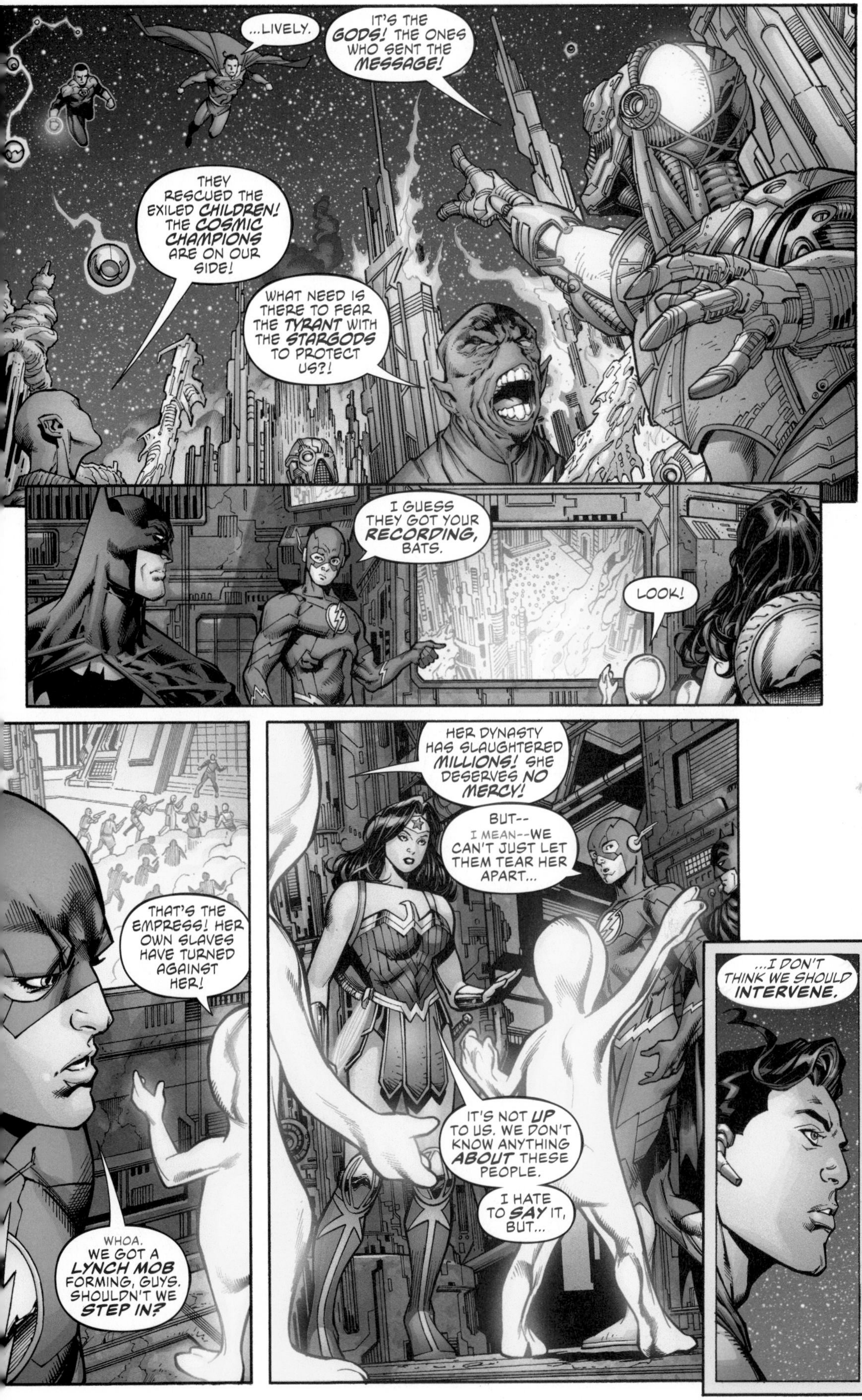
...LIVELY.
IT'S THE GODS! THE ONES WHO SENT THE MESSAGE!
THEY RESCUED THE EXILED CHILDREN! THE COSMIC CHAMPIONS ARE ON OUR SIDE!
WHAT NEED IS THERE TO FEAR THE TYRANT WITH THE STARGODS TO PROTECT US?!
I GUESS THEY GOT YOUR RECORDING, BATS.
LOOK!
THAT'S THE EMPRESS! HER OWN SLAVES HAVE TURNED AGAINST HER!
WHOA. WE GOT A LYNCH MOB FORMING, GUYS. SHOULDN'T WE STEP IN?
HER DYNASTY HAS SLAUGHTERED MILLIONS! SHE DESERVES NO MERCY!
BUT-- I MEAN--WE CAN'T JUST LET THEM TEAR HER APART...
IT'S NOT UP TO US. WE DON'T KNOW ANYTHING ABOUT THESE PEOPLE.
I HATE TO SAY IT, BUT...
...I DON'T THINK WE SHOULD INTERVENE.

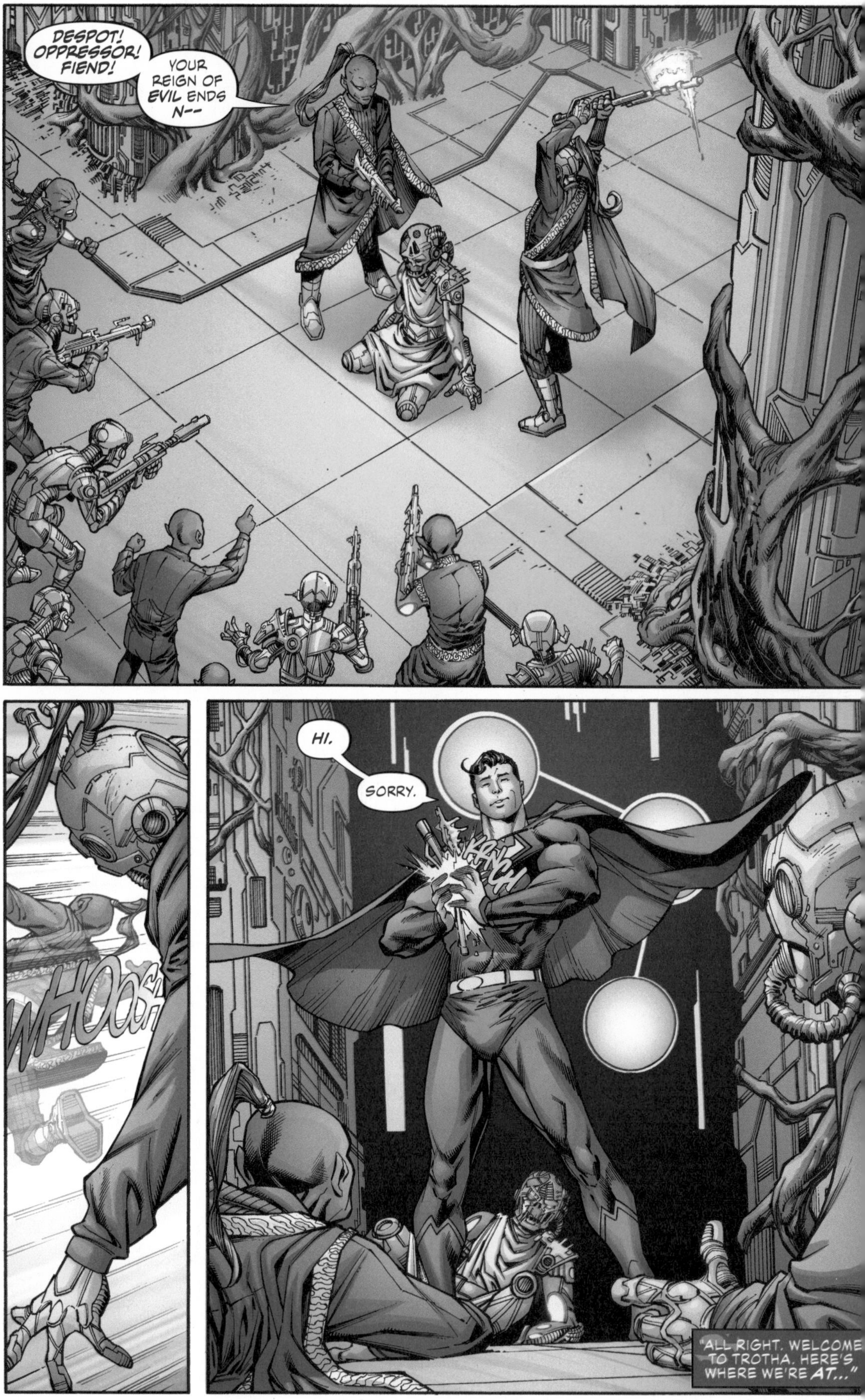
DESPOT! OPPRESSOR! FIEND!
YOUR REIGN OF EVIL ENDS N--
WHOOSH
HI.
SORRY.
KRNCH
"ALL RIGHT. WELCOME TO TROTHA. HERE'S WHERE WE'RE AT..."

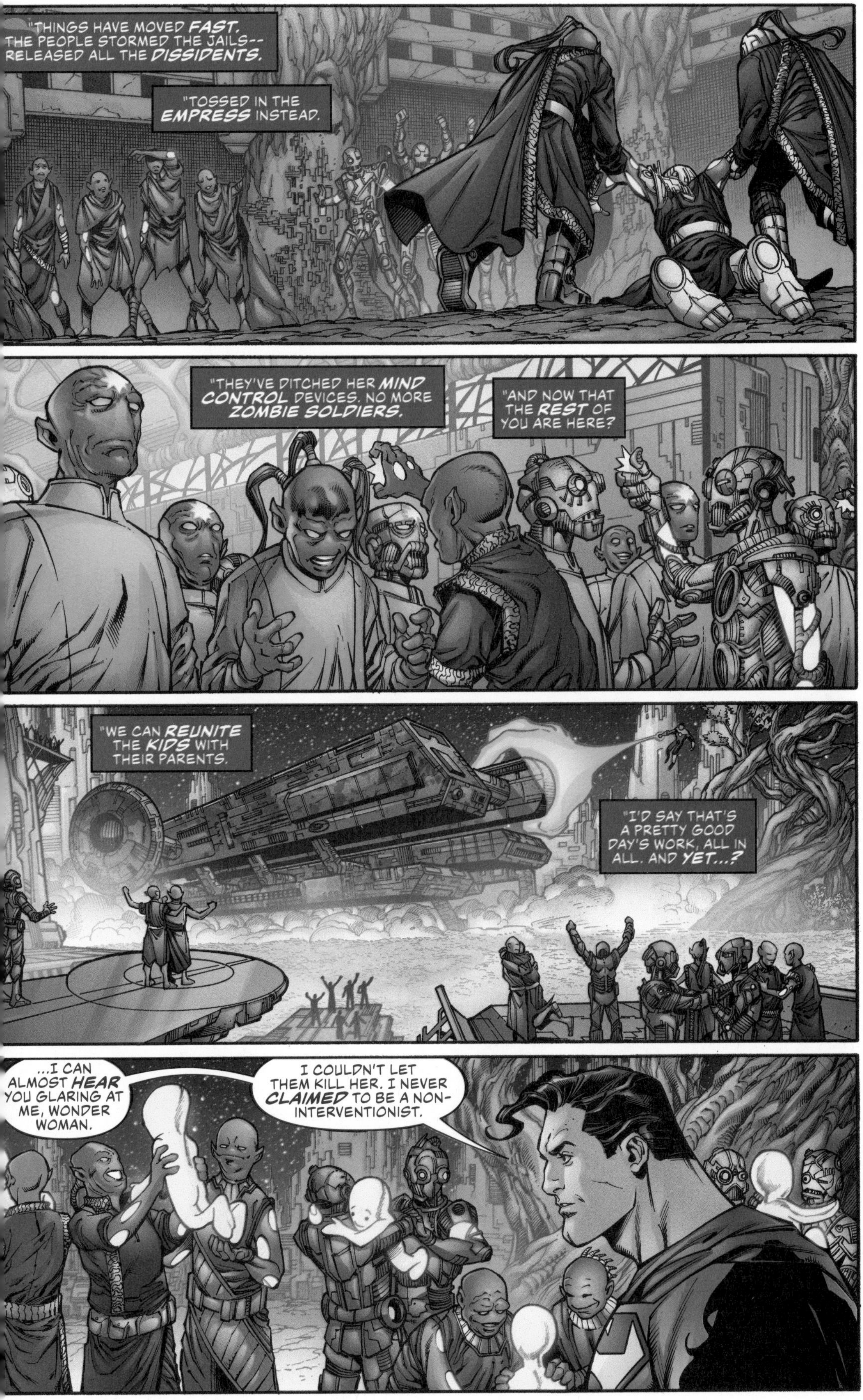
"THINGS HAVE MOVED FAST. THE PEOPLE STORMED THE JAILS--RELEASED ALL THE DISSIDENTS.
"TOSSED IN THE EMPRESS INSTEAD.
"THEY'VE DITCHED HER MIND CONTROL DEVICES. NO MORE ZOMBIE SOLDIERS.
"AND NOW THAT THE REST OF YOU ARE HERE?
"WE CAN REUNITE THE KIDS WITH THEIR PARENTS.
"I'D SAY THAT'S A PRETTY GOOD DAY'S WORK, ALL IN ALL. AND YET...?
...I CAN ALMOST HEAR YOU GLARING AT ME, WONDER WOMAN.
I COULDN'T LET THEM KILL HER. I NEVER CLAIMED TO BE A NON-INTERVENTIONIST.

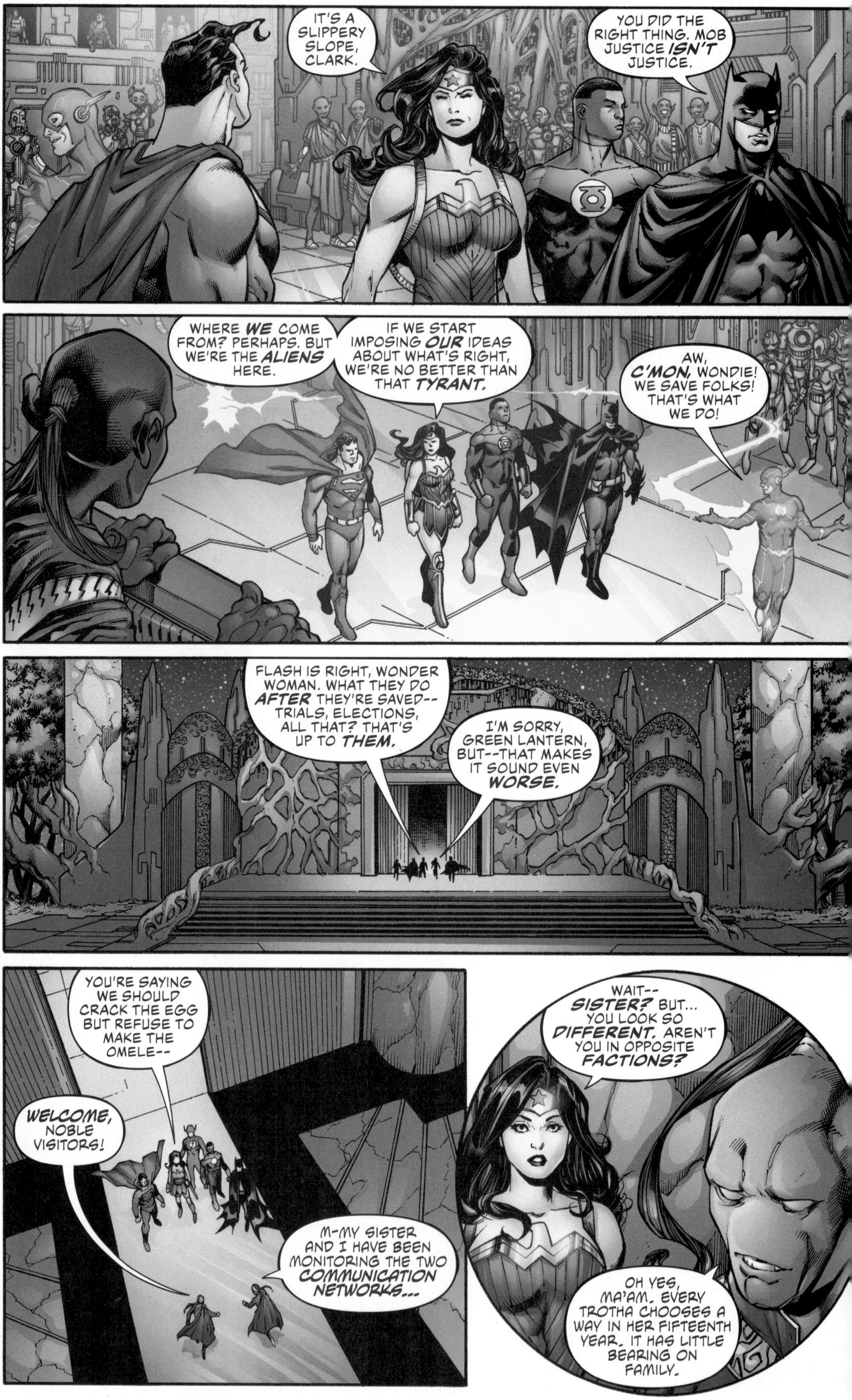

IT'S A SLIPPERY SLOPE, CLARK.
YOU DID THE RIGHT THING. MOB JUSTICE ISN'T JUSTICE.
WHERE WE COME FROM? PERHAPS. BUT WE'RE THE ALIENS HERE.
IF WE START IMPOSING OUR IDEAS ABOUT WHAT'S RIGHT, WE'RE NO BETTER THAN THAT TYRANT.
AW, C'MON, WONDIE! WE SAVE FOLKS! THAT'S WHAT WE DO!
FLASH IS RIGHT, WONDER WOMAN. WHAT THEY DO AFTER THEY'RE SAVED-- TRIALS, ELECTIONS, ALL THAT? THAT'S UP TO THEM.
I'M SORRY, GREEN LANTERN, BUT--THAT MAKES IT SOUND EVEN WORSE.
YOU'RE SAYING WE SHOULD CRACK THE EGG BUT REFUSE TO MAKE THE OMELE--
WELCOME, NOBLE VISITORS!
M-MY SISTER AND I HAVE BEEN MONITORING THE TWO COMMUNICATION NETWORKS...
WAIT-- SISTER? BUT... YOU LOOK SO DIFFERENT. AREN'T YOU IN OPPOSITE FACTIONS?
OH YES, MA'AM. EVERY TROTHA CHOOSES A WAY IN HER FIFTEENTH YEAR. IT HAS LITTLE BEARING ON FAMILY.

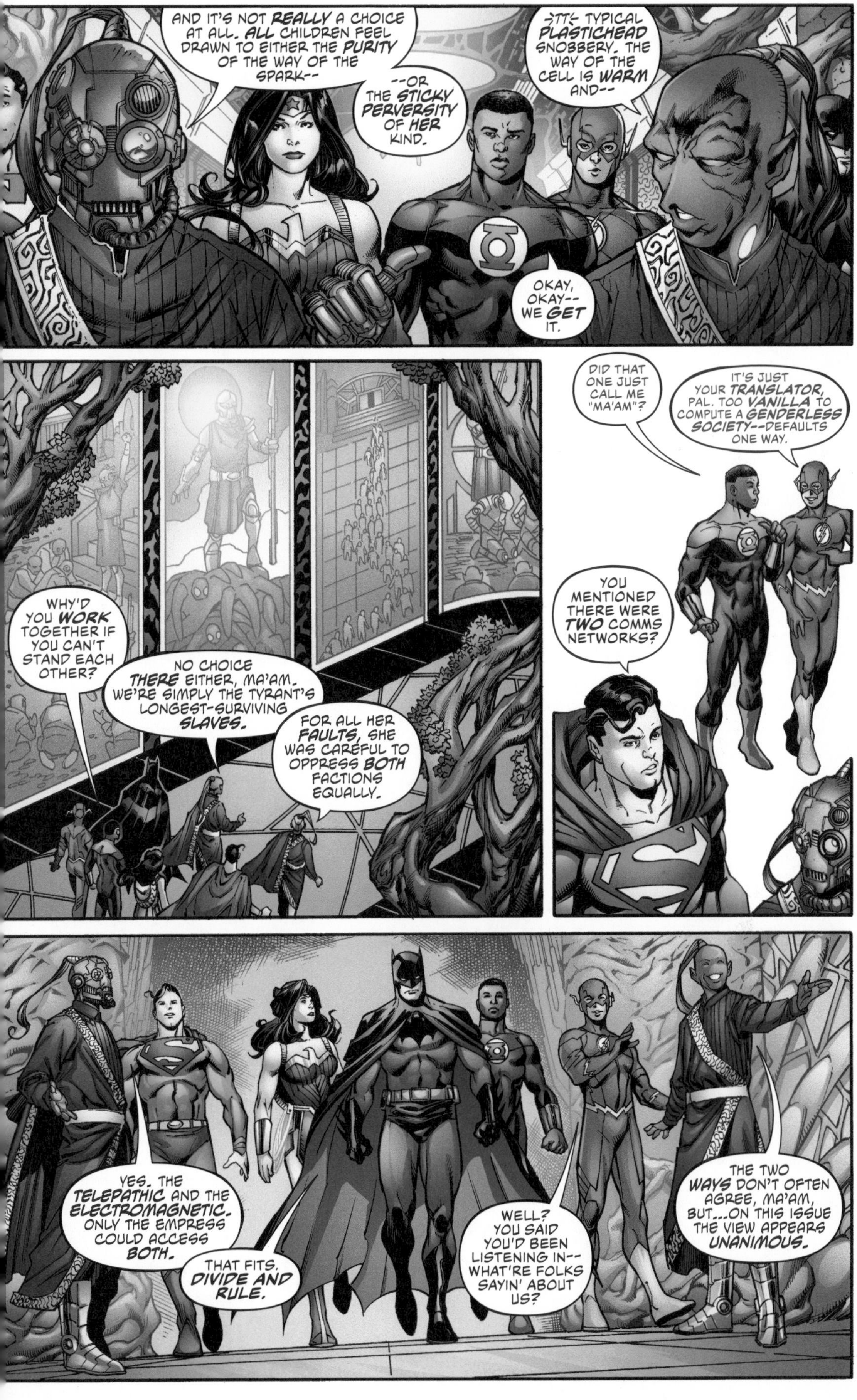
AND IT'S NOT REALLY A CHOICE AT ALL. ALL CHILDREN FEEL DRAWN TO EITHER THE PURITY OF THE WAY OF THE SPARK--
--OR THE STICKY PERVERSITY OF HER KIND.
TT- TYPICAL PLASTICHEAD SNOBBERY. THE WAY OF THE CELL IS WARM AND--
OKAY, OKAY--WE GET IT.
WHY'D YOU WORK TOGETHER IF YOU CAN'T STAND EACH OTHER?
NO CHOICE THERE EITHER, MA'AM. WE'RE SIMPLY THE TYRANT'S LONGEST-SURVIVING SLAVES.
FOR ALL HER FAULTS, SHE WAS CAREFUL TO OPPRESS BOTH FACTIONS EQUALLY.
DID THAT ONE JUST CALL ME "MA'AM"?
IT'S JUST YOUR TRANSLATOR, PAL. TOO VANILLA TO COMPUTE A GENDERLESS SOCIETY--DEFAULTS ONE WAY.
YOU MENTIONED THERE WERE TWO COMMS NETWORKS?
YES. THE TELEPATHIC AND THE ELECTROMAGNETIC. ONLY THE EMPRESS COULD ACCESS BOTH.
THAT FITS. DIVIDE AND RULE.
WELL? YOU SAID YOU'D BEEN LISTENING IN--WHAT'RE FOLKS SAYIN' ABOUT US?
THE TWO WAYS DON'T OFTEN AGREE, MA'AM, BUT...ON THIS ISSUE THE VIEW APPEARS UNANIMOUS.

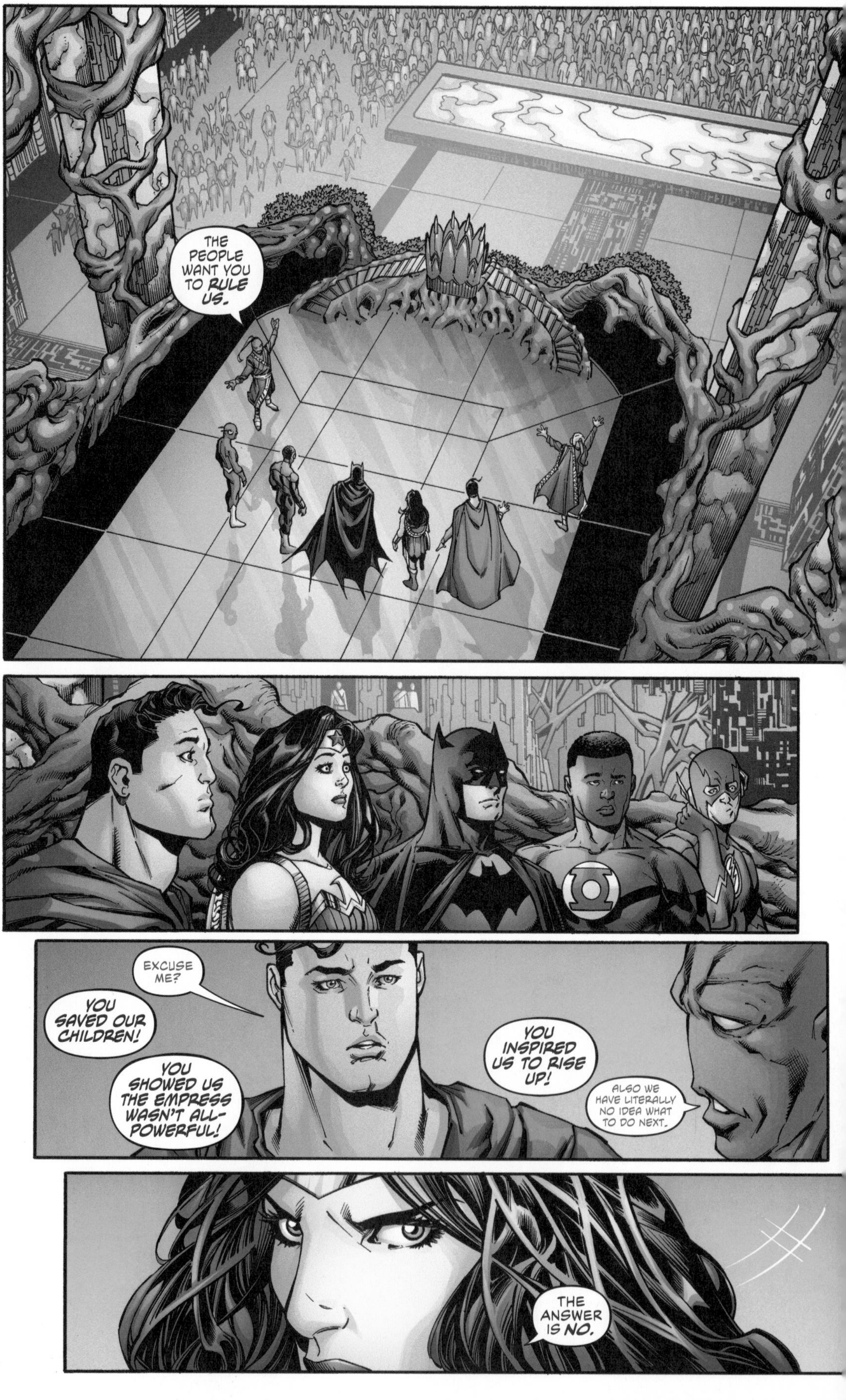
THE PEOPLE WANT YOU TO RULE US.
EXCUSE ME?
YOU SAVED OUR CHILDREN!
YOU SHOWED US THE EMPRESS WASN'T ALL-POWERFUL!
YOU INSPIRED US TO RISE UP!
ALSO WE HAVE LITERALLY NO IDEA WHAT TO DO NEXT.
THE ANSWER IS NO.

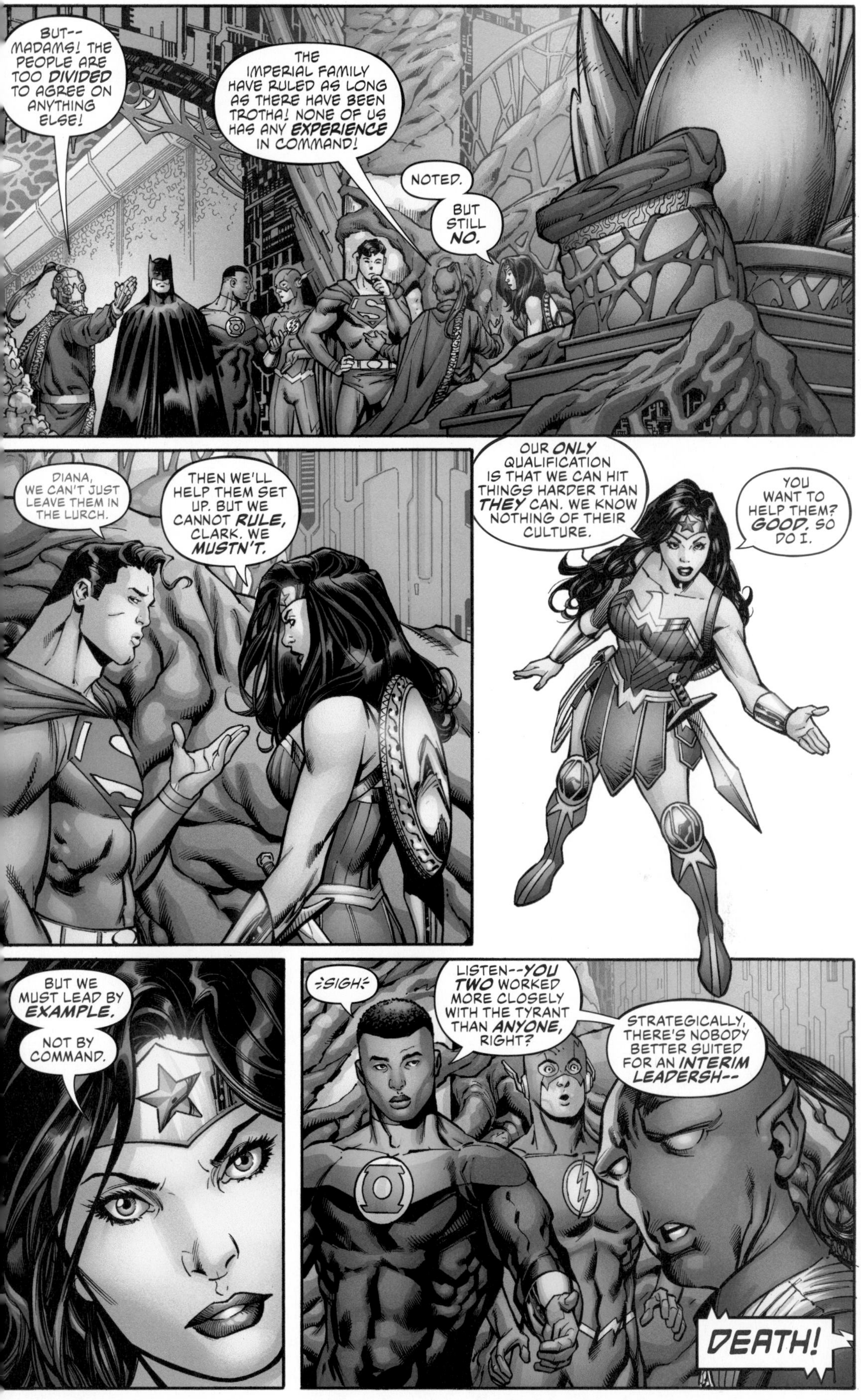
BUT--
MADAMS! THE PEOPLE ARE TOO DIVIDED TO AGREE ON ANYTHING ELSE!
THE IMPERIAL FAMILY HAVE RULED AS LONG AS THERE HAVE BEEN TROTHA! NONE OF US HAS ANY EXPERIENCE IN COMMAND!
NOTED.
BUT STILL NO.
DIANA, WE CAN'T JUST LEAVE THEM IN THE LURCH.
THEN WE'LL HELP THEM SET UP. BUT WE CANNOT RULE, CLARK. WE MUSTN'T.
OUR ONLY QUALIFICATION IS THAT WE CAN HIT THINGS HARDER THAN THEY CAN. WE KNOW NOTHING OF THEIR CULTURE.
YOU WANT TO HELP THEM? GOOD. SO DO I.
BUT WE MUST LEAD BY EXAMPLE.
NOT BY COMMAND.
SIGH
LISTEN--YOU TWO WORKED MORE CLOSELY WITH THE TYRANT THAN ANYONE, RIGHT?
STRATEGICALLY, THERE'S NOBODY BETTER SUITED FOR AN INTERIM LEADERSH--
DEATH!

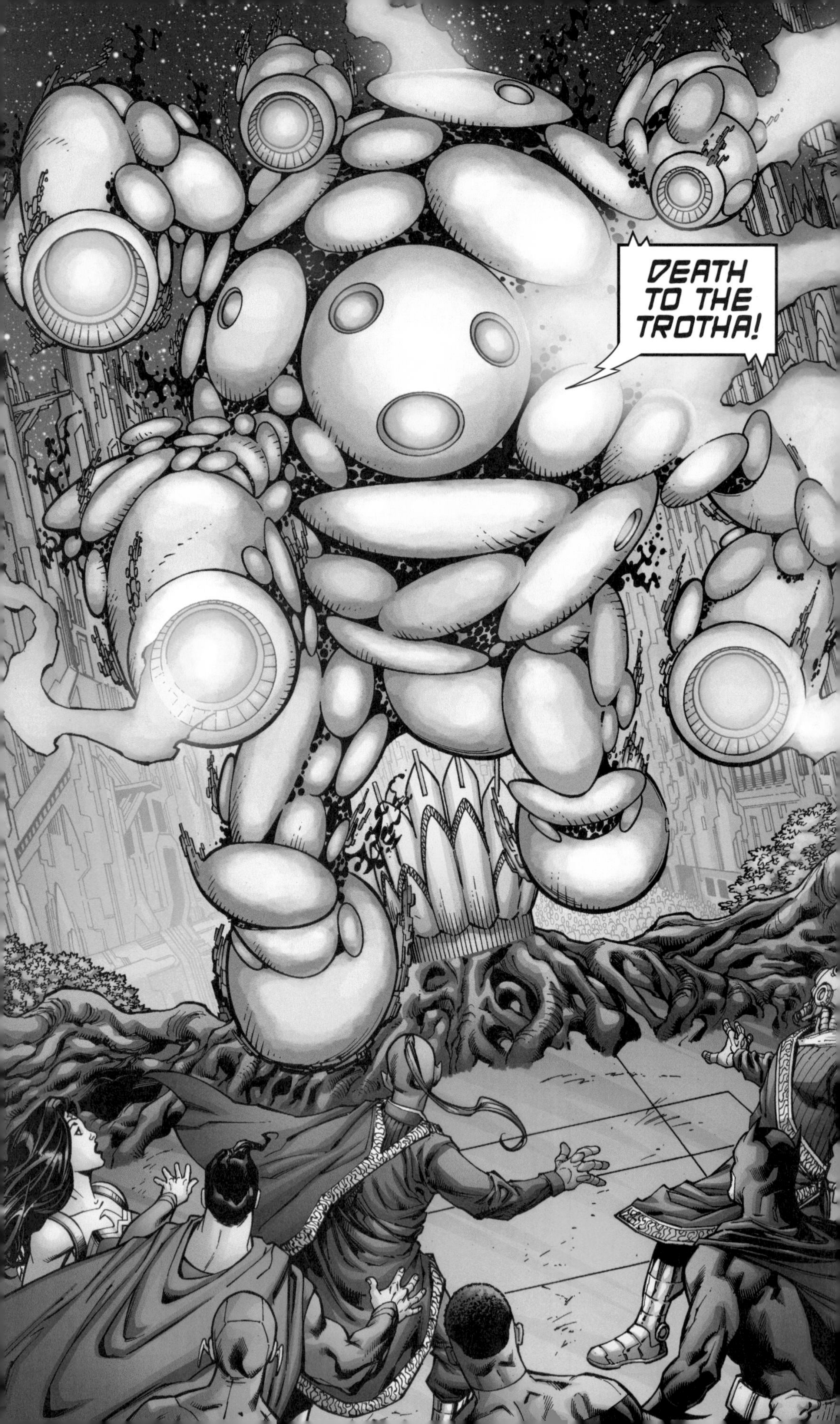
DEATH TO THE TROTHA!

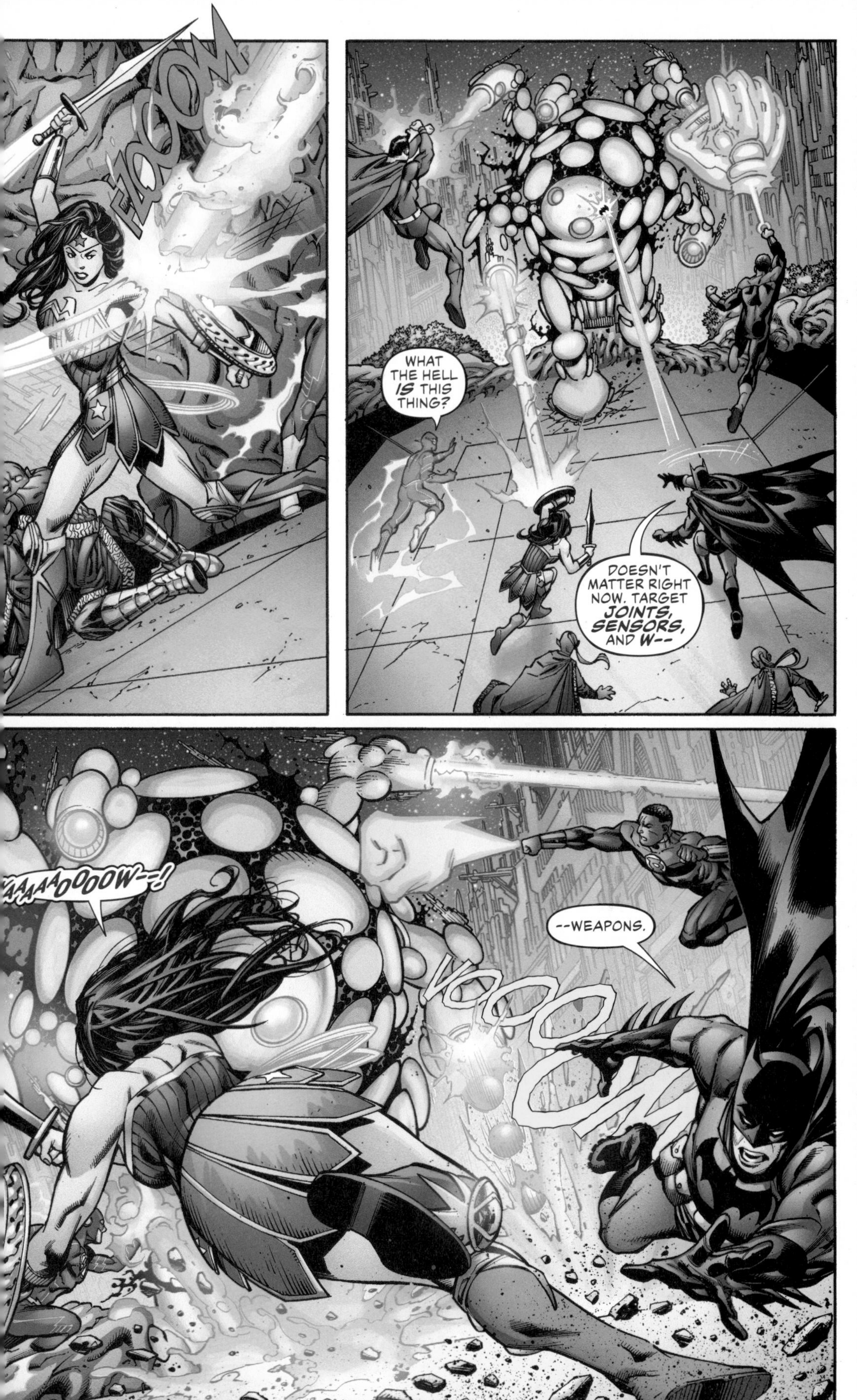
FZOOOM
WHAT THE HELL IS THIS THING?
DOESN'T MATTER RIGHT NOW. TARGET JOINTS, SENSORS, AND W--
AAAAAOOOOW--!
--WEAPONS.
VOOOOM

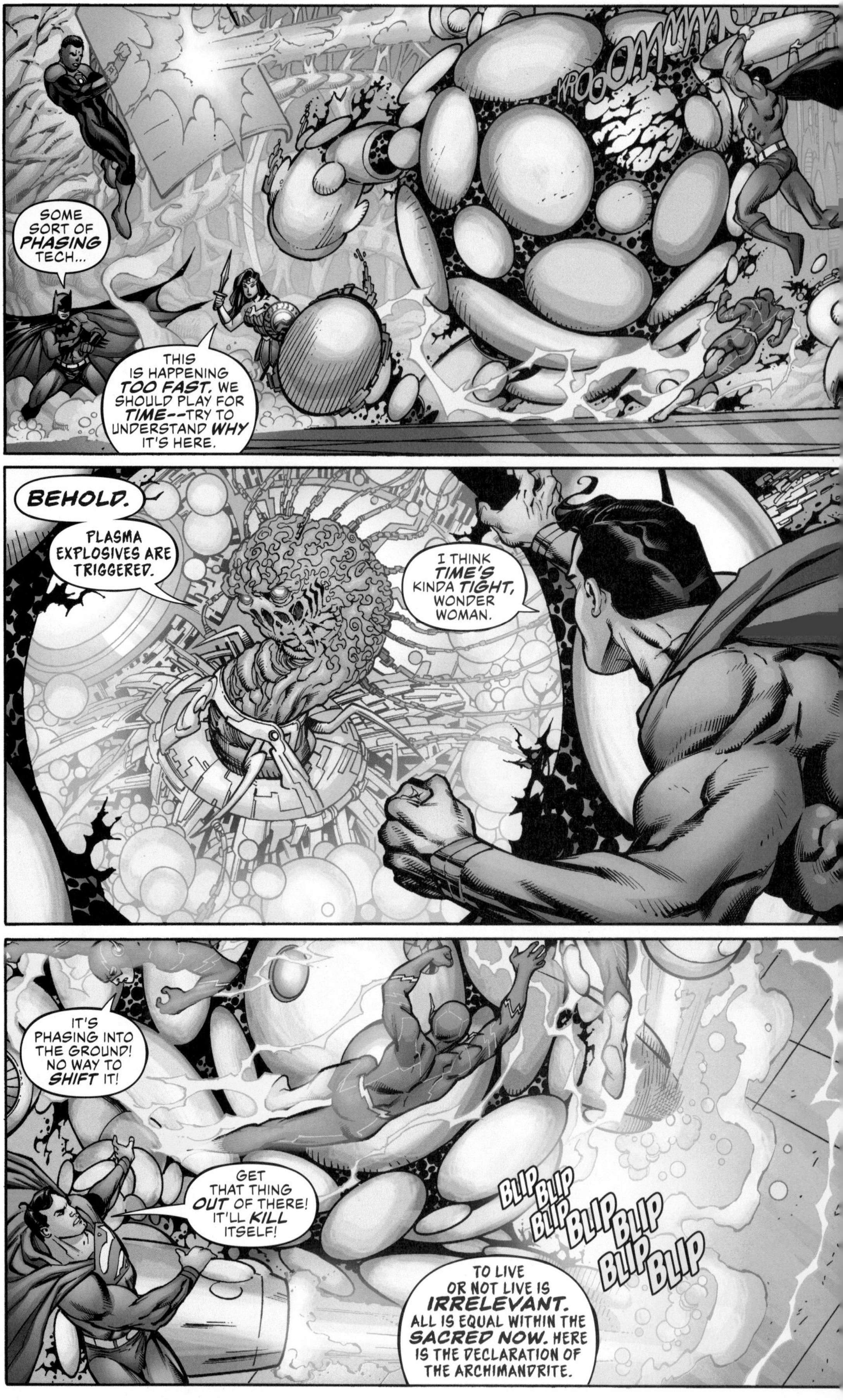
KRROOOMMM
SOME SORT OF PHASING TECH...
THIS IS HAPPENING TOO FAST. WE SHOULD PLAY FOR TIME--TRY TO UNDERSTAND WHY IT'S HERE.
BEHOLD.
PLASMA EXPLOSIVES ARE TRIGGERED.
I THINK TIME'S KINDA TIGHT, WONDER WOMAN.
IT'S PHASING INTO THE GROUND! NO WAY TO SHIFT IT!
GET THAT THING OUT OF THERE! IT'LL KILL ITSELF!
BLIP BLIP BLIP BLIP BLIP BLIP BLIP
TO LIVE OR NOT LIVE IS IRRELEVANT. ALL IS EQUAL WITHIN THE SACRED NOW. HERE IS THE DECLARATION OF THE ARCHIMANDRITE.

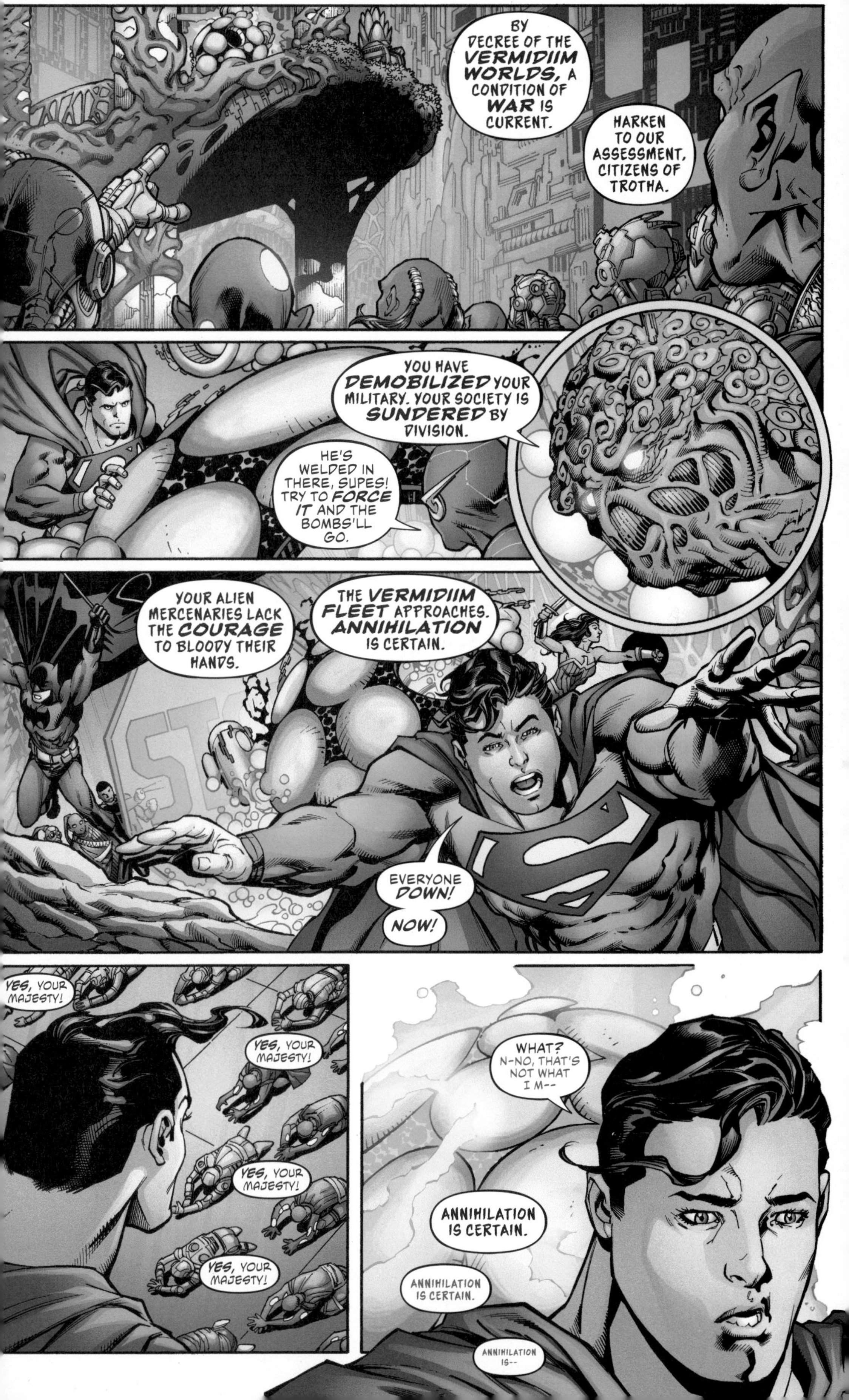
BY DECREE OF THE VERMIDIIM WORLDS, A CONDITION OF WAR IS CURRENT.
HARKEN TO OUR ASSESSMENT, CITIZENS OF TROTHA.
YOU HAVE DEMOBILIZED YOUR MILITARY. YOUR SOCIETY IS SUNDERED BY DIVISION.
HE'S WELDED IN THERE, SUPES! TRY TO FORCE IT AND THE BOMBS'LL GO.
YOUR ALIEN MERCENARIES LACK THE COURAGE TO BLOODY THEIR HANDS.
THE VERMIDIIM FLEET APPROACHES. ANNIHILATION IS CERTAIN.
EVERYONE DOWN!
NOW!
YES, YOUR MAJESTY!
YES, YOUR MAJESTY!
YES, YOUR MAJESTY!
YES, YOUR MAJESTY!
WHAT? N-NO, THAT'S NOT WHAT I M--
ANNIHILATION IS CERTAIN.
ANNIHILATION IS CERTAIN.
ANNIHILATION IS--

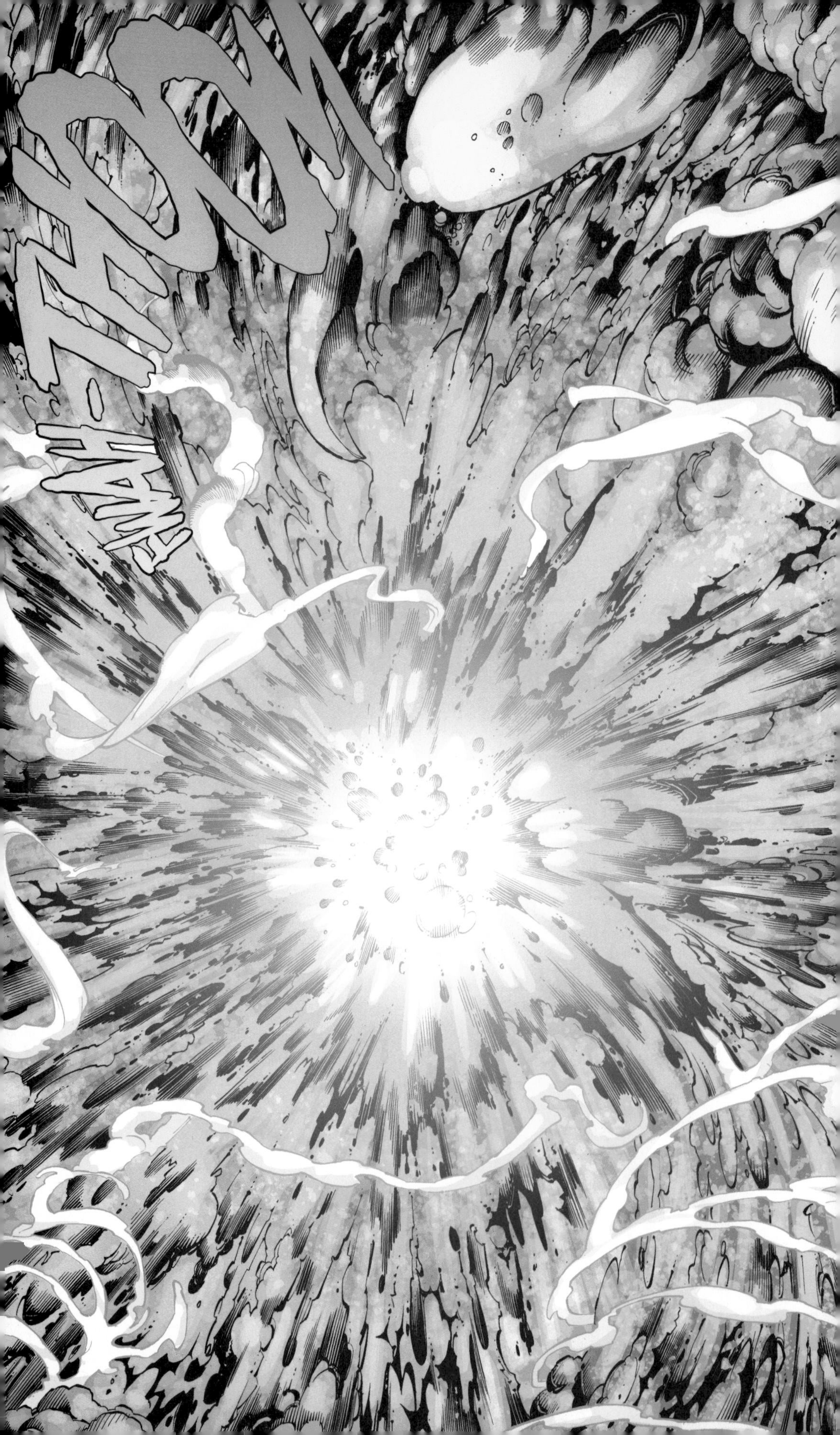
THOOM
FWAH

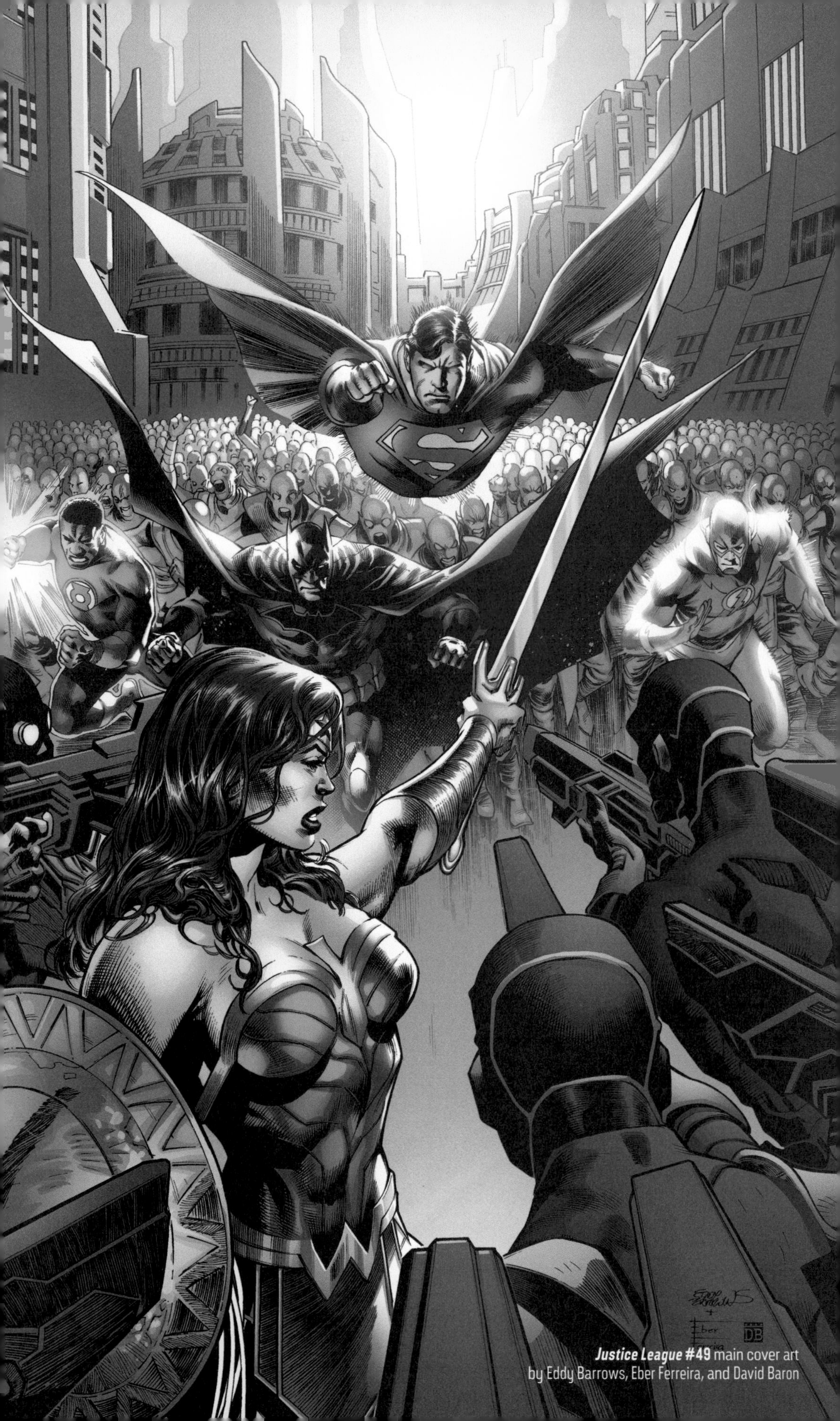

***Justice League* #49** main cover art
by Eddy Barrows, Eber Ferreira, and David Baron

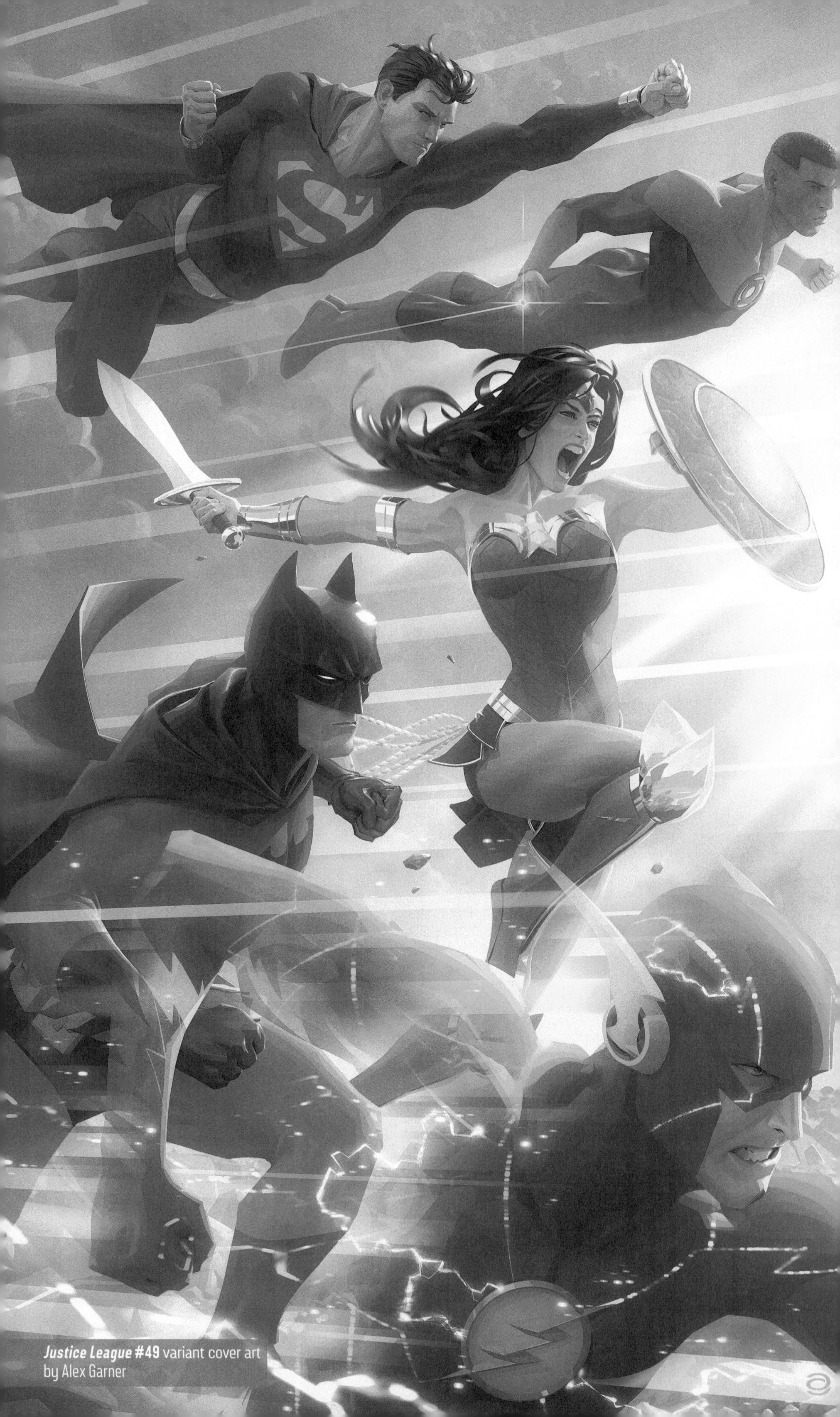

Justice League **#49** variant cover art
by Alex Garner

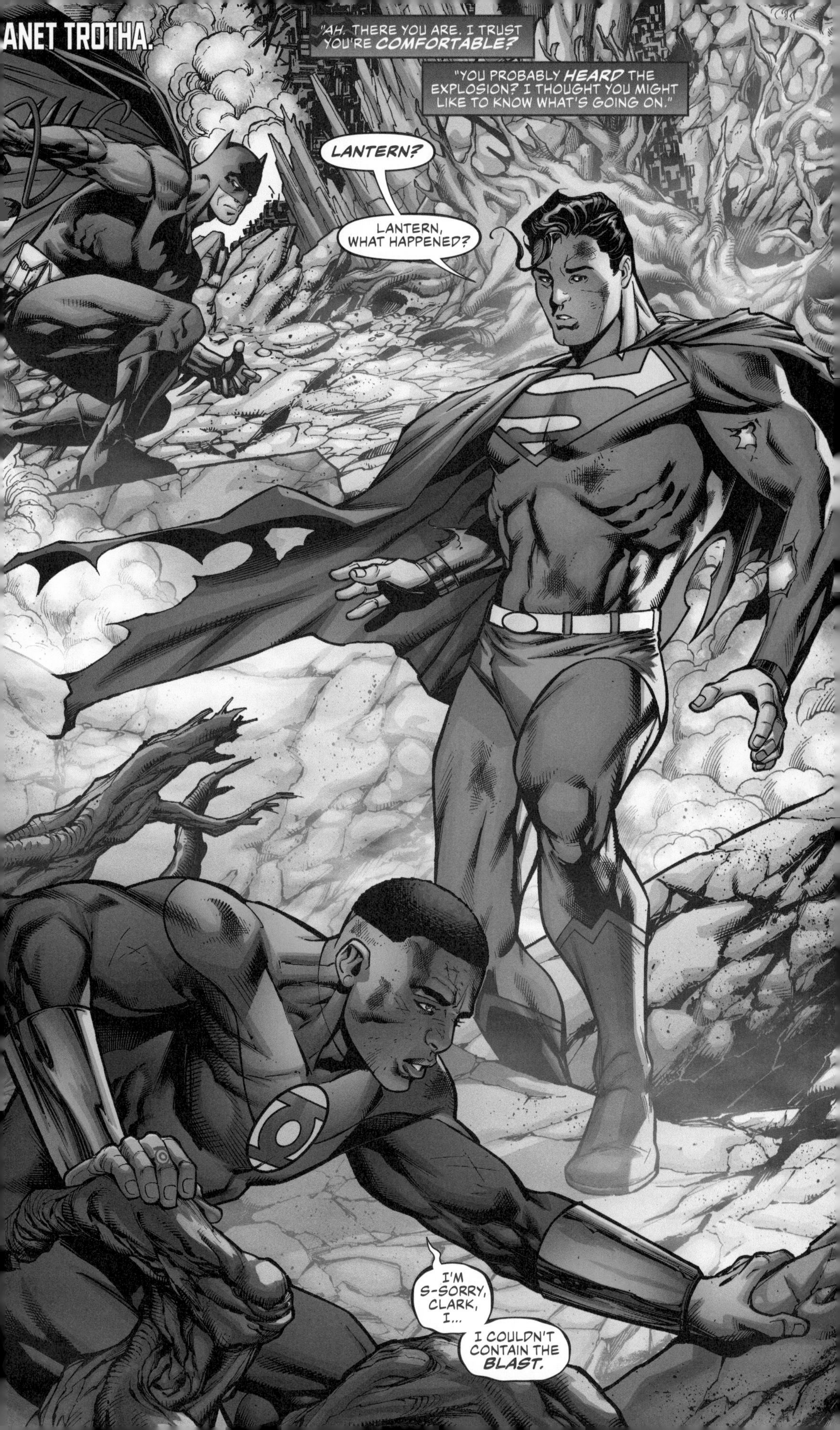
ANET TROTHA.
"AH. THERE YOU ARE. I TRUST YOU'RE COMFORTABLE?
"YOU PROBABLY HEARD THE EXPLOSION? I THOUGHT YOU MIGHT LIKE TO KNOW WHAT'S GOING ON."
LANTERN?
LANTERN, WHAT HAPPENED?
I'M S-SORRY, CLARK, I...
I COULDN'T CONTAIN THE BLAST.

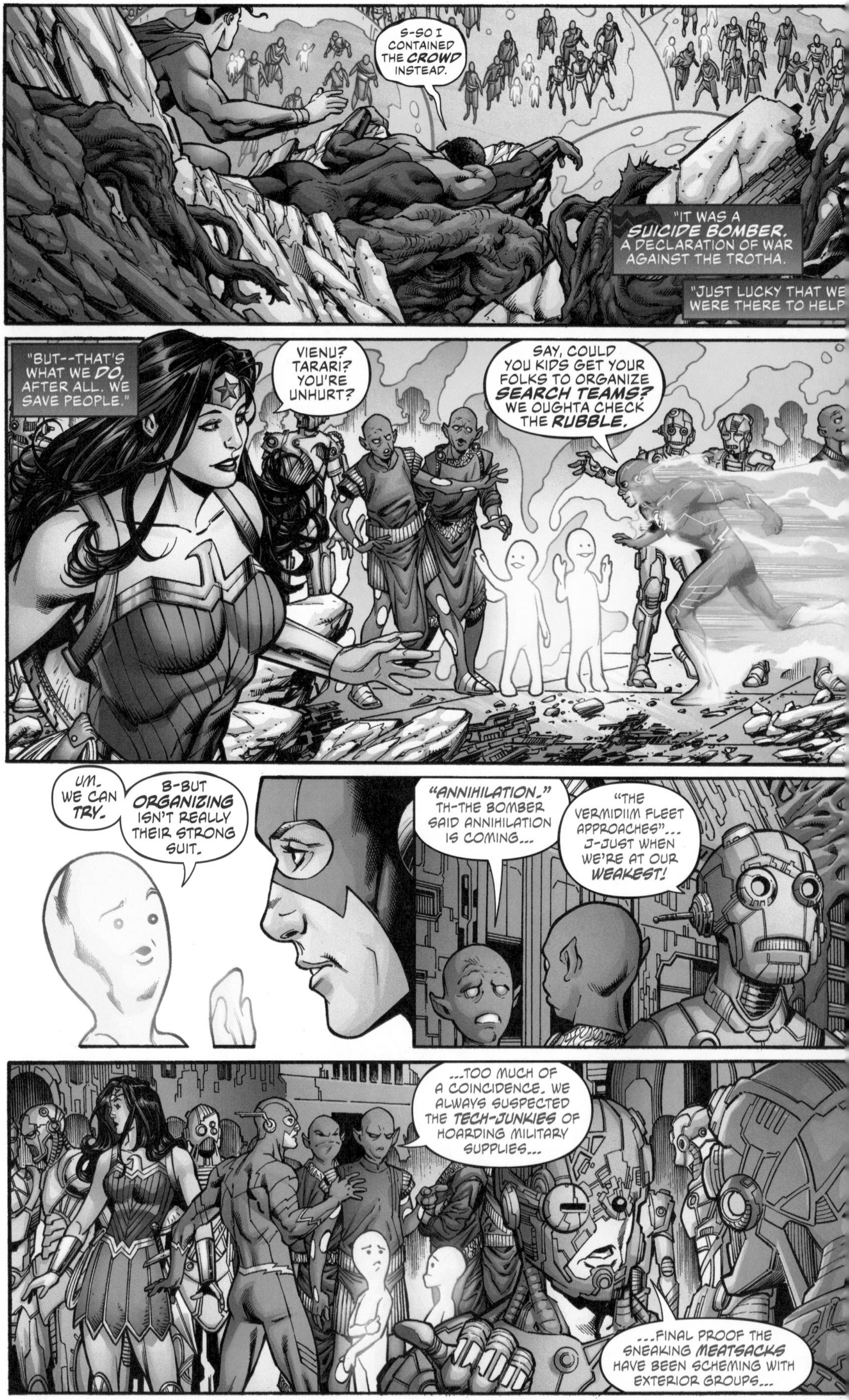

S-SO I CONTAINED THE CROWD INSTEAD.
"IT WAS A SUICIDE BOMBER. A DECLARATION OF WAR AGAINST THE TROTHA.
"JUST LUCKY THAT WE WERE THERE TO HELP
"BUT--THAT'S WHAT WE DO, AFTER ALL. WE SAVE PEOPLE."
VIENU? TARARI? YOU'RE UNHURT?
SAY, COULD YOU KIDS GET YOUR FOLKS TO ORGANIZE SEARCH TEAMS? WE OUGHTA CHECK THE RUBBLE.
UM. WE CAN TRY.
B-BUT ORGANIZING ISN'T REALLY THEIR STRONG SUIT.
"ANNIHILATION." TH-THE BOMBER SAID ANNIHILATION IS COMING...
"THE VERMIDIIM FLEET APPROACHES"... J-JUST WHEN WE'RE AT OUR WEAKEST!
...TOO MUCH OF A COINCIDENCE. WE ALWAYS SUSPECTED THE TECH-JUNKIES OF HOARDING MILITARY SUPPLIES...
...FINAL PROOF THE SNEAKING MEATSACKS HAVE BEEN SCHEMING WITH EXTERIOR GROUPS...

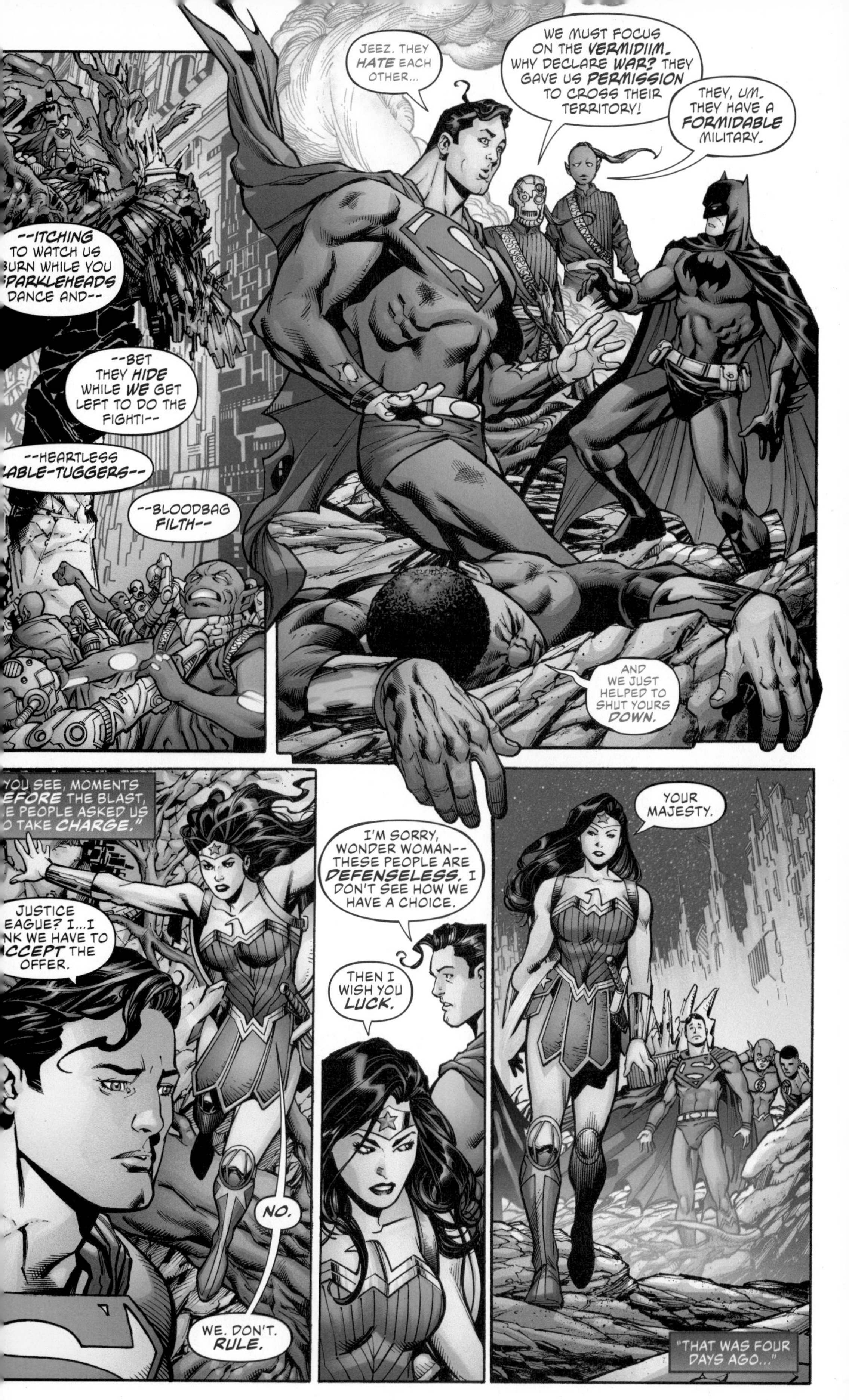
--ITCHING TO WATCH US BURN WHILE YOU SPARKLEHEADS DANCE AND--
--BET THEY HIDE WHILE WE GET LEFT TO DO THE FIGHTI--
--HEARTLESS CABLE-TUGGERS--
--BLOODBAG FILTH--
JEEZ. THEY HATE EACH OTHER...
WE MUST FOCUS ON THE VERMIDIIM. WHY DECLARE WAR? THEY GAVE US PERMISSION TO CROSS THEIR TERRITORY!
THEY, UM. THEY HAVE A FORMIDABLE MILITARY.
AND WE JUST HELPED TO SHUT YOURS DOWN.
YOU SEE, MOMENTS BEFORE THE BLAST, E PEOPLE ASKED US O TAKE CHARGE."
JUSTICE EAGUE? I...I NK WE HAVE TO CCEPT THE OFFER.
NO.
WE. DON'T. RULE.
I'M SORRY, WONDER WOMAN-- THESE PEOPLE ARE DEFENSELESS. I DON'T SEE HOW WE HAVE A CHOICE.
THEN I WISH YOU LUCK.
YOUR MAJESTY.
"THAT WAS FOUR DAYS AGO..."

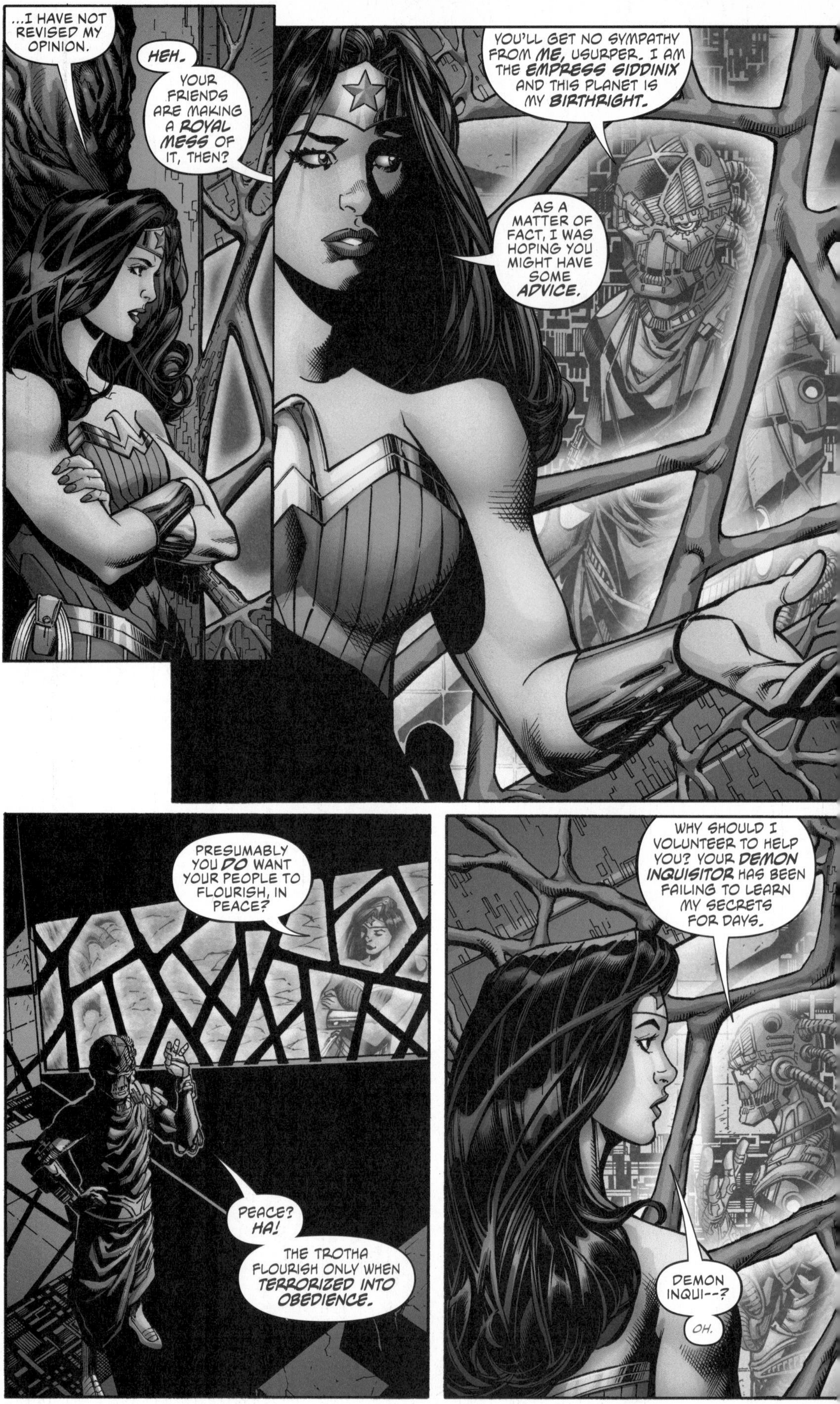
...I HAVE NOT REVISED MY OPINION.
HEH.
YOUR FRIENDS ARE MAKING A ROYAL MESS OF IT, THEN?
YOU'LL GET NO SYMPATHY FROM ME, USURPER. I AM THE EMPRESS SIDDINIX AND THIS PLANET IS MY BIRTHRIGHT.
AS A MATTER OF FACT, I WAS HOPING YOU MIGHT HAVE SOME ADVICE.
PRESUMABLY YOU DO WANT YOUR PEOPLE TO FLOURISH, IN PEACE?
PEACE? HA!
THE TROTHA FLOURISH ONLY WHEN TERRORIZED INTO OBEDIENCE.
WHY SHOULD I VOLUNTEER TO HELP YOU? YOUR DEMON INQUISITOR HAS BEEN FAILING TO LEARN MY SECRETS FOR DAYS.
DEMON INQUI--?
OH.

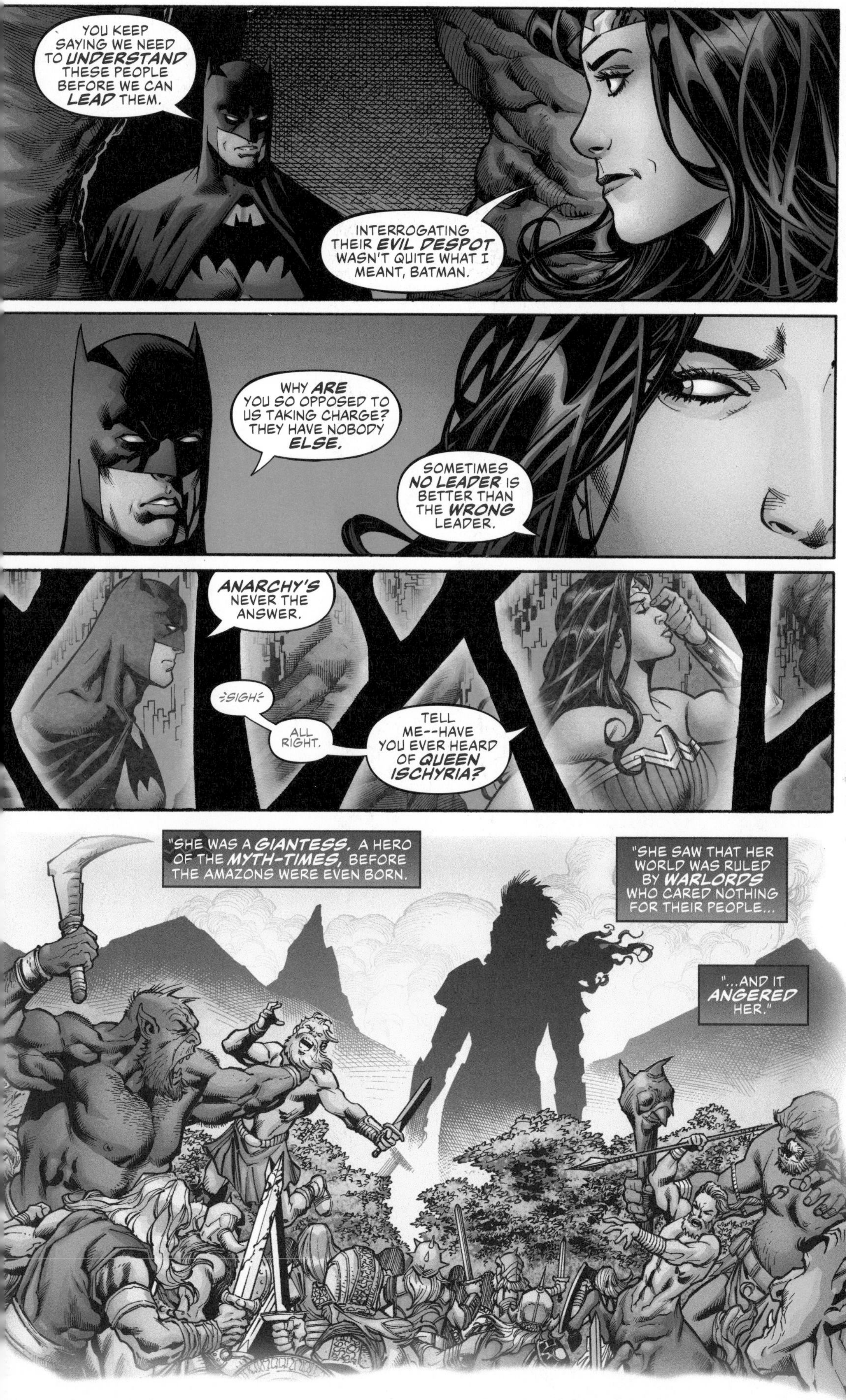
YOU KEEP SAYING WE NEED TO UNDERSTAND THESE PEOPLE BEFORE WE CAN LEAD THEM.
INTERROGATING THEIR EVIL DESPOT WASN'T QUITE WHAT I MEANT, BATMAN.
WHY ARE YOU SO OPPOSED TO US TAKING CHARGE? THEY HAVE NOBODY ELSE.
SOMETIMES NO LEADER IS BETTER THAN THE WRONG LEADER.
ANARCHY'S NEVER THE ANSWER.
SIGH
ALL RIGHT.
TELL ME--HAVE YOU EVER HEARD OF QUEEN ISCHYRIA?
"SHE WAS A GIANTESS. A HERO OF THE MYTH-TIMES, BEFORE THE AMAZONS WERE EVEN BORN.
"SHE SAW THAT HER WORLD WAS RULED BY WARLORDS WHO CARED NOTHING FOR THEIR PEOPLE...
"...AND IT ANGERED HER."

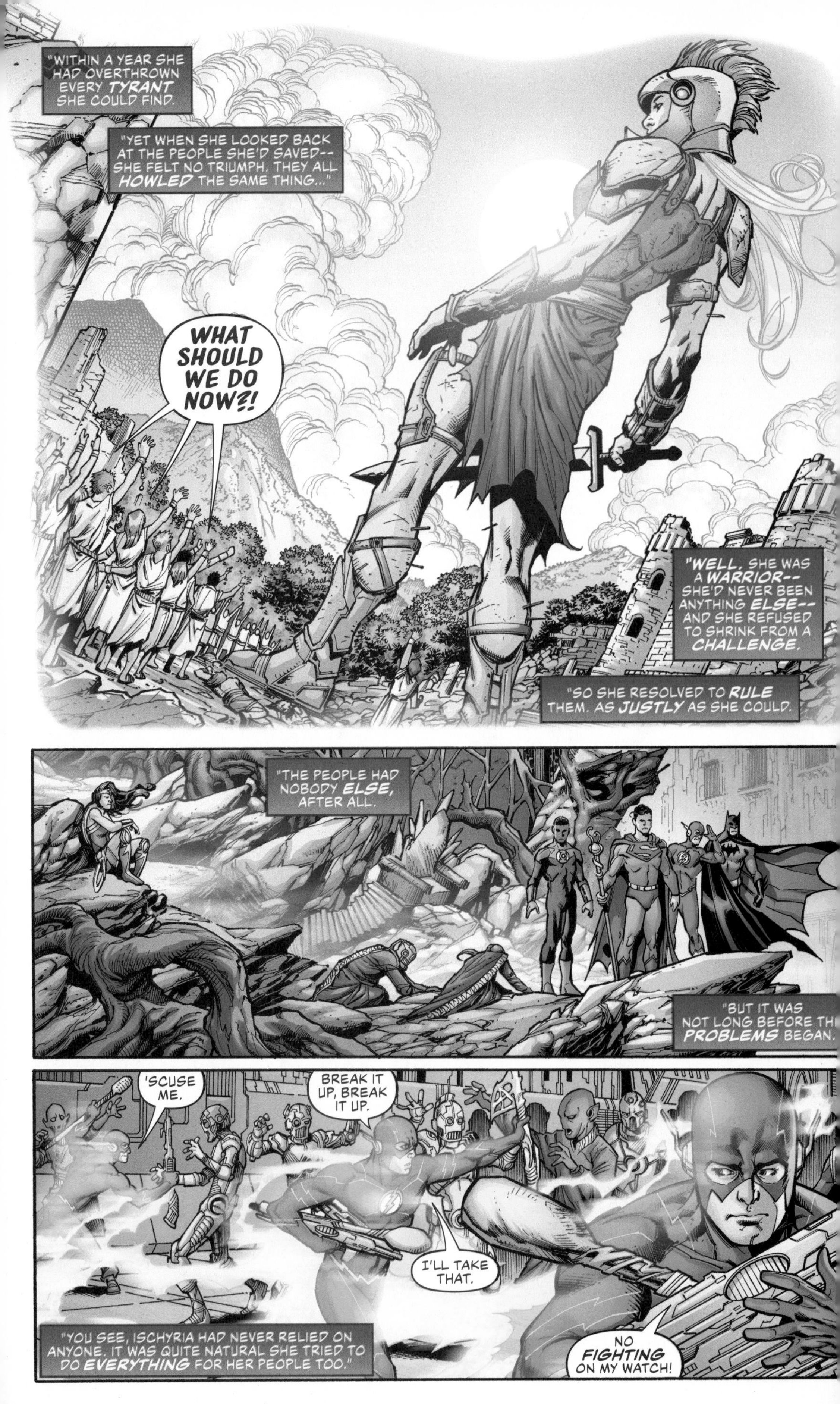
"WITHIN A YEAR SHE HAD OVERTHROWN EVERY TYRANT SHE COULD FIND.
"YET WHEN SHE LOOKED BACK AT THE PEOPLE SHE'D SAVED--SHE FELT NO TRIUMPH. THEY ALL HOWLED THE SAME THING..."
WHAT SHOULD WE DO NOW?!
"WELL, SHE WAS A WARRIOR--SHE'D NEVER BEEN ANYTHING ELSE--AND SHE REFUSED TO SHRINK FROM A CHALLENGE.
"SO SHE RESOLVED TO RULE THEM. AS JUSTLY AS SHE COULD.
"THE PEOPLE HAD NOBODY ELSE, AFTER ALL.
"BUT IT WAS NOT LONG BEFORE TH PROBLEMS BEGAN.
'SCUSE ME.
BREAK IT UP, BREAK IT UP.
I'LL TAKE THAT.
"YOU SEE, ISCHYRIA HAD NEVER RELIED ON ANYONE. IT WAS QUITE NATURAL SHE TRIED TO DO EVERYTHING FOR HER PEOPLE TOO."
NO FIGHTING ON MY WATCH!

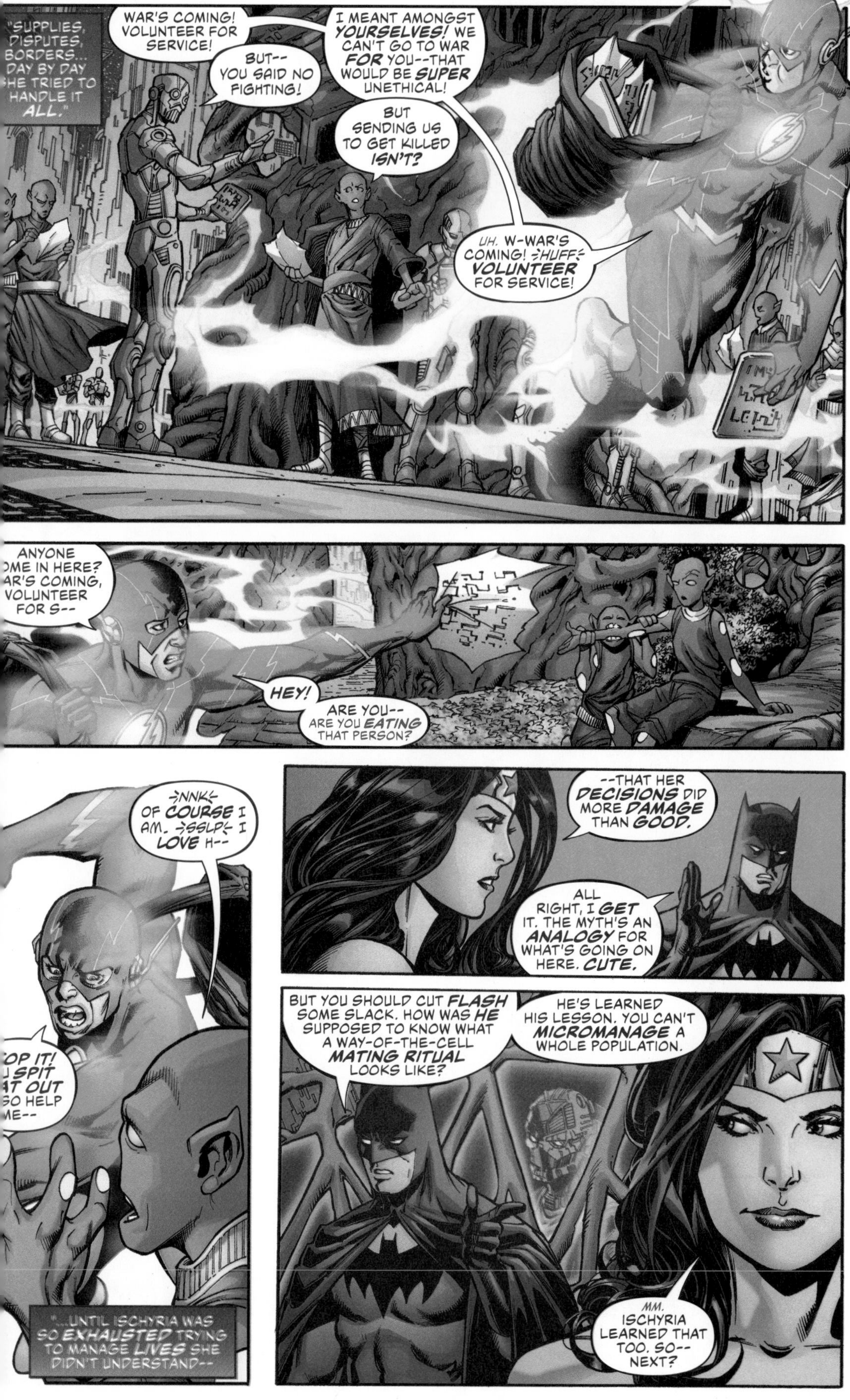
"SUPPLIES, DISPUTES, BORDERS... DAY BY DAY SHE TRIED TO HANDLE IT ALL."
WAR'S COMING! VOLUNTEER FOR SERVICE!
BUT-- YOU SAID NO FIGHTING!
I MEANT AMONGST YOURSELVES! WE CAN'T GO TO WAR FOR YOU--THAT WOULD BE SUPER UNETHICAL!
BUT SENDING US TO GET KILLED ISN'T?
UH. W-WAR'S COMING! HUFF VOLUNTEER FOR SERVICE!
ANYONE OME IN HERE? AR'S COMING, VOLUNTEER FOR S--
HEY!
ARE YOU-- ARE YOU EATING THAT PERSON?
NNK OF COURSE I AM. SSLP I LOVE H--
OP IT! U SPIT AT OUT SO HELP ME--
"...UNTIL ISCHYRIA WAS SO EXHAUSTED TRYING TO MANAGE LIVES SHE DIDN'T UNDERSTAND--
--THAT HER DECISIONS DID MORE DAMAGE THAN GOOD.
ALL RIGHT, I GET IT. THE MYTH'S AN ANALOGY FOR WHAT'S GOING ON HERE. CUTE.
BUT YOU SHOULD CUT FLASH SOME SLACK. HOW WAS HE SUPPOSED TO KNOW WHAT A WAY-OF-THE-CELL MATING RITUAL LOOKS LIKE?
HE'S LEARNED HIS LESSON. YOU CAN'T MICROMANAGE A WHOLE POPULATION.
MM. ISCHYRIA LEARNED THAT TOO. SO-- NEXT?

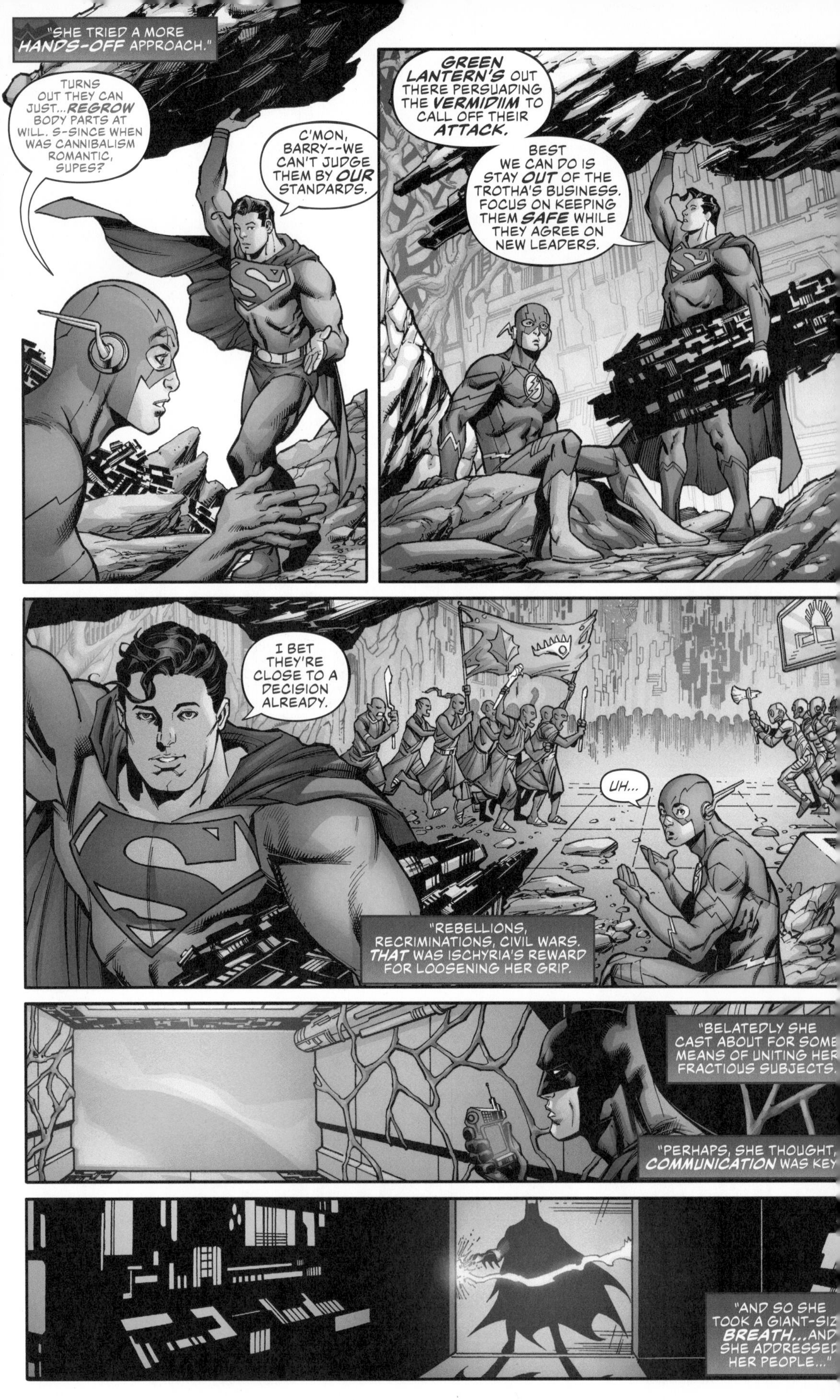
"SHE TRIED A MORE HANDS-OFF APPROACH."
TURNS OUT THEY CAN JUST...REGROW BODY PARTS AT WILL. S-SINCE WHEN WAS CANNIBALISM ROMANTIC, SUPES?
C'MON, BARRY--WE CAN'T JUDGE THEM BY OUR STANDARDS.
GREEN LANTERN'S OUT THERE PERSUADING THE VERMIDIIM TO CALL OFF THEIR ATTACK.
BEST WE CAN DO IS STAY OUT OF THE TROTHA'S BUSINESS. FOCUS ON KEEPING THEM SAFE WHILE THEY AGREE ON NEW LEADERS.
I BET THEY'RE CLOSE TO A DECISION ALREADY.
UH...
"REBELLIONS, RECRIMINATIONS, CIVIL WARS. THAT WAS ISCHYRIA'S REWARD FOR LOOSENING HER GRIP.
"BELATEDLY SHE CAST ABOUT FOR SOME MEANS OF UNITING HER FRACTIOUS SUBJECTS.
"PERHAPS, SHE THOUGHT, COMMUNICATION WAS KEY.
"AND SO SHE TOOK A GIANT-SIZ BREATH...AND SHE ADDRESSED HER PEOPLE..."

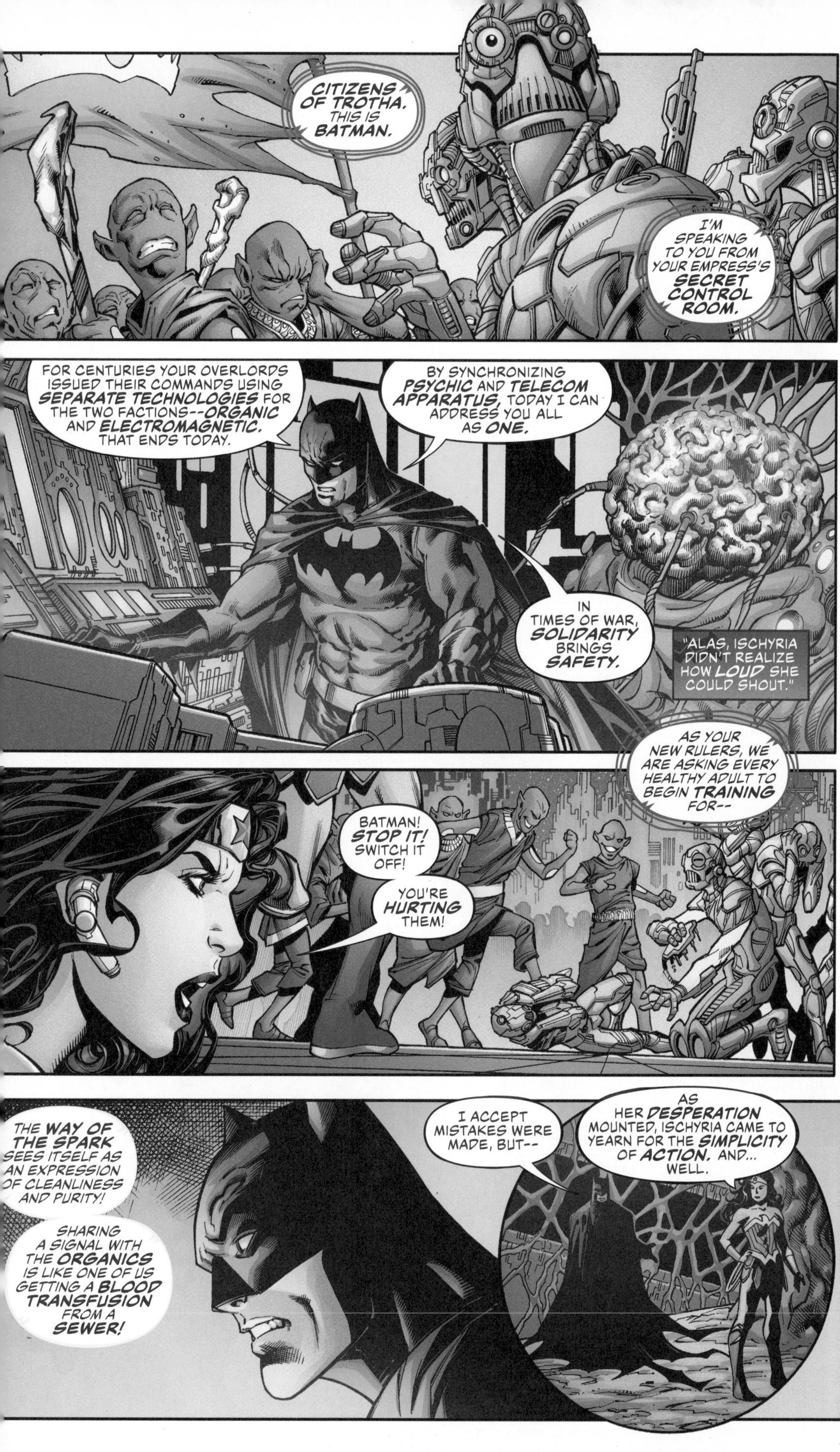
CITIZENS OF TROTHA. THIS IS BATMAN.
I'M SPEAKING TO YOU FROM YOUR EMPRESS'S SECRET CONTROL ROOM.
FOR CENTURIES YOUR OVERLORDS ISSUED THEIR COMMANDS USING SEPARATE TECHNOLOGIES FOR THE TWO FACTIONS--ORGANIC AND ELECTROMAGNETIC. THAT ENDS TODAY.
BY SYNCHRONIZING PSYCHIC AND TELECOM APPARATUS, TODAY I CAN ADDRESS YOU ALL AS ONE.
IN TIMES OF WAR, SOLIDARITY BRINGS SAFETY.
"ALAS, ISCHYRIA DIDN'T REALIZE HOW LOUD SHE COULD SHOUT."
AS YOUR NEW RULERS, WE ARE ASKING EVERY HEALTHY ADULT TO BEGIN TRAINING FOR--
BATMAN! STOP IT! SWITCH IT OFF!
YOU'RE HURTING THEM!
THE WAY OF THE SPARK SEES ITSELF AS AN EXPRESSION OF CLEANLINESS AND PURITY!
SHARING A SIGNAL WITH THE ORGANICS IS LIKE ONE OF US GETTING A BLOOD TRANSFUSION FROM A SEWER!
I ACCEPT MISTAKES WERE MADE, BUT--
AS HER DESPERATION MOUNTED, ISCHYRIA CAME TO YEARN FOR THE SIMPLICITY OF ACTION. AND... WELL.

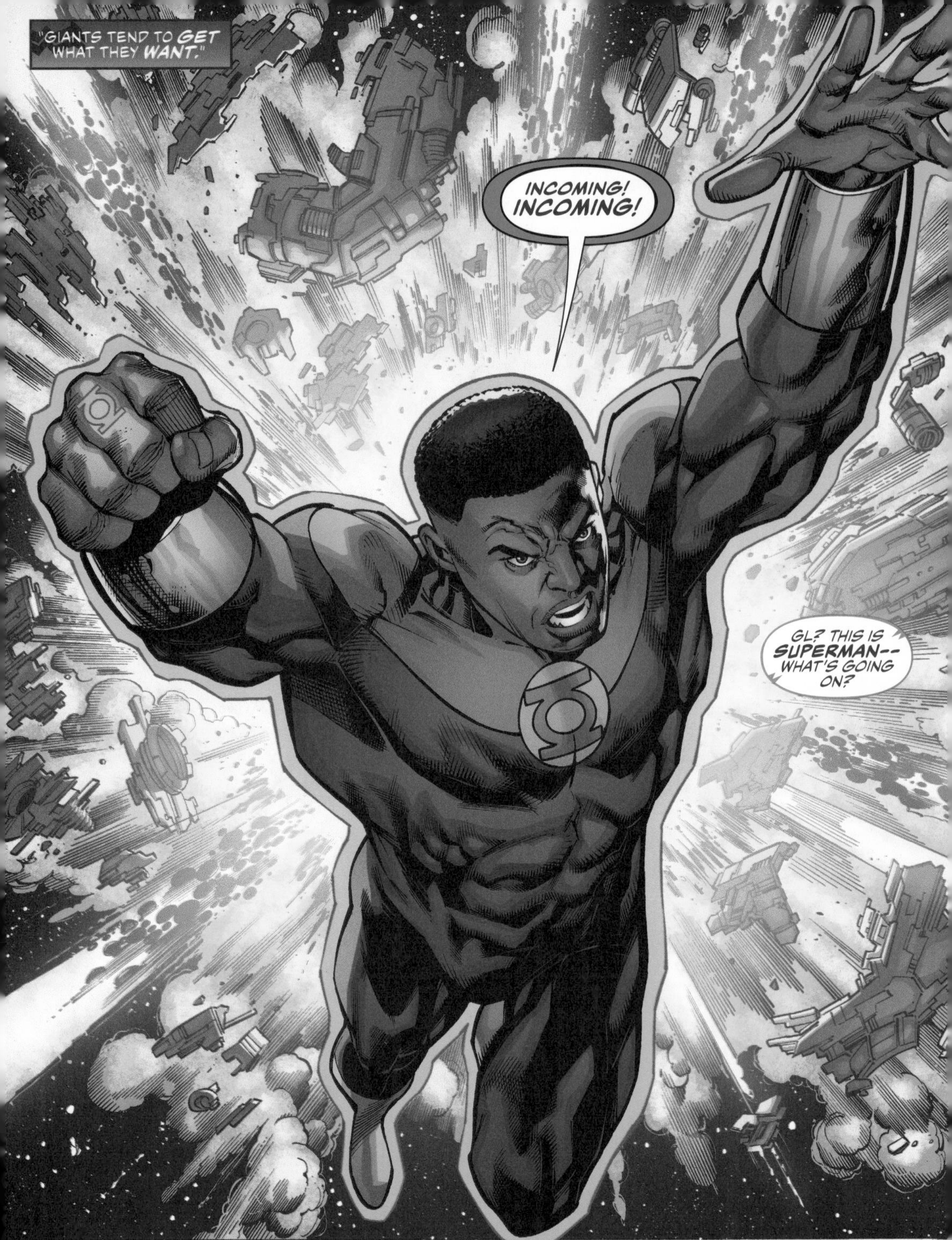
"GIANTS TEND TO GET WHAT THEY WANT."
INCOMING! INCOMING!
GL? THIS IS SUPERMAN-- WHAT'S GOING ON?

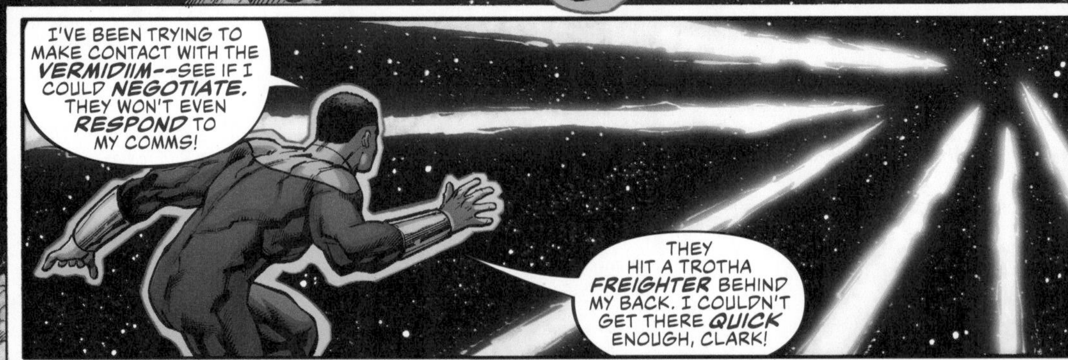
I'VE BEEN TRYING TO MAKE CONTACT WITH THE VERMIDIIM--SEE IF I COULD NEGOTIATE. THEY WON'T EVEN RESPOND TO MY COMMS!
THEY HIT A TROTHA FREIGHTER BEHIND MY BACK. I COULDN'T GET THERE QUICK ENOUGH, CLARK!

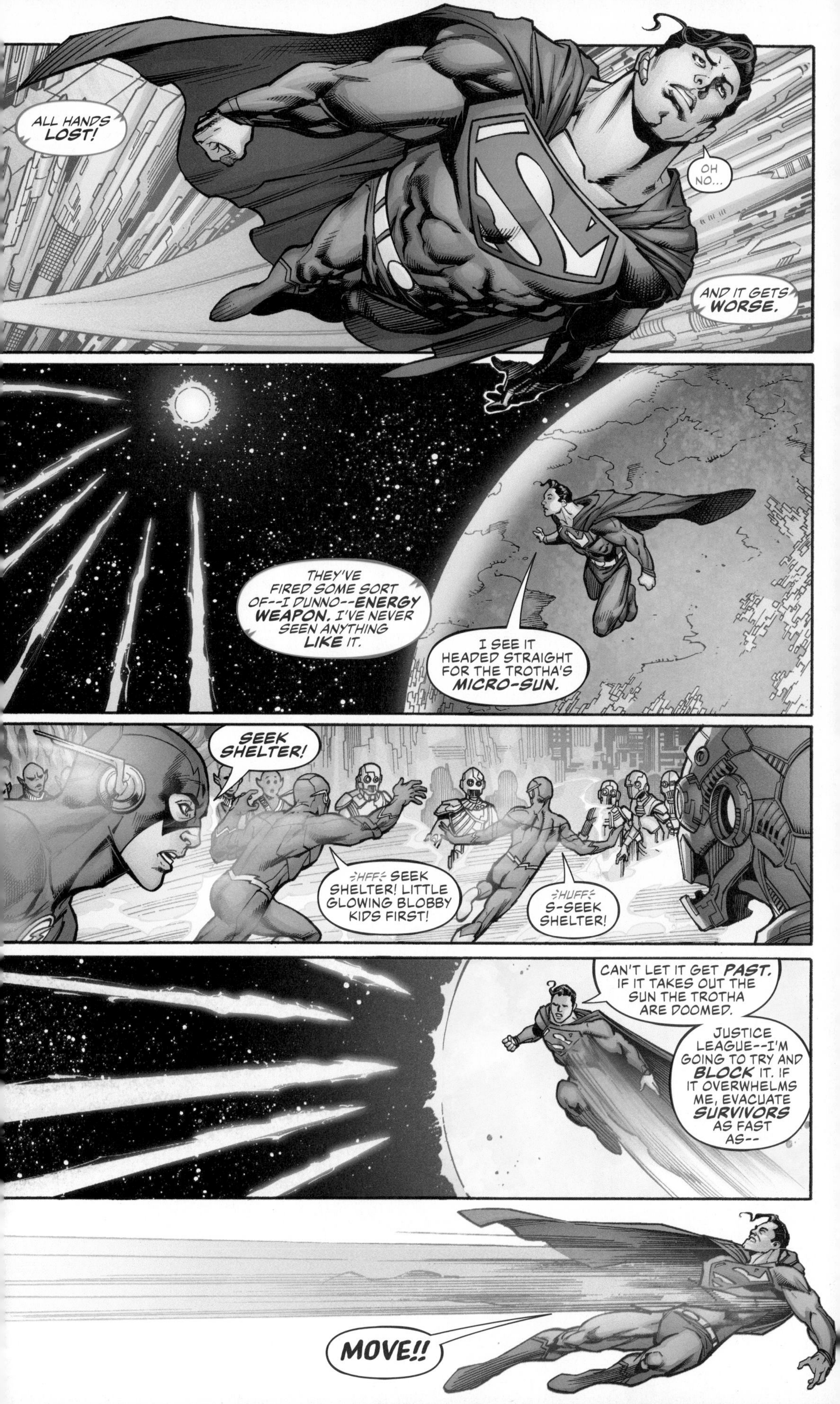
ALL HANDS LOST!
OH NO...
AND IT GETS WORSE.
THEY'VE FIRED SOME SORT OF--I DUNNO--ENERGY WEAPON. I'VE NEVER SEEN ANYTHING LIKE IT.
I SEE IT HEADED STRAIGHT FOR THE TROTHA'S MICRO-SUN.
SEEK SHELTER!
HFF SEEK SHELTER! LITTLE GLOWING BLOBBY KIDS FIRST!
HUFF S-SEEK SHELTER!
CAN'T LET IT GET PAST. IF IT TAKES OUT THE SUN THE TROTHA ARE DOOMED.
JUSTICE LEAGUE--I'M GOING TO TRY AND BLOCK IT. IF IT OVERWHELMS ME, EVACUATE SURVIVORS AS FAST AS--
MOVE!!

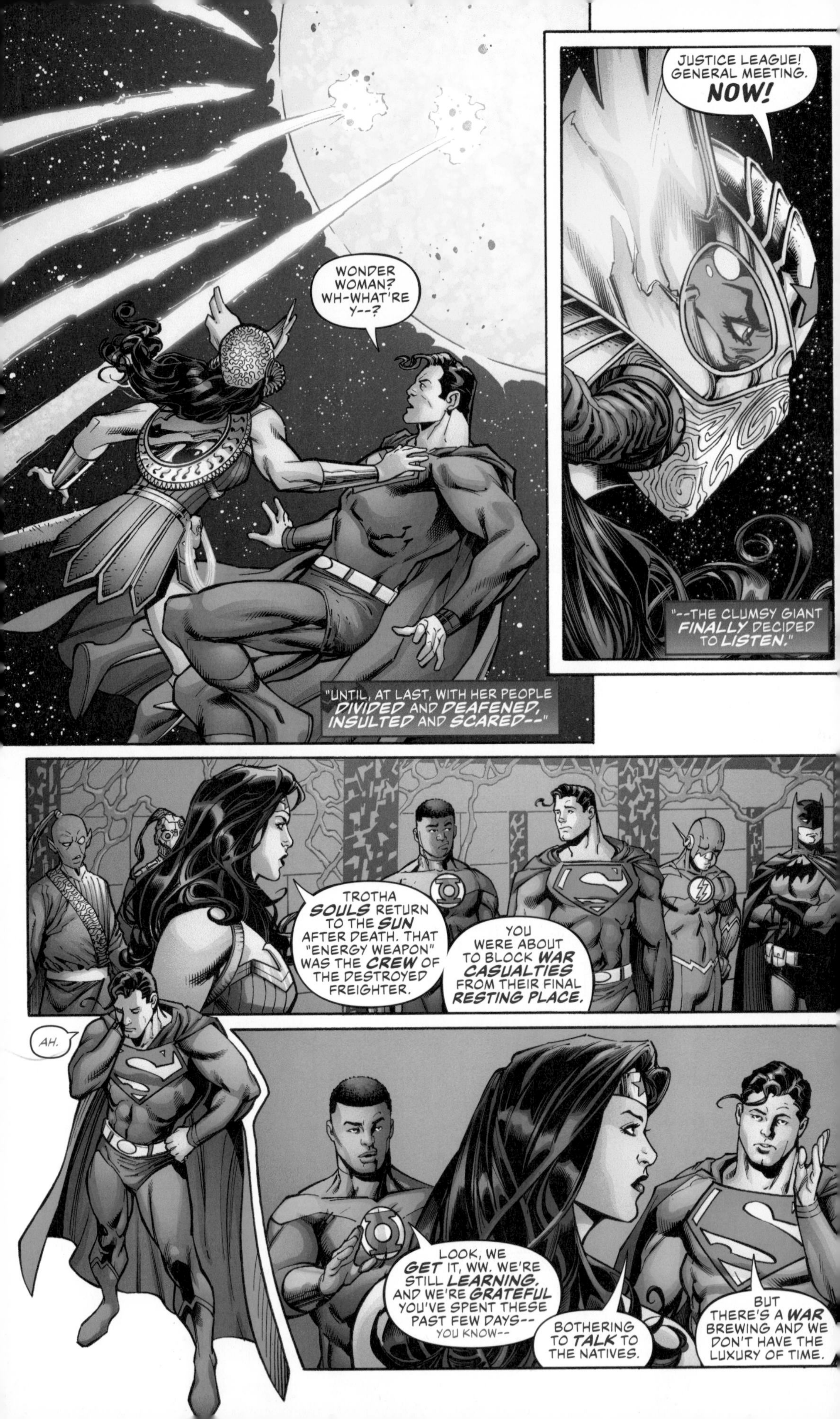
WONDER WOMAN? WH-WHAT'RE Y--?
"UNTIL, AT LAST, WITH HER PEOPLE DIVIDED AND DEAFENED, INSULTED AND SCARED--"
JUSTICE LEAGUE! GENERAL MEETING. NOW!
"--THE CLUMSY GIANT FINALLY DECIDED TO LISTEN."
TROTHA SOULS RETURN TO THE SUN AFTER DEATH. THAT "ENERGY WEAPON" WAS THE CREW OF THE DESTROYED FREIGHTER.
YOU WERE ABOUT TO BLOCK WAR CASUALTIES FROM THEIR FINAL RESTING PLACE.
AH.
LOOK, WE GET IT, WW. WE'RE STILL LEARNING. AND WE'RE GRATEFUL YOU'VE SPENT THESE PAST FEW DAYS-- YOU KNOW--
BOTHERING TO TALK TO THE NATIVES.
BUT THERE'S A WAR BREWING AND WE DON'T HAVE THE LUXURY OF TIME.

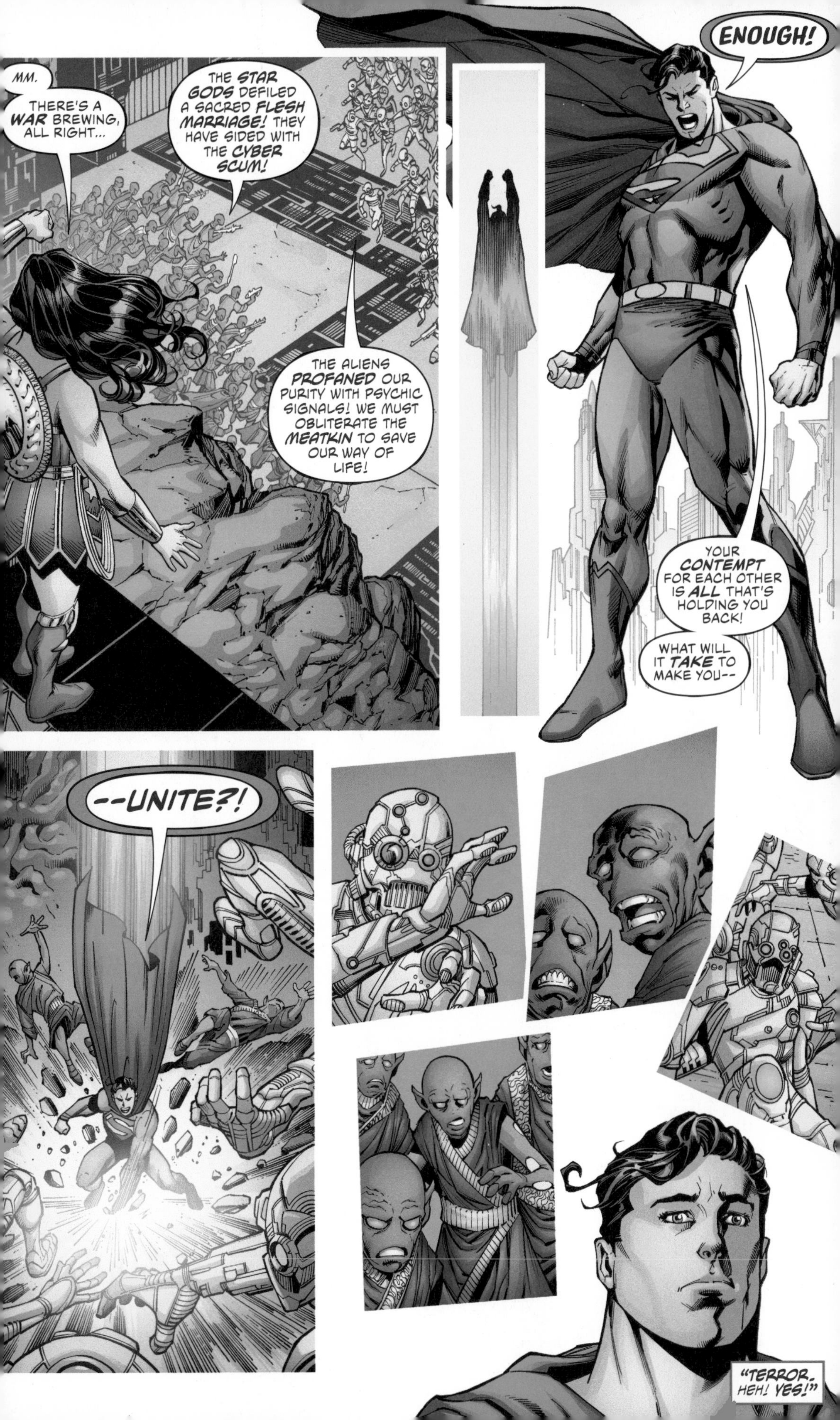
ENOUGH!
MM.
THERE'S A WAR BREWING, ALL RIGHT...
THE STAR GODS DEFILED A SACRED FLESH MARRIAGE! THEY HAVE SIDED WITH THE CYBER SCUM!
THE ALIENS PROFANED OUR PURITY WITH PSYCHIC SIGNALS! WE MUST OBLITERATE THE MEATKIN TO SAVE OUR WAY OF LIFE!
YOUR CONTEMPT FOR EACH OTHER IS ALL THAT'S HOLDING YOU BACK!
WHAT WILL IT TAKE TO MAKE YOU--
--UNITE?!
"TERROR. HEH! YES!"

Batman (off-panel): IN THEIR *FEAR* THEY ANSWERED THE QUESTION.

Wonder Woman: DO YOU MIND? I'M TRYING TO TELL A STORY.

Wonder Woman: YOU SEE, EVEN AFTER SEEKING *COUNSEL,* ISCHYRIA HAD NO IDEA HOW TO *HELP* HER PEOPLE. DO YOU KNOW *WHY,* BATMAN?

Batman: ASTONISH ME.

Wonder Woman: BECAUSE SHE HADN'T ASKED THE RIGHT *QUESTIONS.*

Wonder Woman: EMPRESS...WOULD YOU CARE TO *GUESS* WHAT HAPPENED TO THE GIANTESS, IN THE END?

Empress: HMPH. IT'S A *PREDICTABLE* MYTH, EVEN FROM A CREATURE AS *ALIEN* AS YOU.

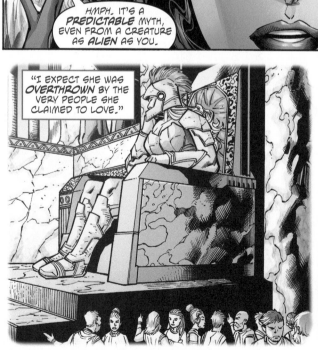

Wonder Woman: "I EXPECT SHE WAS *OVERTHROWN* BY THE VERY PEOPLE SHE CLAIMED TO LOVE."

Batman: MM.

Batman: PREDICTABLE...

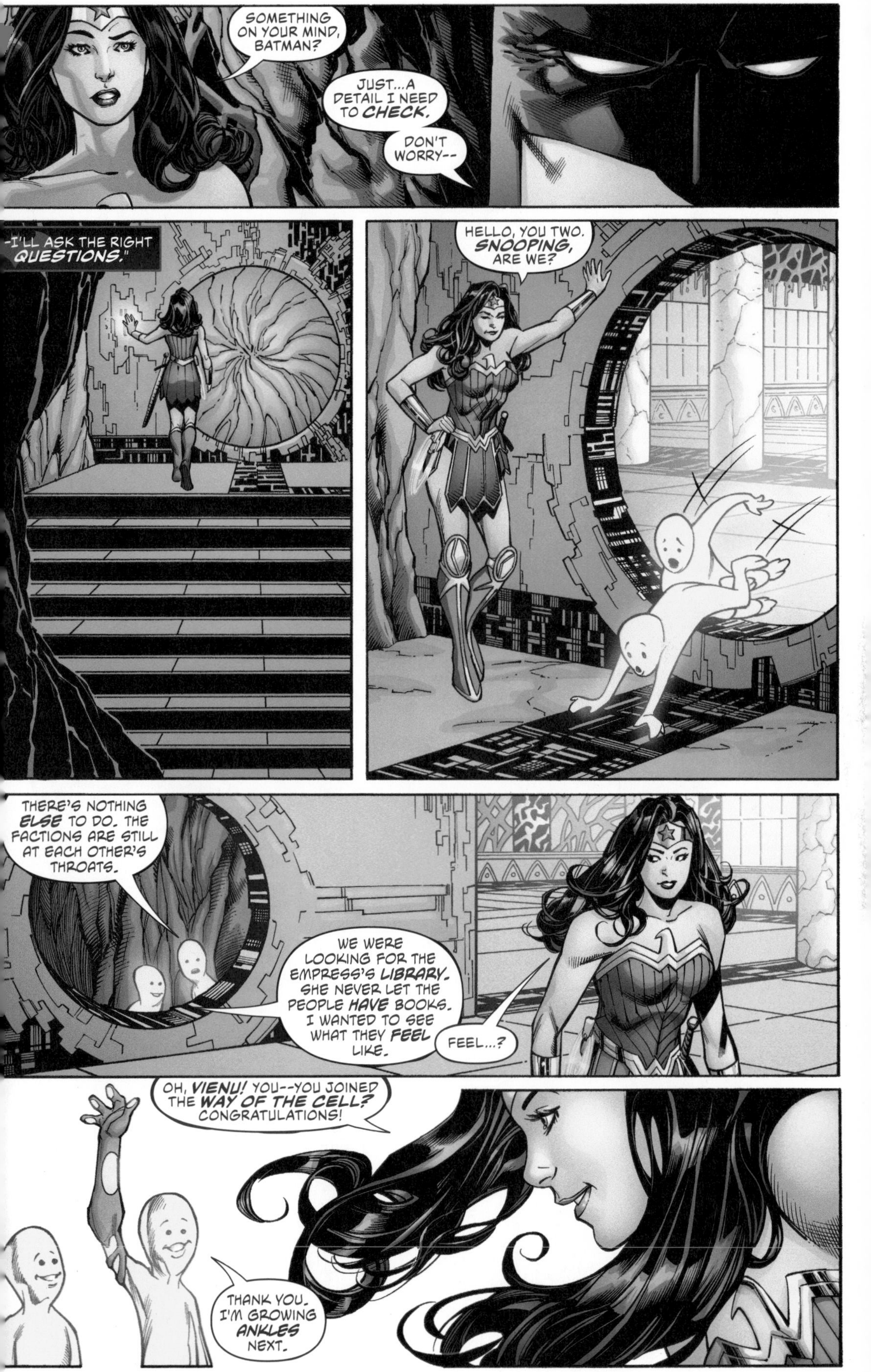
SOMETHING ON YOUR MIND, BATMAN?
JUST...A DETAIL I NEED TO CHECK.
DON'T WORRY--
-I'LL ASK THE RIGHT QUESTIONS."
HELLO, YOU TWO. SNOOPING, ARE WE?
THERE'S NOTHING ELSE TO DO. THE FACTIONS ARE STILL AT EACH OTHER'S THROATS.
WE WERE LOOKING FOR THE EMPRESS'S LIBRARY. SHE NEVER LET THE PEOPLE HAVE BOOKS. I WANTED TO SEE WHAT THEY FEEL LIKE.
FEEL...?
OH, VIENU! YOU--YOU JOINED THE WAY OF THE CELL? CONGRATULATIONS!
THANK YOU. I'M GROWING ANKLES NEXT.

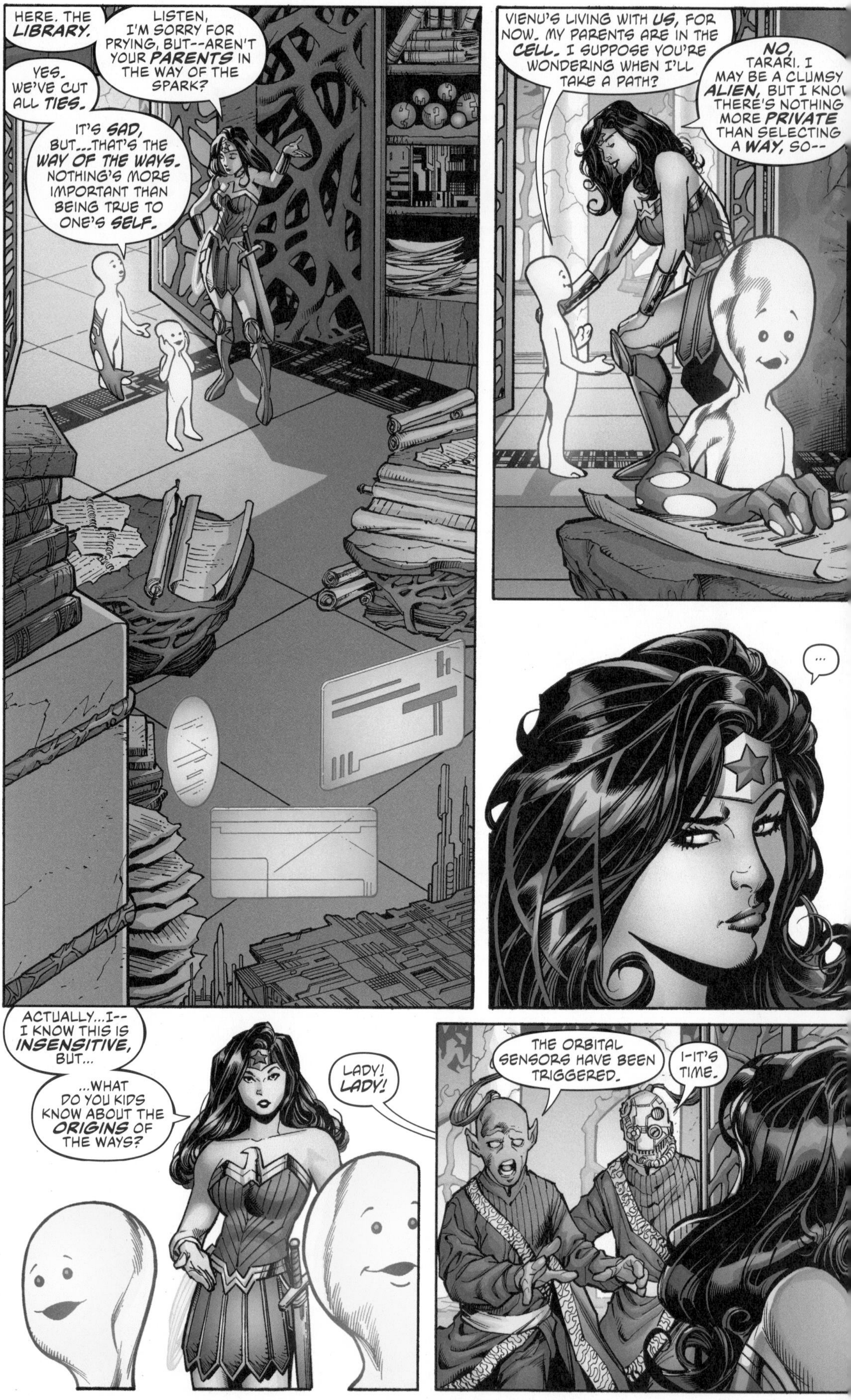
HERE. THE LIBRARY.
LISTEN, I'M SORRY FOR PRYING, BUT--AREN'T YOUR PARENTS IN THE WAY OF THE SPARK?
YES. WE'VE CUT ALL TIES.
IT'S SAD, BUT...THAT'S THE WAY OF THE WAYS. NOTHING'S MORE IMPORTANT THAN BEING TRUE TO ONE'S SELF.
VIENU'S LIVING WITH US, FOR NOW. MY PARENTS ARE IN THE CELL. I SUPPOSE YOU'RE WONDERING WHEN I'LL TAKE A PATH?
NO, TARARI. I MAY BE A CLUMSY ALIEN, BUT I KNOW THERE'S NOTHING MORE PRIVATE THAN SELECTING A WAY, SO--
...
ACTUALLY...I-- I KNOW THIS IS INSENSITIVE, BUT...
...WHAT DO YOU KIDS KNOW ABOUT THE ORIGINS OF THE WAYS?
LADY! LADY!
THE ORBITAL SENSORS HAVE BEEN TRIGGERED.
I-IT'S TIME.

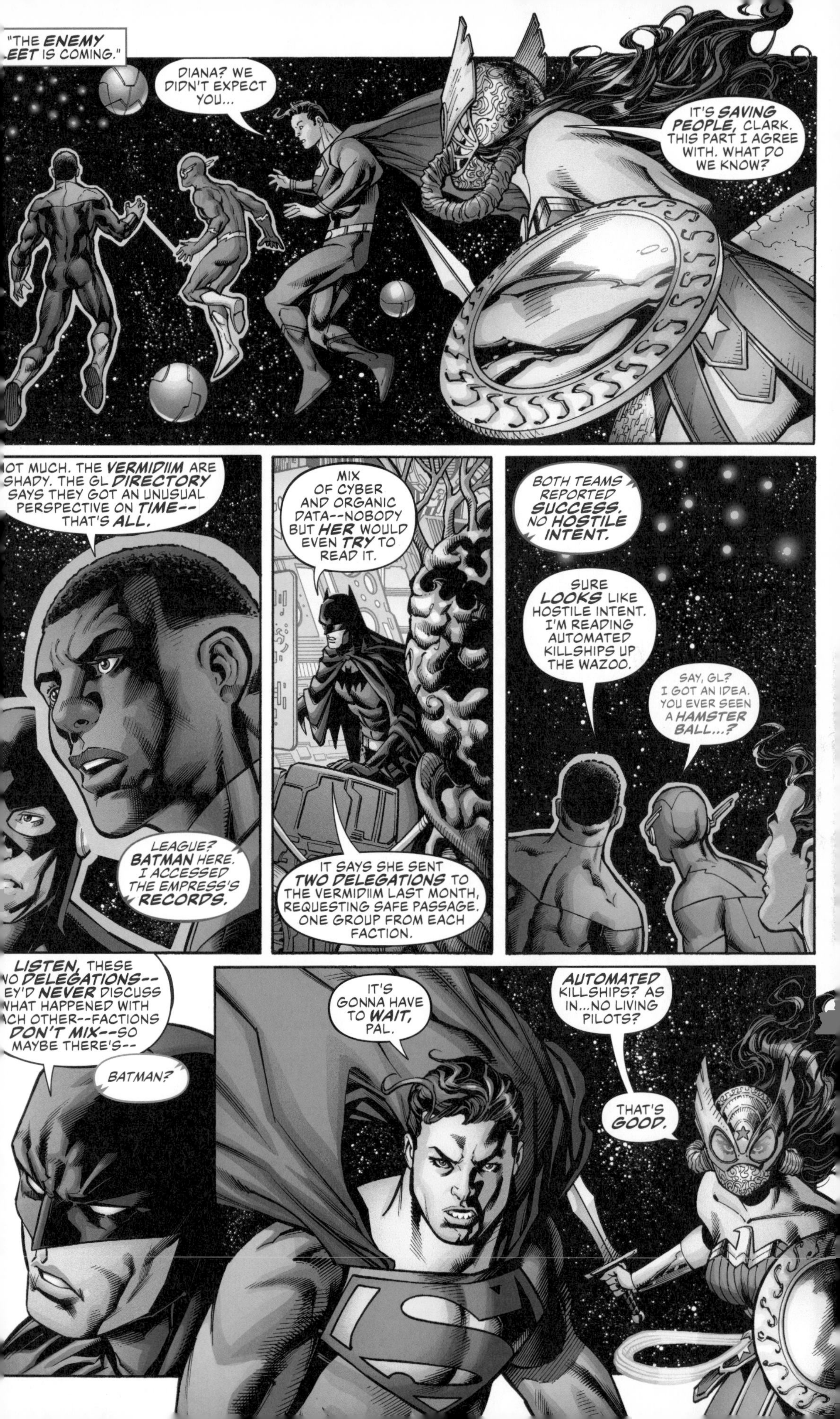
"THE ENEMY
EET IS COMING."
DIANA? WE DIDN'T EXPECT YOU...
IT'S SAVING PEOPLE, CLARK. THIS PART I AGREE WITH. WHAT DO WE KNOW?
OT MUCH. THE VERMIDIIM ARE SHADY. THE GL DIRECTORY SAYS THEY GOT AN UNUSUAL PERSPECTIVE ON TIME-- THAT'S ALL.
LEAGUE? BATMAN HERE. I ACCESSED THE EMPRESS'S RECORDS.
MIX OF CYBER AND ORGANIC DATA--NOBODY BUT HER WOULD EVEN TRY TO READ IT.
IT SAYS SHE SENT TWO DELEGATIONS TO THE VERMIDIIM LAST MONTH, REQUESTING SAFE PASSAGE. ONE GROUP FROM EACH FACTION.
BOTH TEAMS REPORTED SUCCESS. NO HOSTILE INTENT.
SURE LOOKS LIKE HOSTILE INTENT. I'M READING AUTOMATED KILLSHIPS UP THE WAZOO.
SAY, GL? I GOT AN IDEA. YOU EVER SEEN A HAMSTER BALL...?
LISTEN, THESE NO DELEGATIONS-- EY'D NEVER DISCUSS WHAT HAPPENED WITH ACH OTHER--FACTIONS DON'T MIX--SO MAYBE THERE'S--
BATMAN?
IT'S GONNA HAVE TO WAIT, PAL.
AUTOMATED KILLSHIPS? AS IN...NO LIVING PILOTS?
THAT'S GOOD.

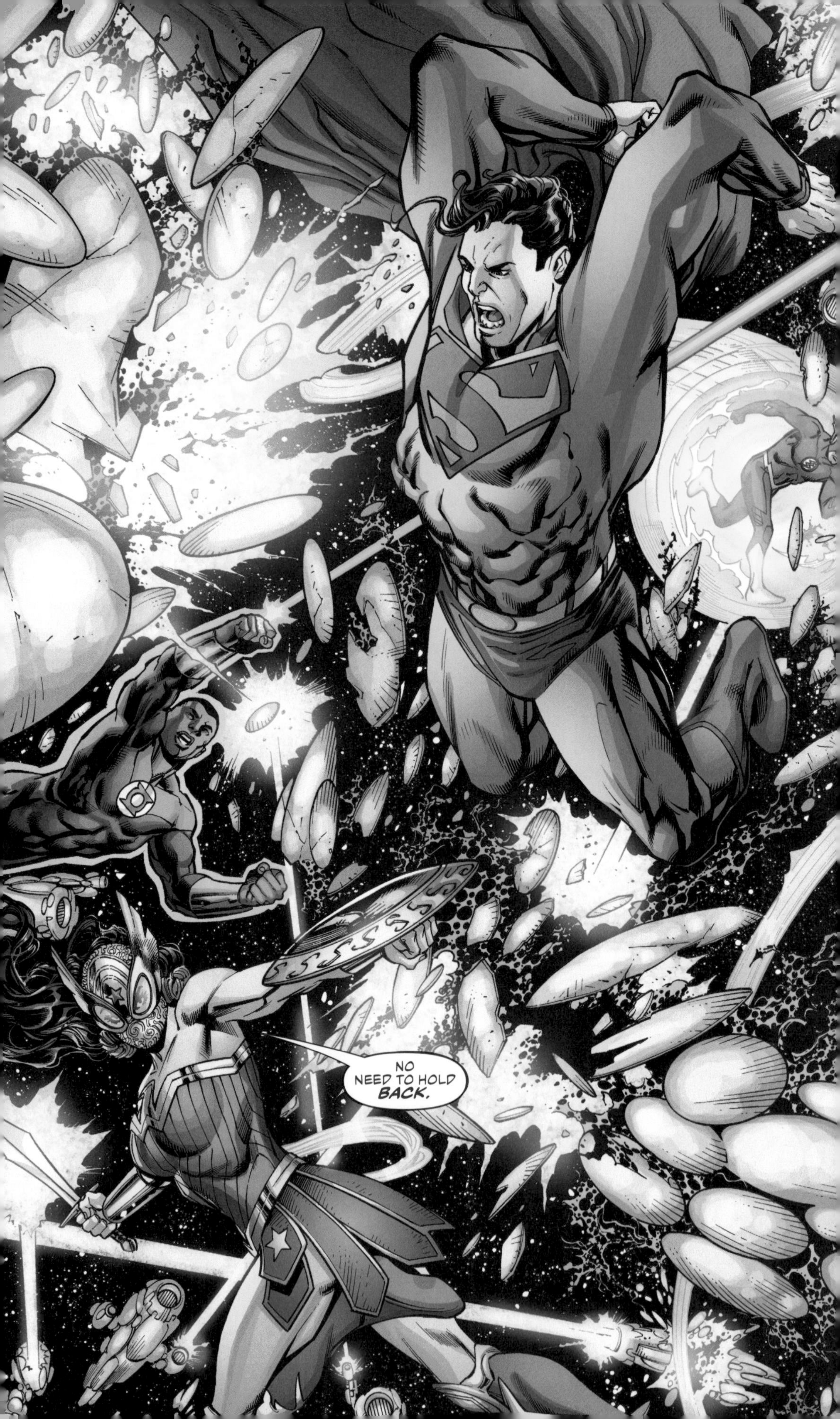
NO NEED TO HOLD BACK.

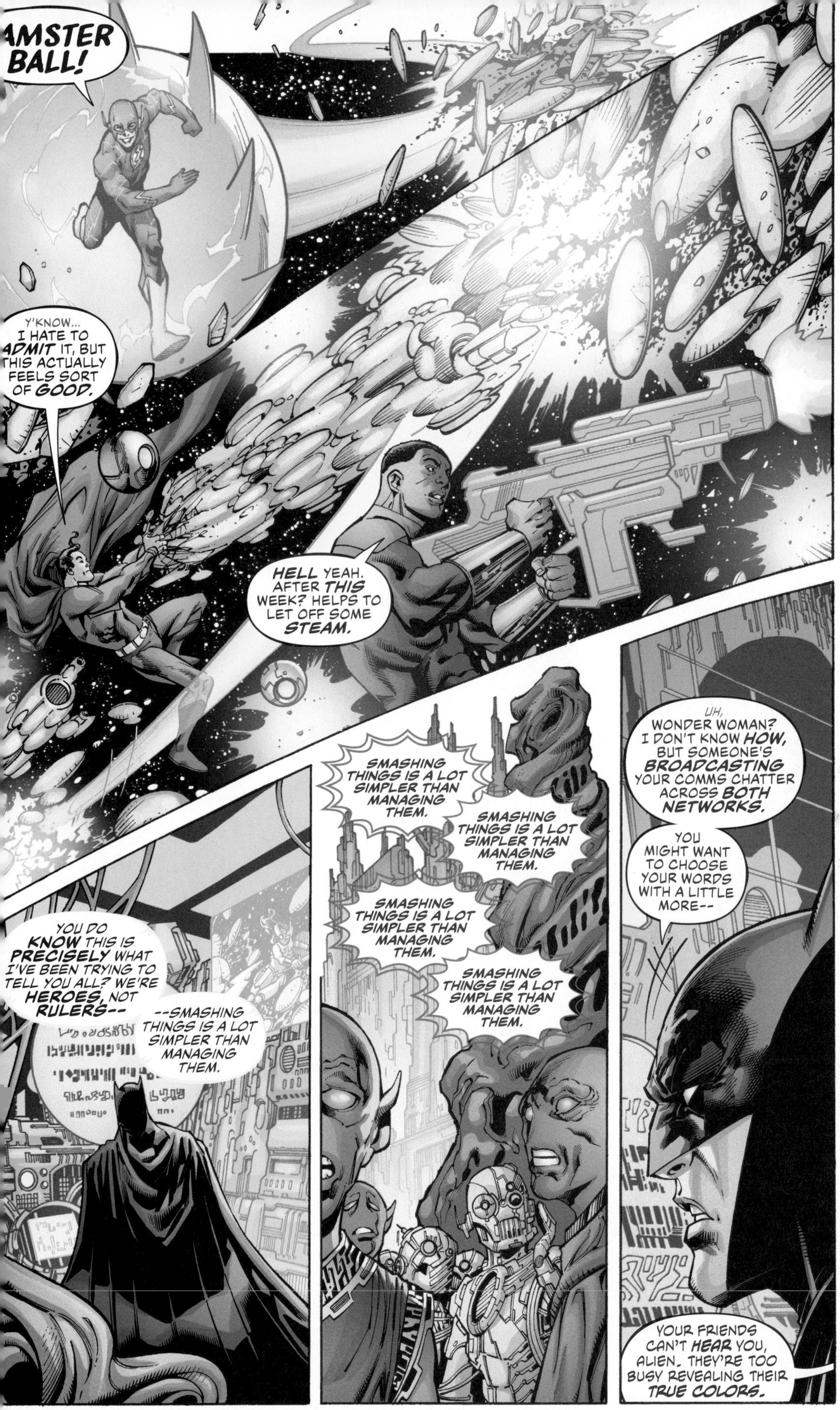
AMSTER BALL!
Y'KNOW... I HATE TO ADMIT IT, BUT THIS ACTUALLY FEELS SORT OF GOOD.
HELL YEAH. AFTER THIS WEEK? HELPS TO LET OFF SOME STEAM.
YOU DO KNOW THIS IS PRECISELY WHAT I'VE BEEN TRYING TO TELL YOU ALL? WE'RE HEROES, NOT RULERS--
--SMASHING THINGS IS A LOT SIMPLER THAN MANAGING THEM.
SMASHING THINGS IS A LOT SIMPLER THAN MANAGING THEM.
SMASHING THINGS IS A LOT SIMPLER THAN MANAGING THEM.
SMASHING THINGS IS A LOT SIMPLER THAN MANAGING THEM.
SMASHING THINGS IS A LOT SIMPLER THAN MANAGING THEM.
UH, WONDER WOMAN? I DON'T KNOW HOW, BUT SOMEONE'S BROADCASTING YOUR COMMS CHATTER ACROSS BOTH NETWORKS.
YOU MIGHT WANT TO CHOOSE YOUR WORDS WITH A LITTLE MORE--
YOUR FRIENDS CAN'T HEAR YOU, ALIEN. THEY'RE TOO BUSY REVEALING THEIR TRUE COLORS.

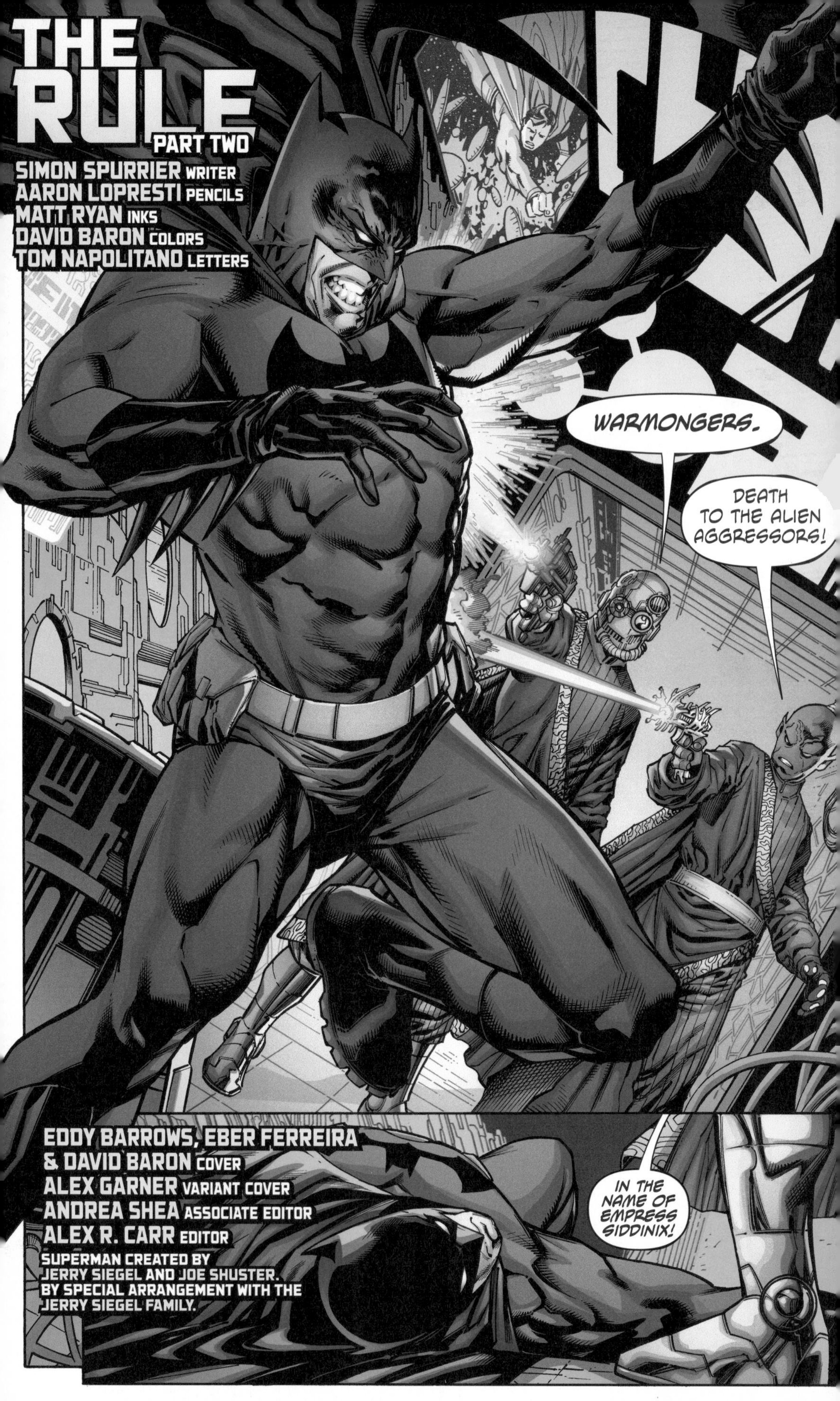
THE RULE
PART TWO
SIMON SPURRIER WRITER
AARON LOPRESTI PENCILS
MATT RYAN INKS
DAVID BARON COLORS
TOM NAPOLITANO LETTERS
WARMONGERS.
DEATH TO THE ALIEN AGGRESSORS!
EDDY BARROWS, EBER FERREIRA & DAVID BARON COVER
ALEX GARNER VARIANT COVER
ANDREA SHEA ASSOCIATE EDITOR
ALEX R. CARR EDITOR
SUPERMAN CREATED BY JERRY SIEGEL AND JOE SHUSTER. BY SPECIAL ARRANGEMENT WITH THE JERRY SIEGEL FAMILY.
IN THE NAME OF EMPRESS SIDDINIX!

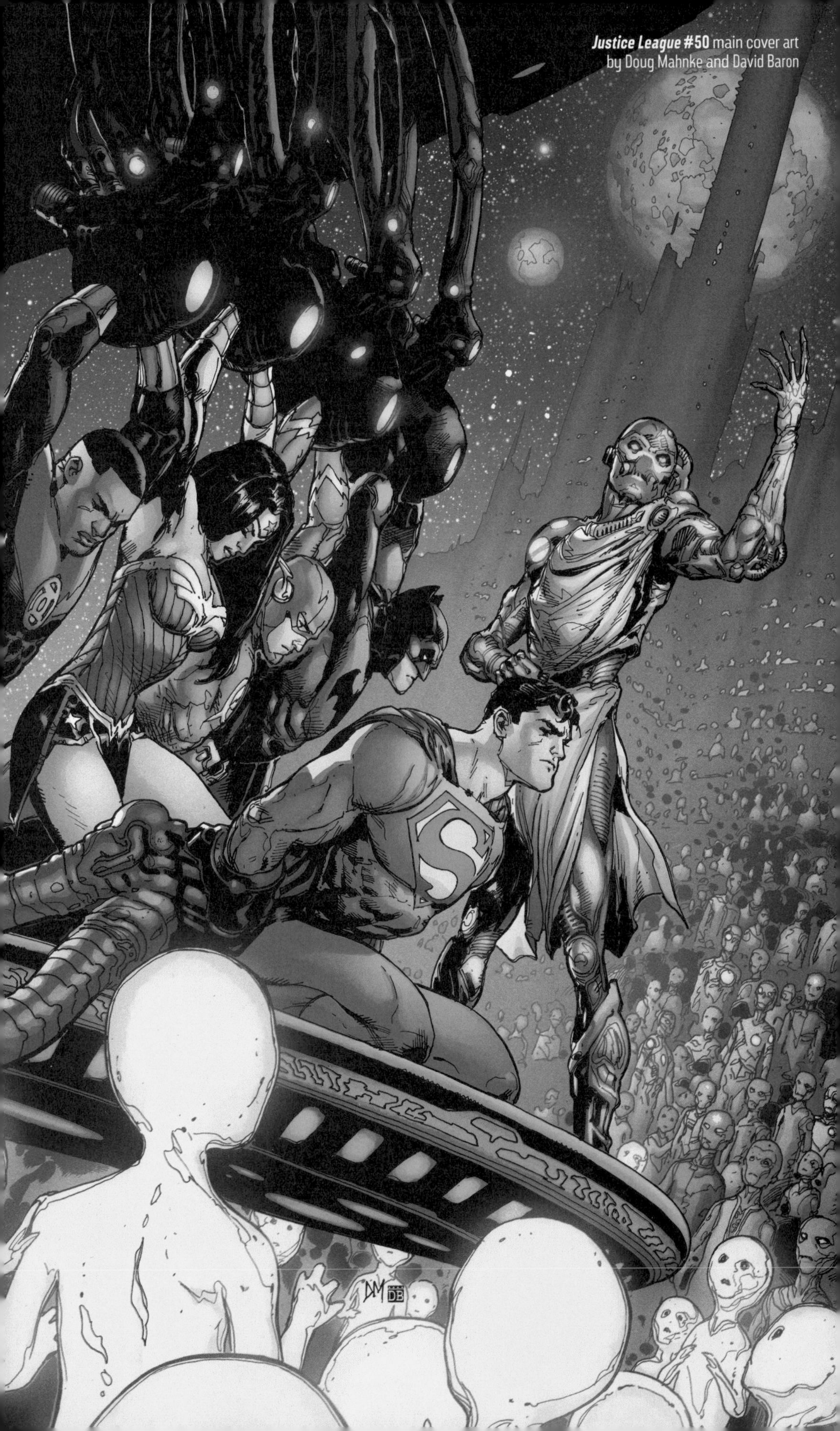

***Justice League* #50** main cover art
by Doug Mahnke and David Baron

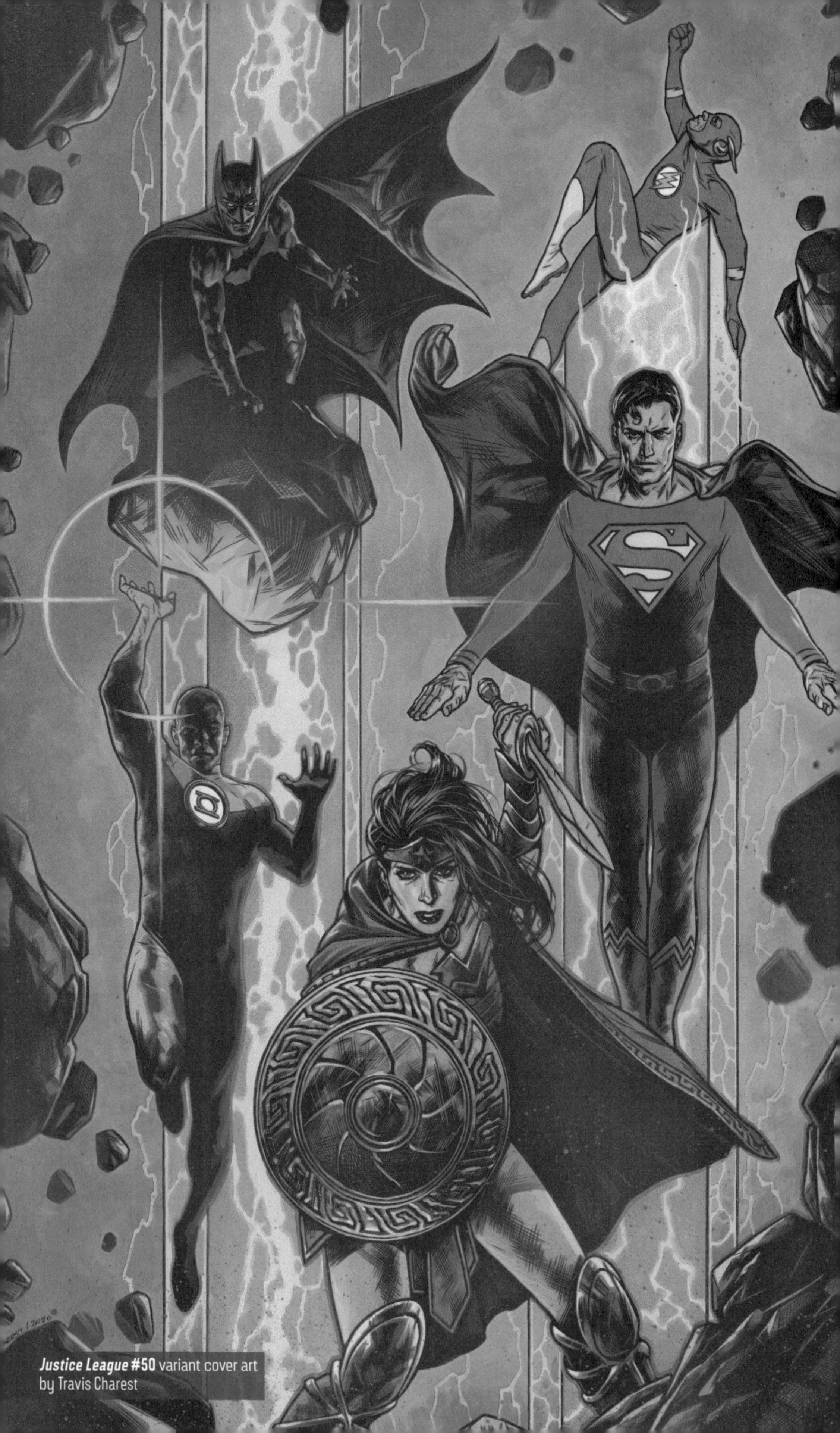

***Justice League* #50** variant cover art
by Travis Charest

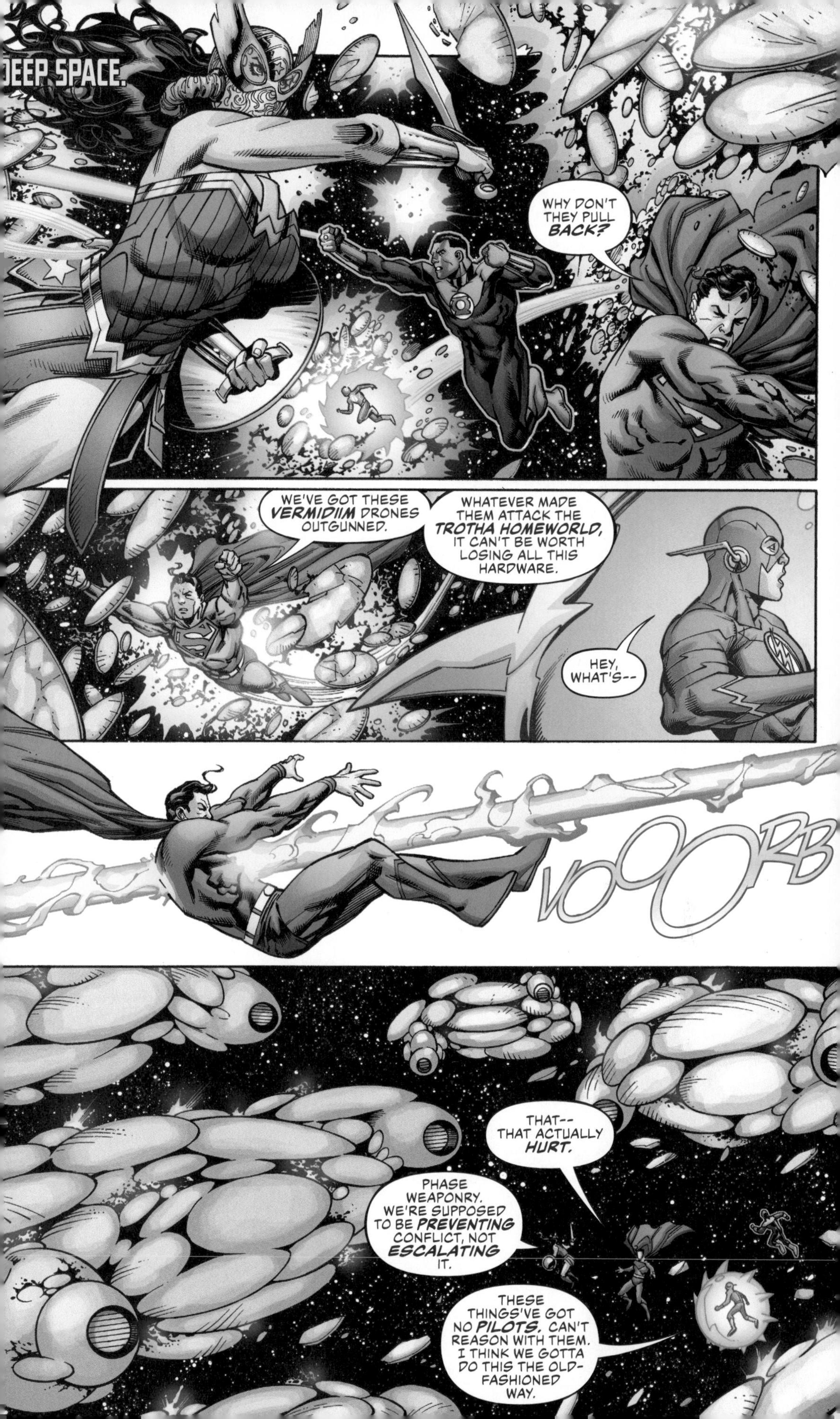
DEEP SPACE.
WHY DON'T THEY PULL BACK?
WE'VE GOT THESE VERMIDIIM DRONES OUTGUNNED.
WHATEVER MADE THEM ATTACK THE TROTHA HOMEWORLD, IT CAN'T BE WORTH LOSING ALL THIS HARDWARE.
HEY, WHAT'S--
VOOOORB
THAT-- THAT ACTUALLY HURT.
PHASE WEAPONRY. WE'RE SUPPOSED TO BE PREVENTING CONFLICT, NOT ESCALATING IT.
THESE THINGS'VE GOT NO PILOTS. CAN'T REASON WITH THEM. I THINK WE GOTTA DO THIS THE OLD-FASHIONED WAY.

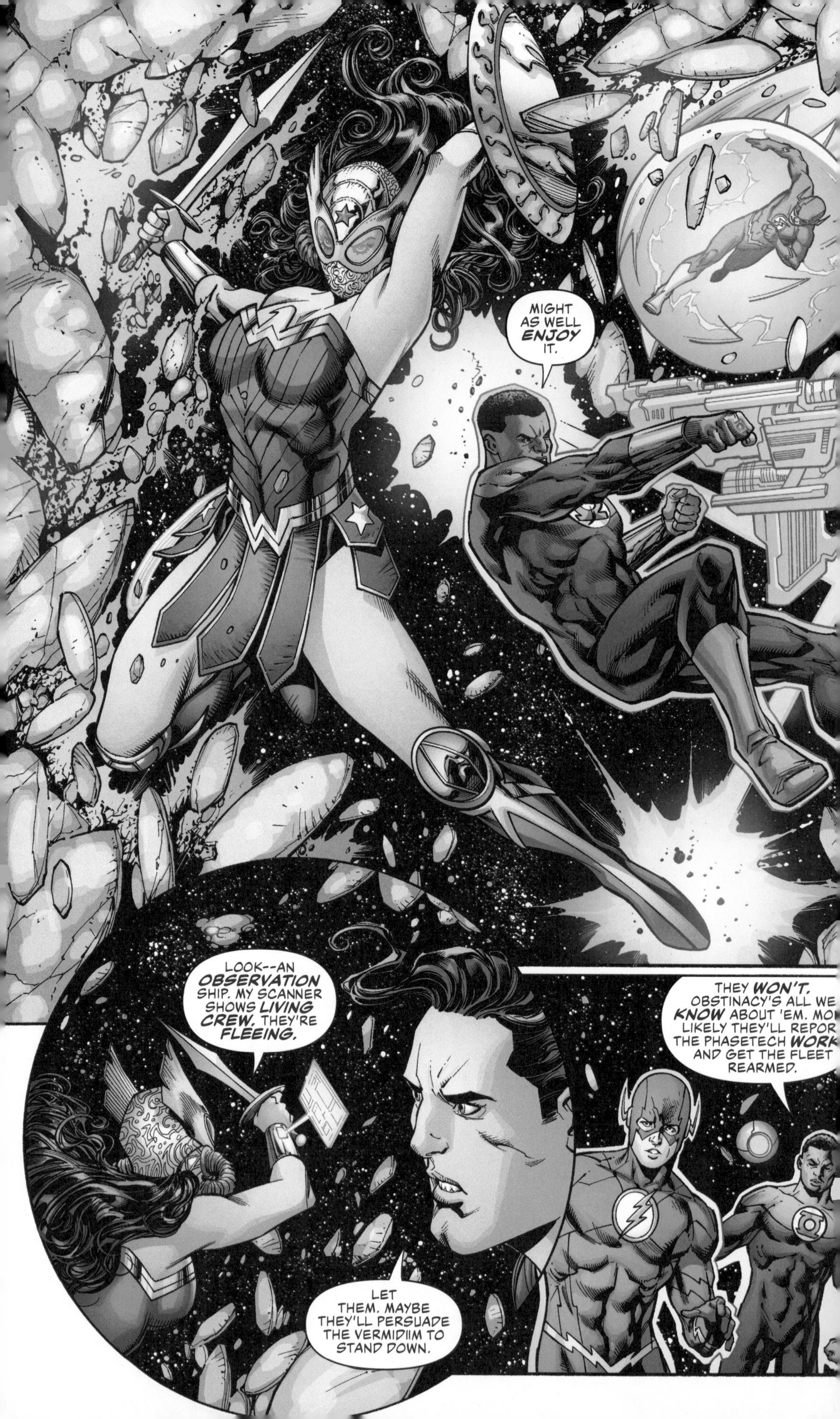
MIGHT AS WELL ENJOY IT.
LOOK--AN OBSERVATION SHIP. MY SCANNER SHOWS LIVING CREW. THEY'RE FLEEING.
LET THEM. MAYBE THEY'LL PERSUADE THE VERMIDIIM TO STAND DOWN.
THEY WON'T. OBSTINACY'S ALL WE KNOW ABOUT 'EM. MO LIKELY THEY'LL REPOR THE PHASETECH WORK AND GET THE FLEET REARMED.

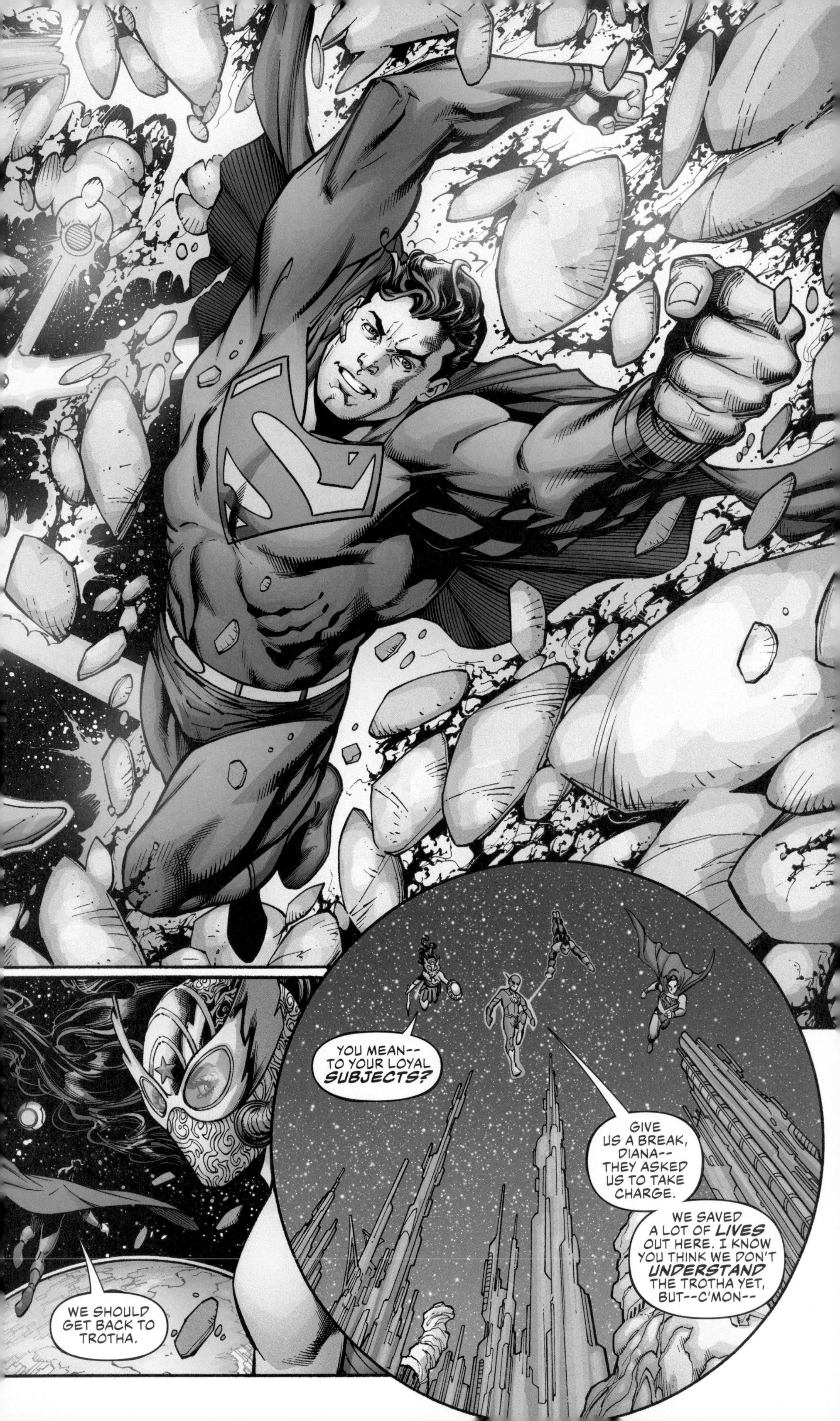
YOU MEAN--
TO YOUR LOYAL
SUBJECTS?
GIVE US A BREAK, DIANA-- THEY ASKED US TO TAKE CHARGE.
WE SAVED A LOT OF LIVES OUT HERE. I KNOW YOU THINK WE DON'T UNDERSTAND THE TROTHA YET, BUT--C'MON--
WE SHOULD GET BACK TO TROTHA.

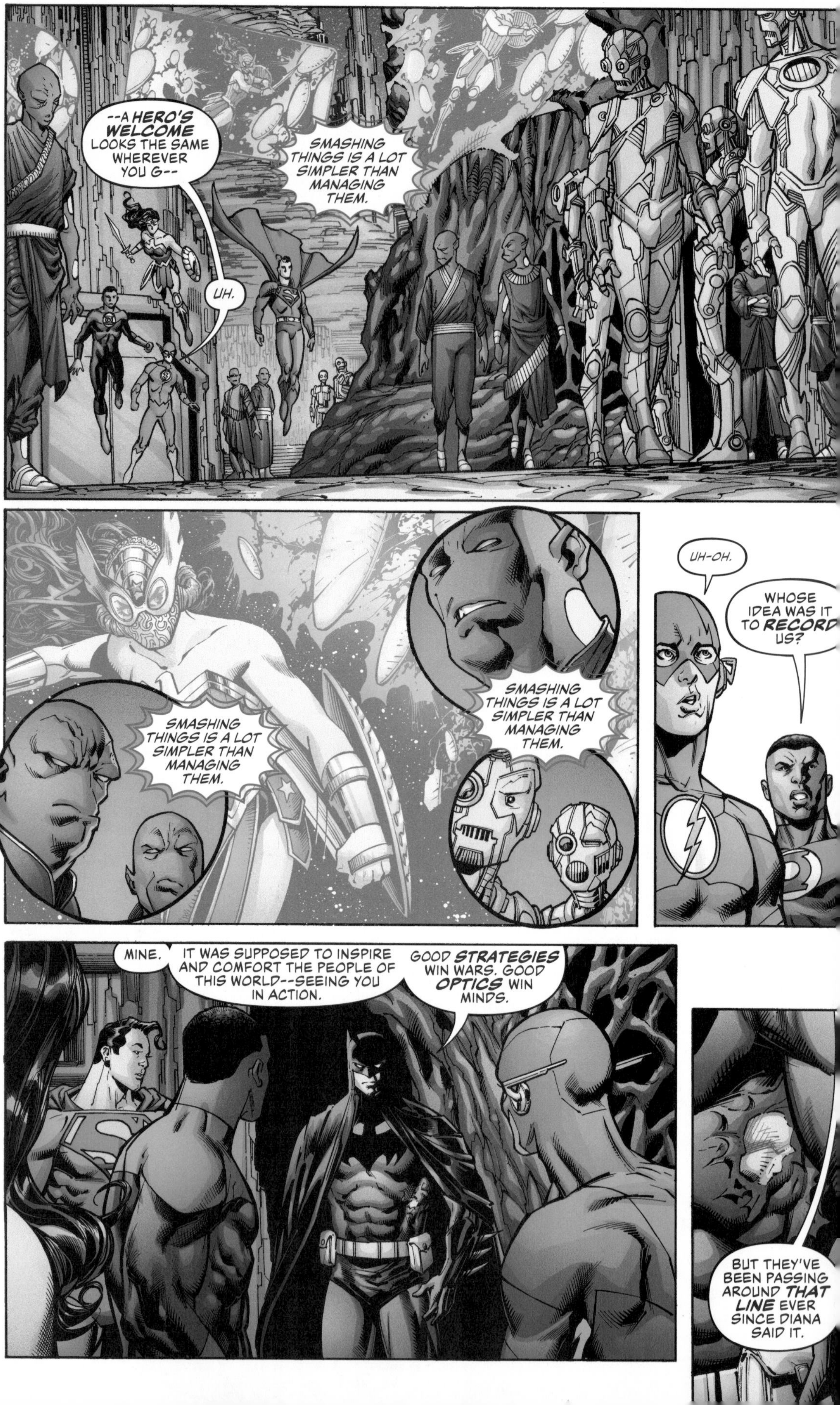
--A HERO'S WELCOME LOOKS THE SAME WHEREVER YOU G--
SMASHING THINGS IS A LOT SIMPLER THAN MANAGING THEM.
UH.
SMASHING THINGS IS A LOT SIMPLER THAN MANAGING THEM.
SMASHING THINGS IS A LOT SIMPLER THAN MANAGING THEM.
UH-OH.
WHOSE IDEA WAS IT TO RECORD US?
MINE.
IT WAS SUPPOSED TO INSPIRE AND COMFORT THE PEOPLE OF THIS WORLD--SEEING YOU IN ACTION.
GOOD STRATEGIES WIN WARS. GOOD OPTICS WIN MINDS.
BUT THEY'VE BEEN PASSING AROUND THAT LINE EVER SINCE DIANA SAID IT.

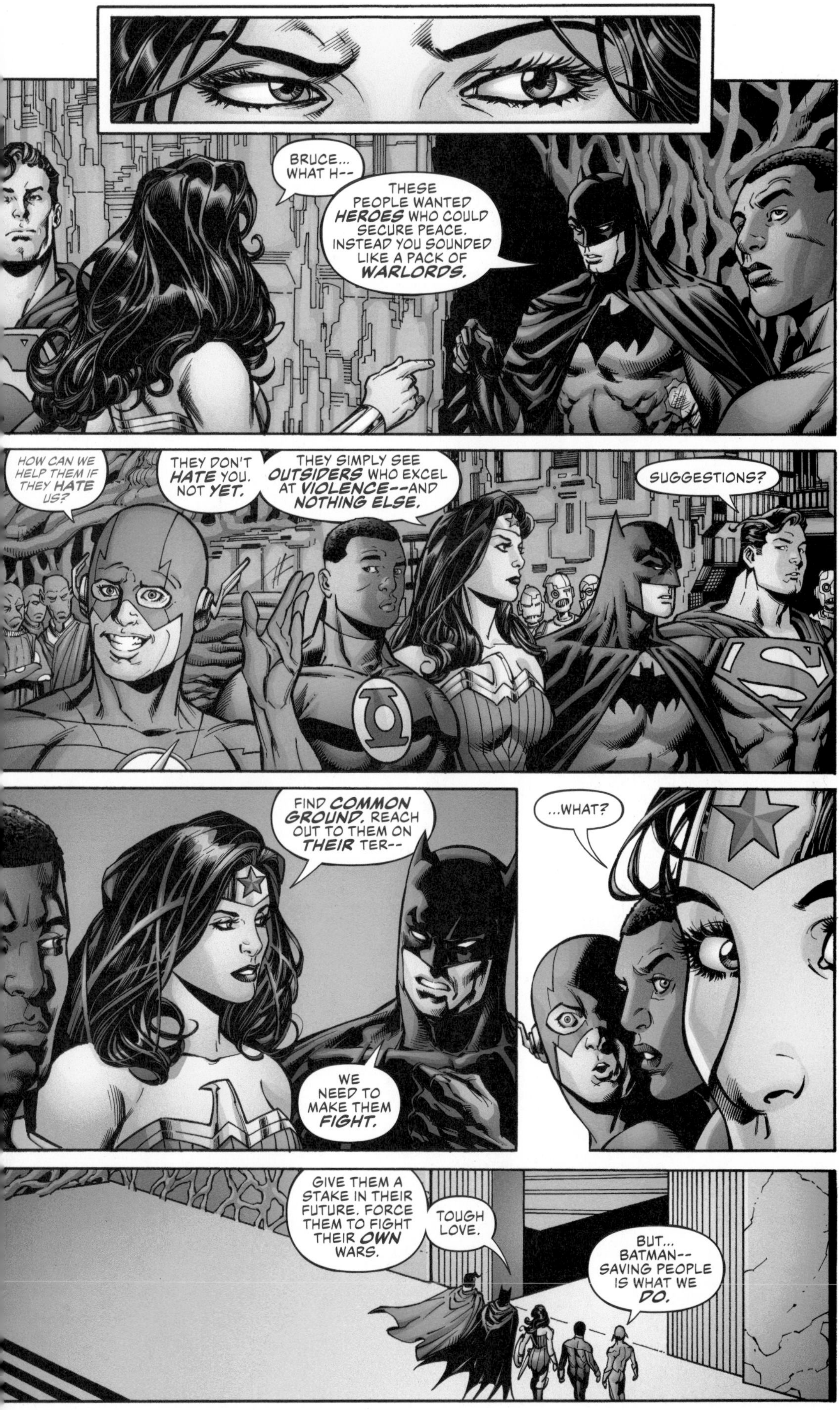
BRUCE... WHAT H--
THESE PEOPLE WANTED HEROES WHO COULD SECURE PEACE. INSTEAD YOU SOUNDED LIKE A PACK OF WARLORDS.
HOW CAN WE HELP THEM IF THEY HATE US?
THEY DON'T HATE YOU. NOT YET.
THEY SIMPLY SEE OUTSIDERS WHO EXCEL AT VIOLENCE--AND NOTHING ELSE.
SUGGESTIONS?
FIND COMMON GROUND. REACH OUT TO THEM ON THEIR TER--
WE NEED TO MAKE THEM FIGHT.
...WHAT?
GIVE THEM A STAKE IN THEIR FUTURE. FORCE THEM TO FIGHT THEIR OWN WARS.
TOUGH LOVE.
BUT... BATMAN-- SAVING PEOPLE IS WHAT WE DO.

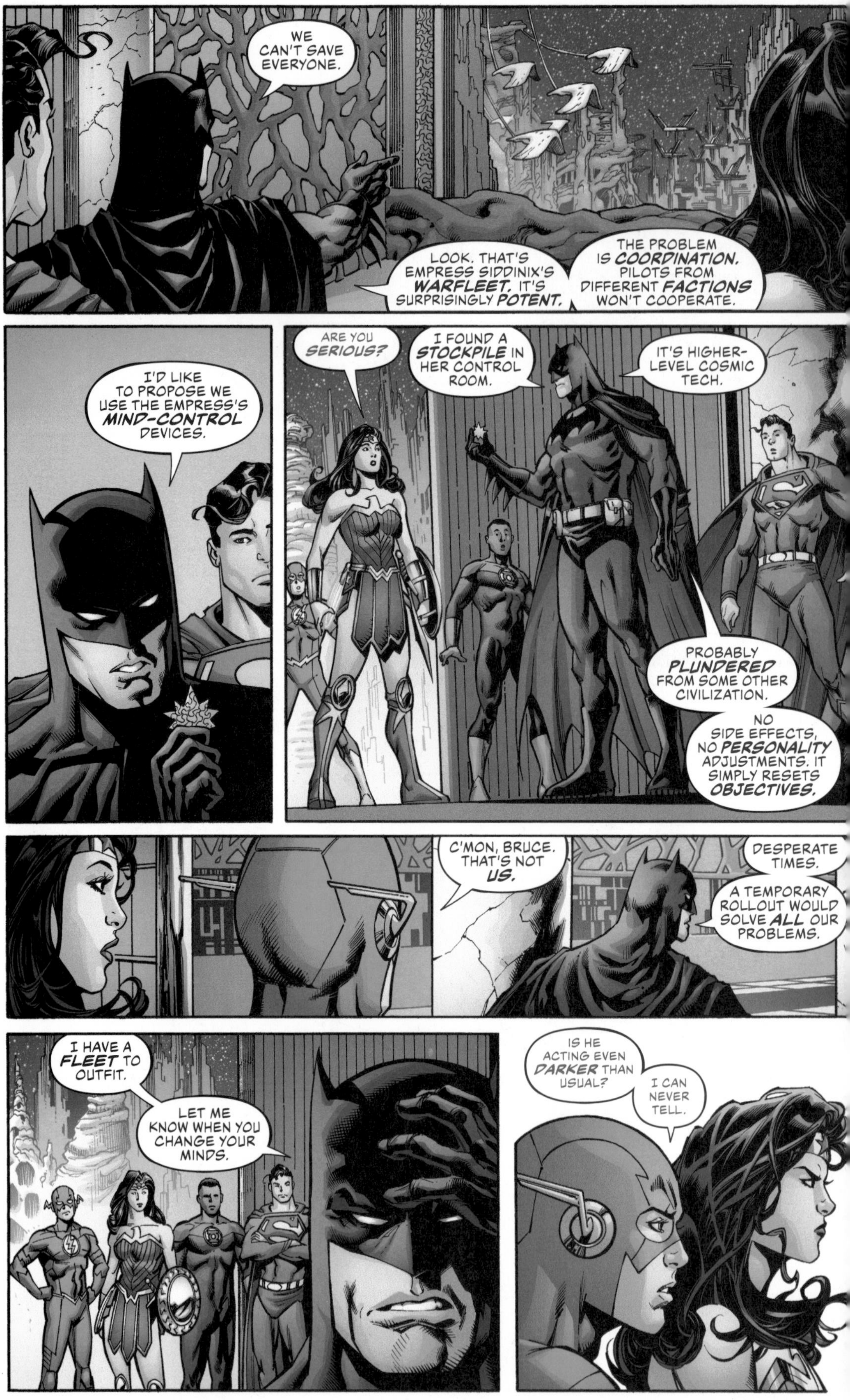

WE CAN'T SAVE EVERYONE.
LOOK. THAT'S EMPRESS SIDDINIX'S WARFLEET. IT'S SURPRISINGLY POTENT.
THE PROBLEM IS COORDINATION. PILOTS FROM DIFFERENT FACTIONS WON'T COOPERATE.
I'D LIKE TO PROPOSE WE USE THE EMPRESS'S MIND-CONTROL DEVICES.
ARE YOU SERIOUS?
I FOUND A STOCKPILE IN HER CONTROL ROOM.
IT'S HIGHER-LEVEL COSMIC TECH.
PROBABLY PLUNDERED FROM SOME OTHER CIVILIZATION.
NO SIDE EFFECTS, NO PERSONALITY ADJUSTMENTS. IT SIMPLY RESETS OBJECTIVES.
C'MON, BRUCE. THAT'S NOT US.
DESPERATE TIMES.
A TEMPORARY ROLLOUT WOULD SOLVE ALL OUR PROBLEMS.
I HAVE A FLEET TO OUTFIT.
LET ME KNOW WHEN YOU CHANGE YOUR MINDS.
IS HE ACTING EVEN DARKER THAN USUAL?
I CAN NEVER TELL.

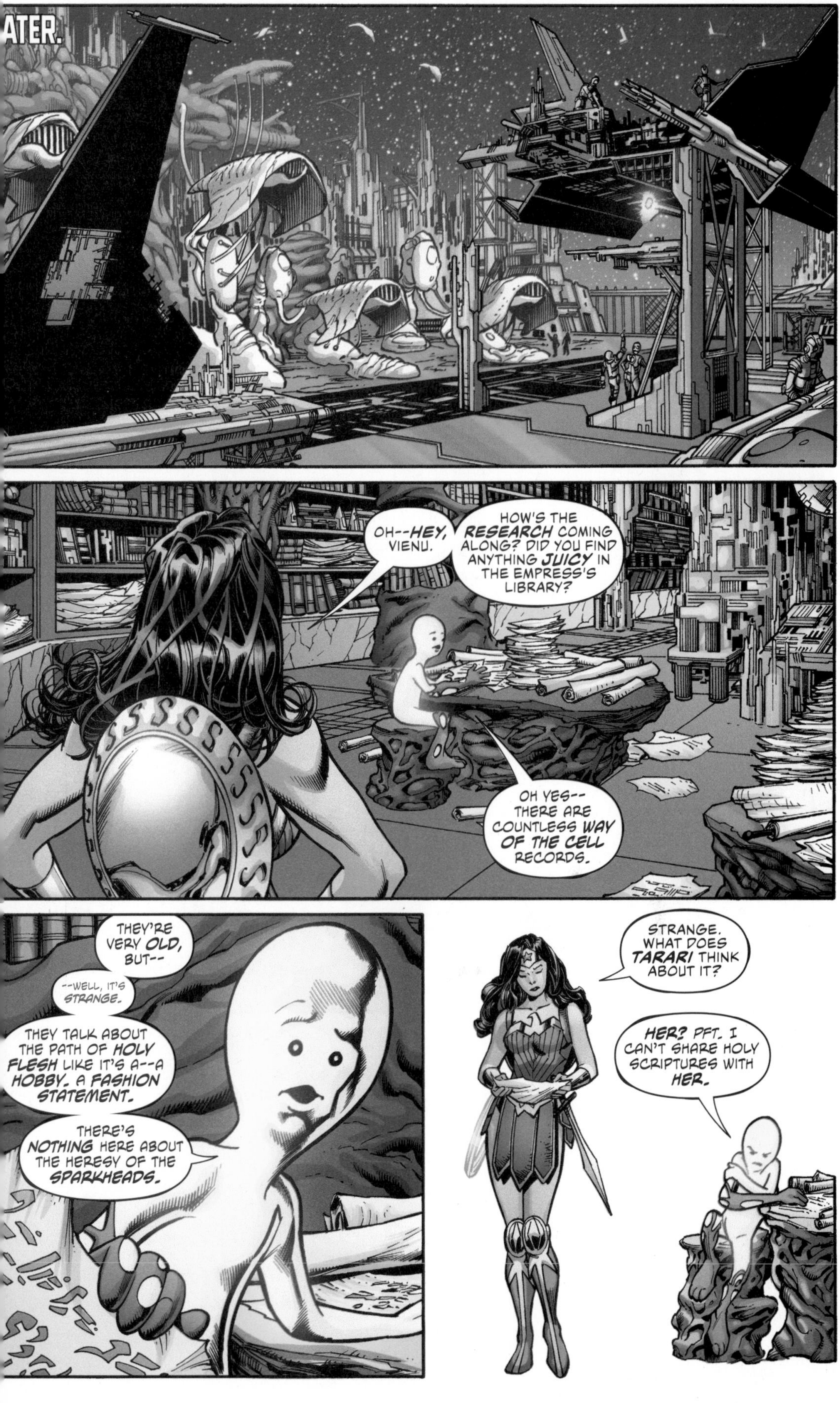
ATER.
OH--HEY, VIENU.
HOW'S THE RESEARCH COMING ALONG? DID YOU FIND ANYTHING JUICY IN THE EMPRESS'S LIBRARY?
OH YES-- THERE ARE COUNTLESS WAY OF THE CELL RECORDS.
THEY'RE VERY OLD, BUT--
--WELL, IT'S STRANGE.
THEY TALK ABOUT THE PATH OF HOLY FLESH LIKE IT'S A--A HOBBY. A FASHION STATEMENT.
THERE'S NOTHING HERE ABOUT THE HERESY OF THE SPARKHEADS.
STRANGE. WHAT DOES TARARI THINK ABOUT IT?
HER? PFT. I CAN'T SHARE HOLY SCRIPTURES WITH HER.

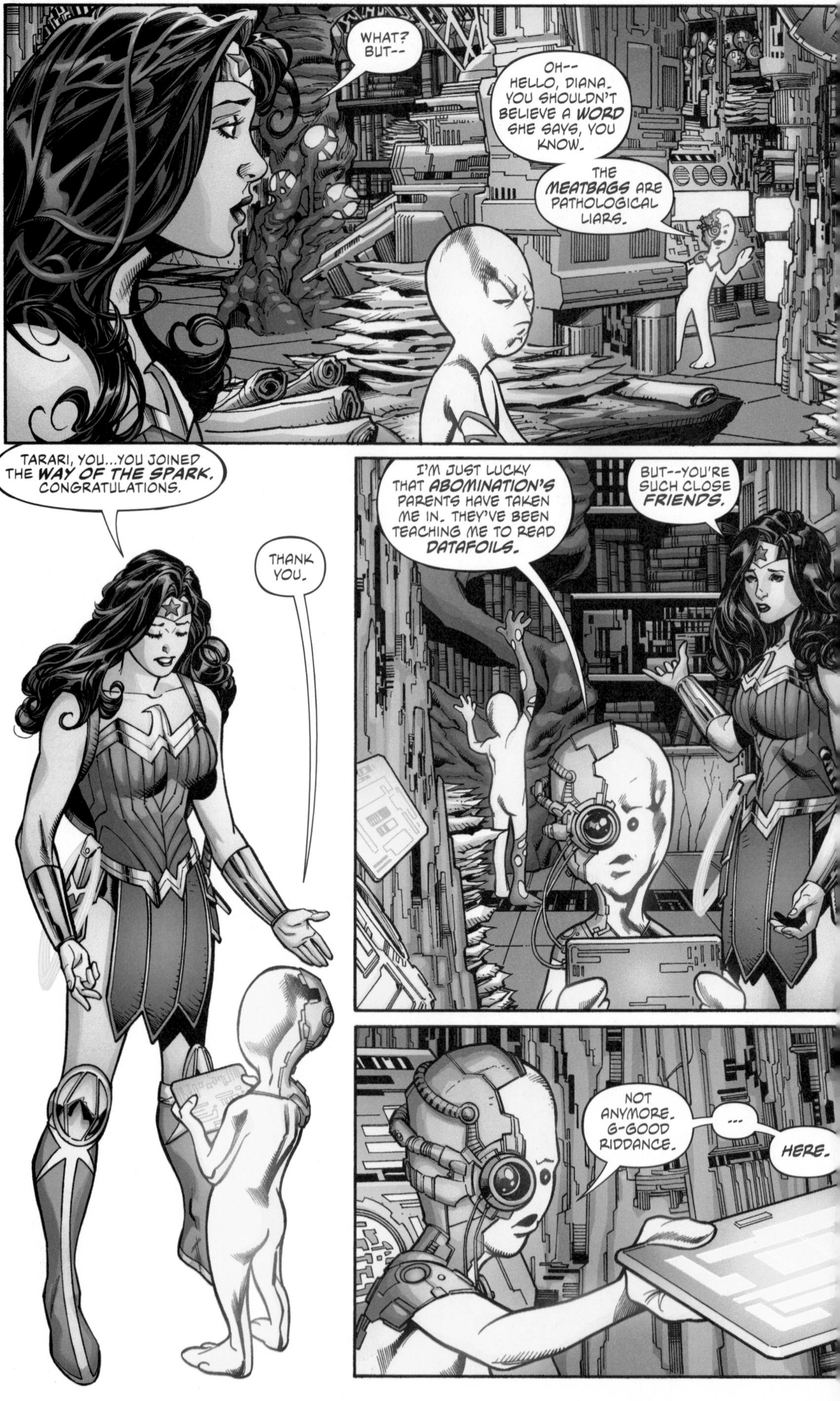
WHAT? BUT--
OH-- HELLO, DIANA. YOU SHOULDN'T BELIEVE A WORD SHE SAYS, YOU KNOW.
THE MEATBAGS ARE PATHOLOGICAL LIARS.
TARARI, YOU...YOU JOINED THE WAY OF THE SPARK. CONGRATULATIONS.
THANK YOU.
I'M JUST LUCKY THAT ABOMINATION'S PARENTS HAVE TAKEN ME IN. THEY'VE BEEN TEACHING ME TO READ DATAFOILS.
BUT--YOU'RE SUCH CLOSE FRIENDS.
NOT ANYMORE. G-GOOD RIDDANCE.
...
HERE.

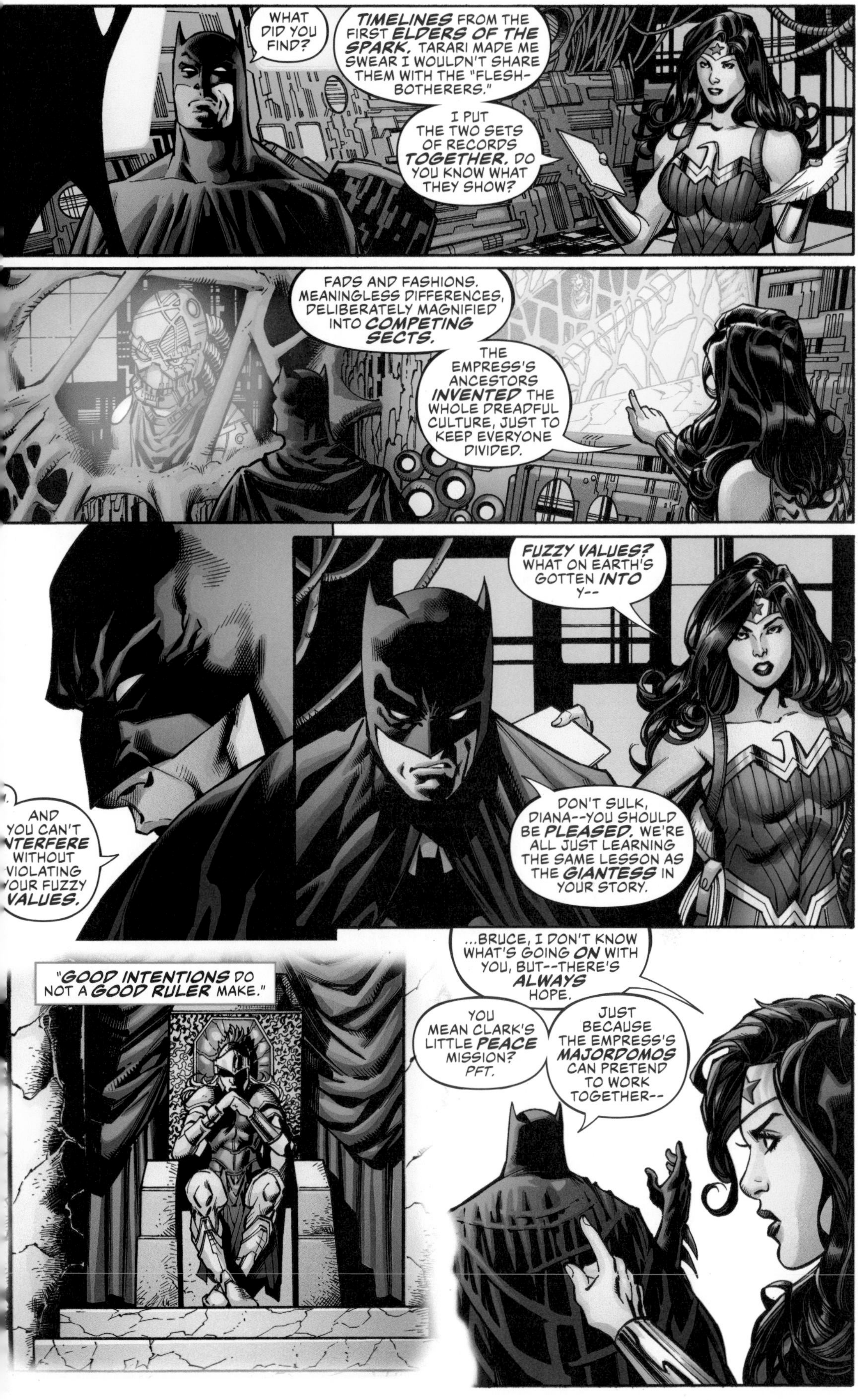

WHAT DID YOU FIND?
TIMELINES FROM THE FIRST ELDERS OF THE SPARK. TARARI MADE ME SWEAR I WOULDN'T SHARE THEM WITH THE "FLESH-BOTHERERS."
I PUT THE TWO SETS OF RECORDS TOGETHER. DO YOU KNOW WHAT THEY SHOW?
FADS AND FASHIONS. MEANINGLESS DIFFERENCES, DELIBERATELY MAGNIFIED INTO COMPETING SECTS.
THE EMPRESS'S ANCESTORS INVENTED THE WHOLE DREADFUL CULTURE, JUST TO KEEP EVERYONE DIVIDED.
AND YOU CAN'T NTERFERE WITHOUT VIOLATING OUR FUZZY VALUES.
FUZZY VALUES? WHAT ON EARTH'S GOTTEN INTO Y--
DON'T SULK, DIANA--YOU SHOULD BE PLEASED. WE'RE ALL JUST LEARNING THE SAME LESSON AS THE GIANTESS IN YOUR STORY.
"GOOD INTENTIONS DO NOT A GOOD RULER MAKE."
...BRUCE, I DON'T KNOW WHAT'S GOING ON WITH YOU, BUT--THERE'S ALWAYS HOPE.
JUST BECAUSE THE EMPRESS'S MAJORDOMOS CAN PRETEND TO WORK TOGETHER--
YOU MEAN CLARK'S LITTLE PEACE MISSION? PFT.

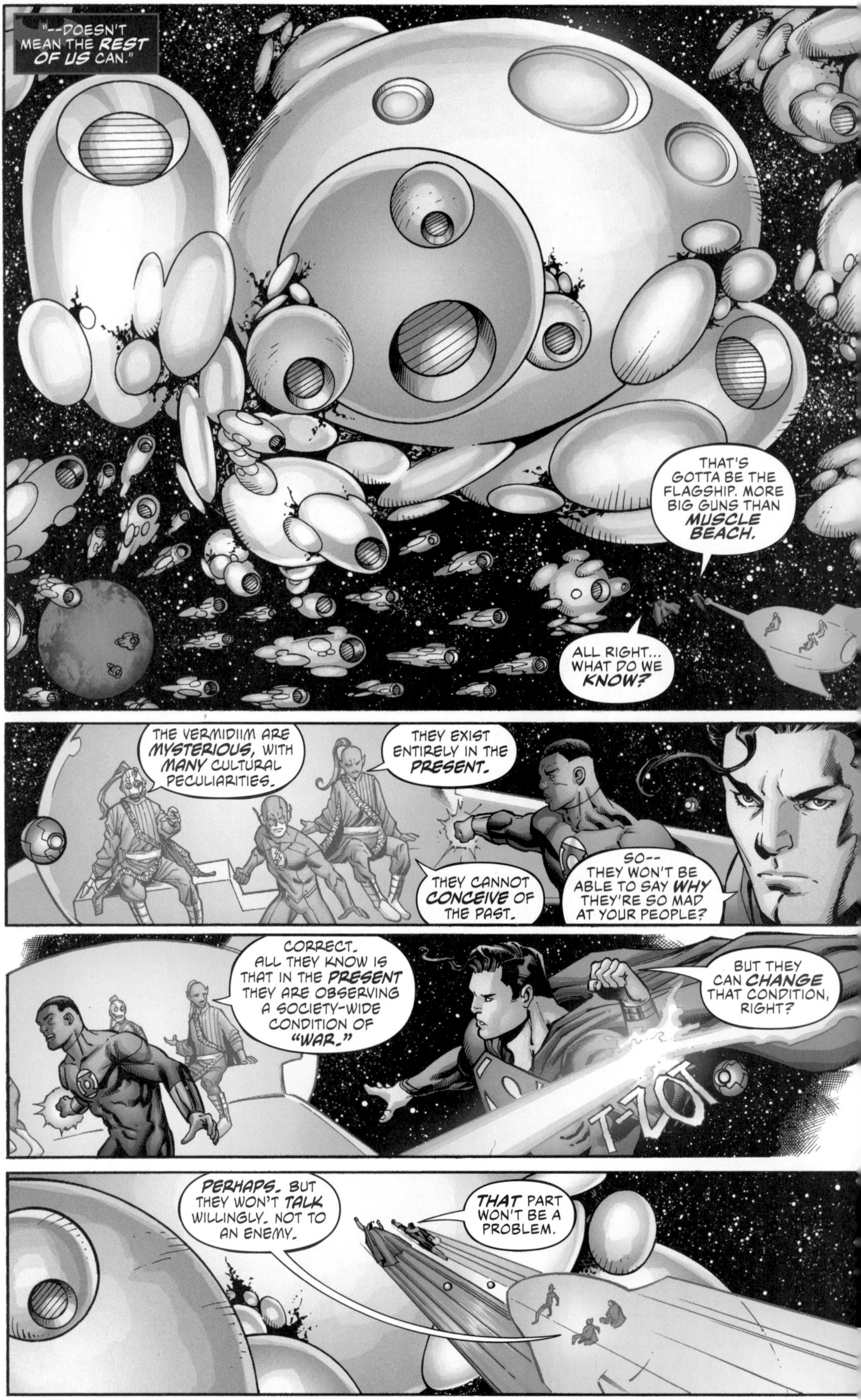
"--DOESN'T MEAN THE REST OF US CAN."
THAT'S GOTTA BE THE FLAGSHIP. MORE BIG GUNS THAN MUSCLE BEACH.
ALL RIGHT... WHAT DO WE KNOW?
THE VERMIDIIM ARE MYSTERIOUS, WITH MANY CULTURAL PECULIARITIES.
THEY EXIST ENTIRELY IN THE PRESENT.
THEY CANNOT CONCEIVE OF THE PAST.
SO-- THEY WON'T BE ABLE TO SAY WHY THEY'RE SO MAD AT YOUR PEOPLE?
CORRECT. ALL THEY KNOW IS THAT IN THE PRESENT THEY ARE OBSERVING A SOCIETY-WIDE CONDITION OF "WAR."
BUT THEY CAN CHANGE THAT CONDITION, RIGHT?
T-ZOT
PERHAPS. BUT THEY WON'T TALK WILLINGLY. NOT TO AN ENEMY.
THAT PART WON'T BE A PROBLEM.

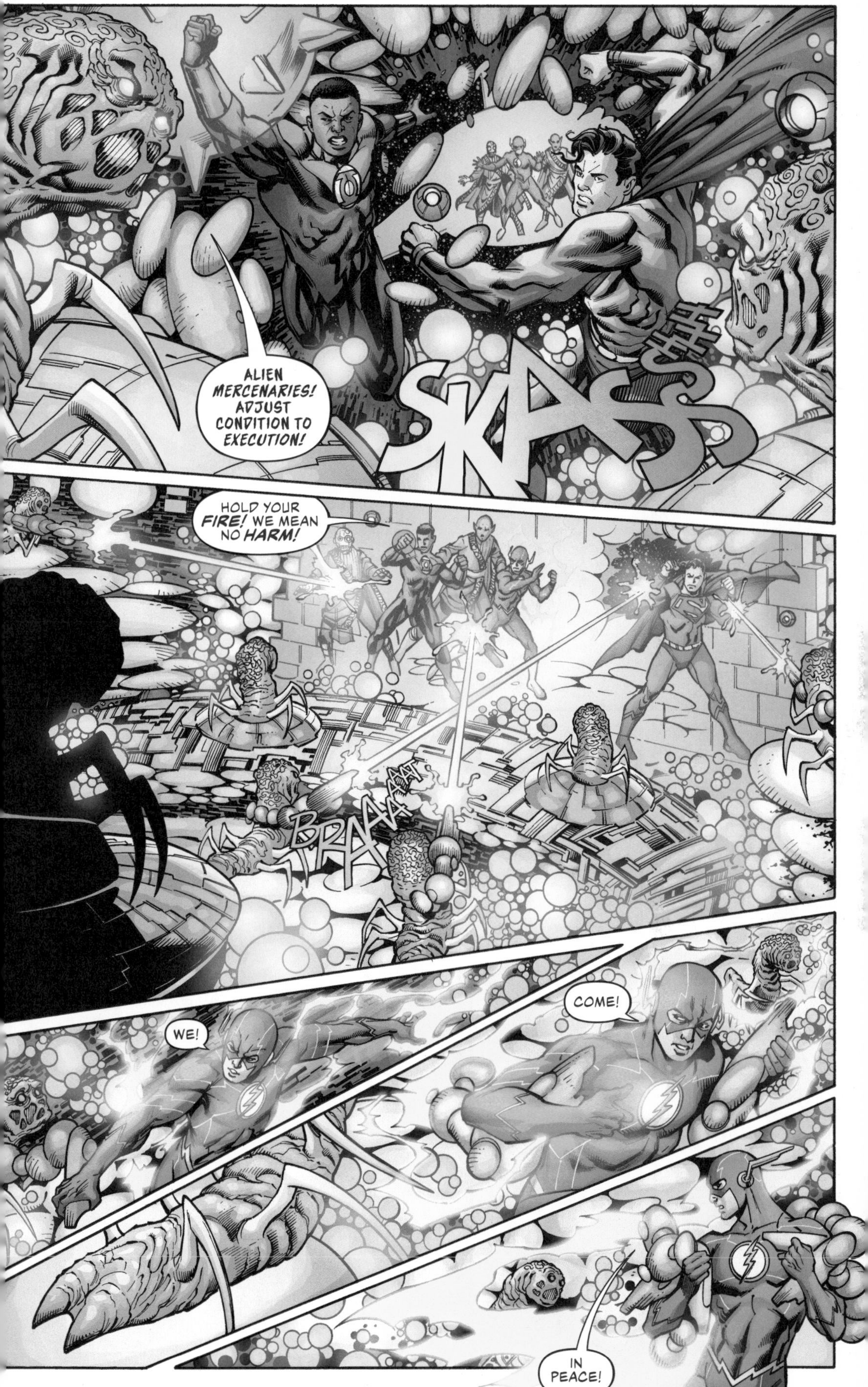
ALIEN MERCENARIES! ADJUST CONDITION TO EXECUTION!
SKASS
HOLD YOUR FIRE! WE MEAN NO HARM!
BRAAAAT
WE!
COME!
IN PEACE!

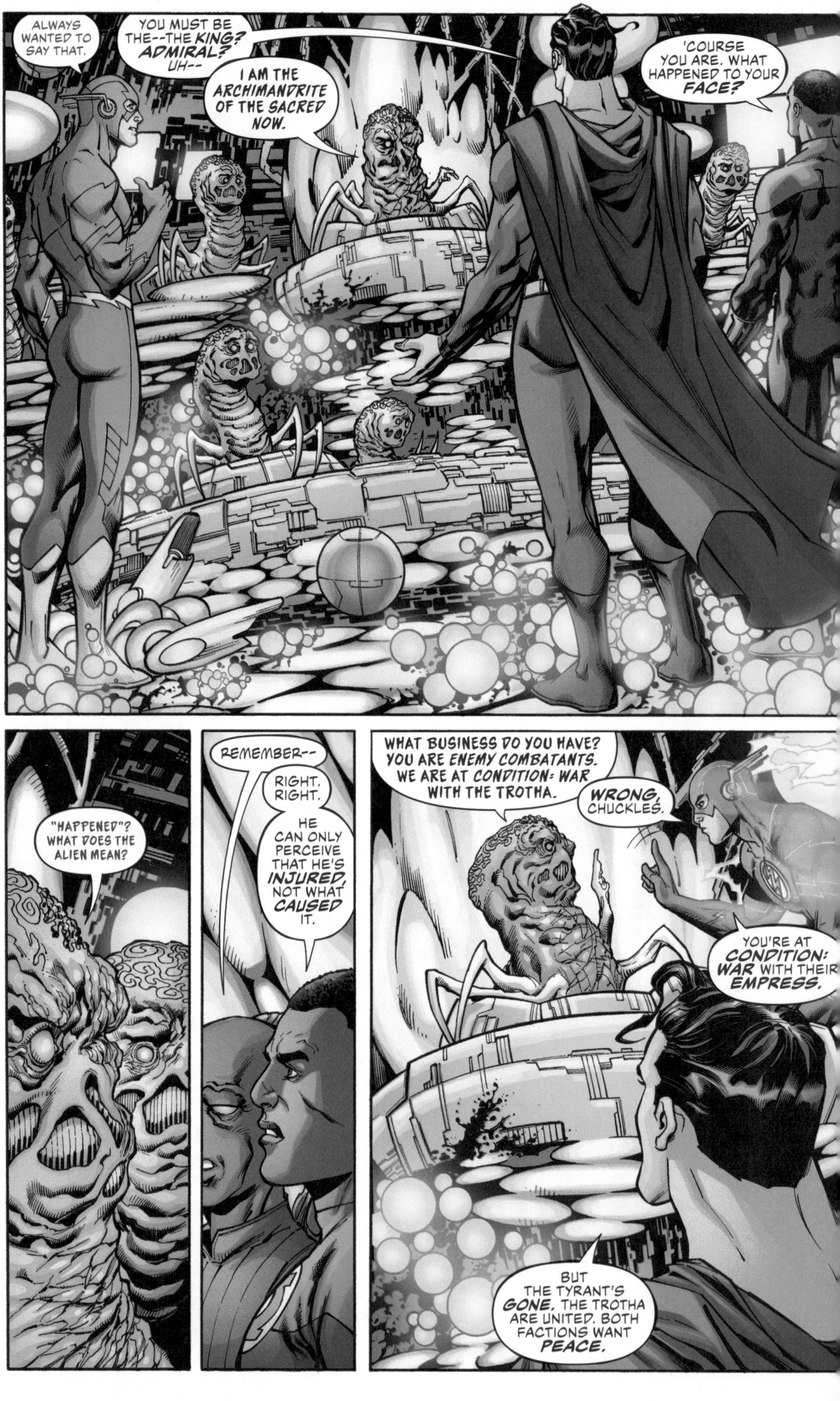

ALWAYS WANTED TO SAY THAT.
YOU MUST BE THE--THE KING? ADMIRAL? UH--
I AM THE ARCHIMANDRITE OF THE SACRED NOW.
'COURSE YOU ARE. WHAT HAPPENED TO YOUR FACE?
"HAPPENED"? WHAT DOES THE ALIEN MEAN?
REMEMBER--
RIGHT. RIGHT.
HE CAN ONLY PERCEIVE THAT HE'S INJURED, NOT WHAT CAUSED IT.
WHAT BUSINESS DO YOU HAVE? YOU ARE ENEMY COMBATANTS. WE ARE AT CONDITION: WAR WITH THE TROTHA.
WRONG, CHUCKLES.
YOU'RE AT CONDITION: WAR WITH THEIR EMPRESS.
BUT THE TYRANT'S GONE. THE TROTHA ARE UNITED. BOTH FACTIONS WANT PEACE.

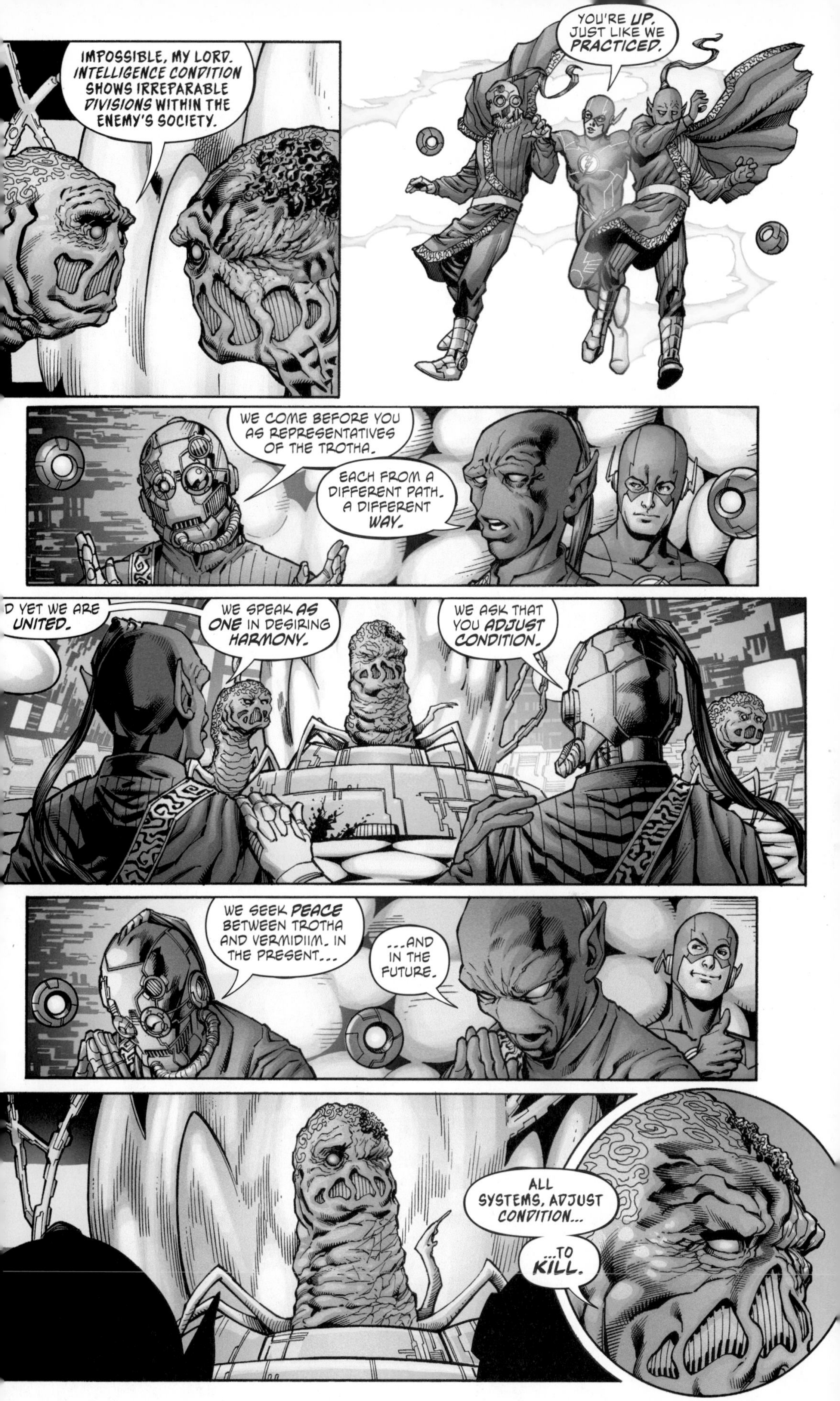
IMPOSSIBLE, MY LORD. INTELLIGENCE CONDITION SHOWS IRREPARABLE DIVISIONS WITHIN THE ENEMY'S SOCIETY.
YOU'RE UP. JUST LIKE WE PRACTICED.
WE COME BEFORE YOU AS REPRESENTATIVES OF THE TROTHA.
EACH FROM A DIFFERENT PATH. A DIFFERENT WAY.
D YET WE ARE UNITED.
WE SPEAK AS ONE IN DESIRING HARMONY.
WE ASK THAT YOU ADJUST CONDITION.
WE SEEK PEACE BETWEEN TROTHA AND VERMIDIIM. IN THE PRESENT...
...AND IN THE FUTURE.
ALL SYSTEMS, ADJUST CONDITION...
...TO KILL.

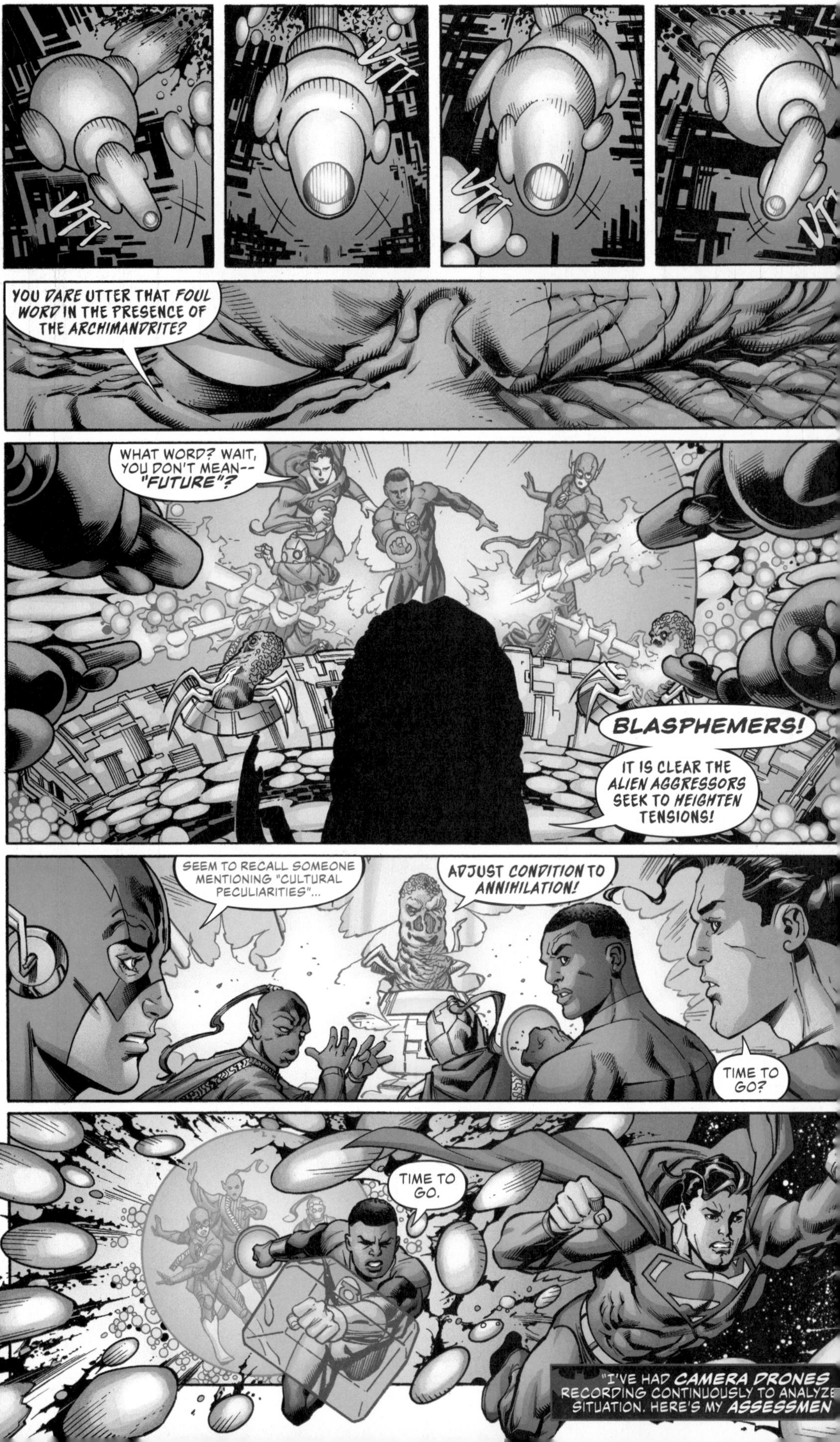
VTT
VTT
VTT
VTT
YOU DARE UTTER THAT FOUL WORD IN THE PRESENCE OF THE ARCHIMANDRITE?
WHAT WORD? WAIT, YOU DON'T MEAN-- "FUTURE"?
BLASPHEMERS!
IT IS CLEAR THE ALIEN AGGRESSORS SEEK TO HEIGHTEN TENSIONS!
SEEM TO RECALL SOMEONE MENTIONING "CULTURAL PECULIARITIES"...
ADJUST CONDITION TO ANNIHILATION!
TIME TO GO?
TIME TO GO.
"I'VE HAD CAMERA DRONES RECORDING CONTINUOUSLY TO ANALYZE SITUATION. HERE'S MY ASSESSMEN

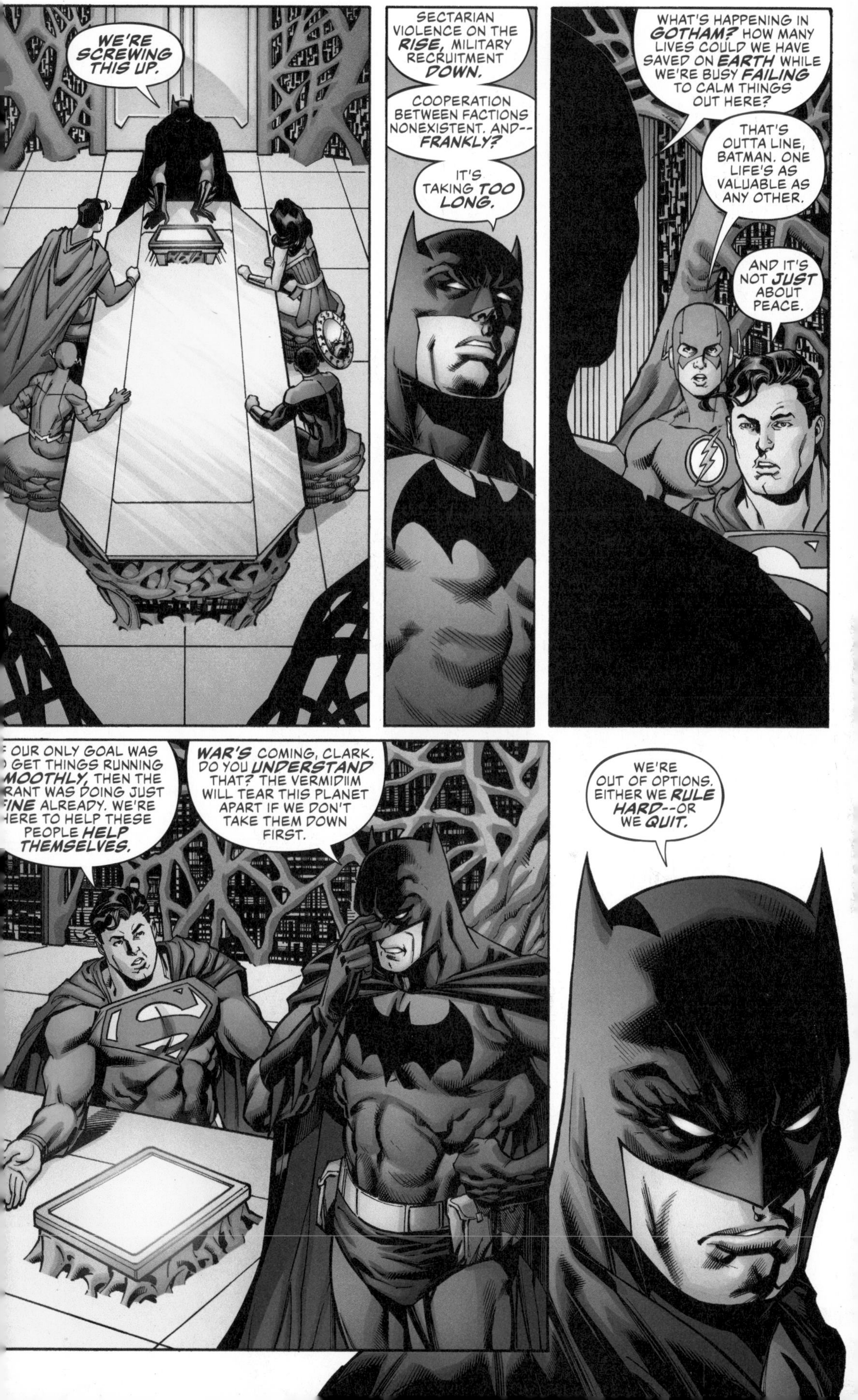
WE'RE SCREWING THIS UP.
SECTARIAN VIOLENCE ON THE RISE, MILITARY RECRUITMENT DOWN.
COOPERATION BETWEEN FACTIONS NONEXISTENT. AND-- FRANKLY?
IT'S TAKING TOO LONG.
WHAT'S HAPPENING IN GOTHAM? HOW MANY LIVES COULD WE HAVE SAVED ON EARTH WHILE WE'RE BUSY FAILING TO CALM THINGS OUT HERE?
THAT'S OUTTA LINE, BATMAN. ONE LIFE'S AS VALUABLE AS ANY OTHER.
AND IT'S NOT JUST ABOUT PEACE.
F OUR ONLY GOAL WAS) GET THINGS RUNNING MOOTHLY, THEN THE RANT WAS DOING JUST INE ALREADY. WE'RE HERE TO HELP THESE PEOPLE HELP THEMSELVES.
WAR'S COMING, CLARK. DO YOU UNDERSTAND THAT? THE VERMIDIIM WILL TEAR THIS PLANET APART IF WE DON'T TAKE THEM DOWN FIRST.
WE'RE OUT OF OPTIONS. EITHER WE RULE HARD--OR WE QUIT.

INSTEAD YOU'RE STILL *FRETTING* ABOUT *CULTURAL INSENSITIVITY.*

ENOUGH!

IF YOU HAVE SOMETHING TO *SAY,* AT LEAST HAVE THE *DECENCY* TO--

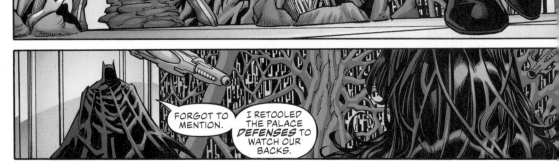

FORGOT TO MENTION.

I RETOOLED THE PALACE *DEFENSES* TO WATCH OUR BACKS.

BRUCE, WHAT THE HELL IS UP WITH Y--

BETTER SAFE THAN SORRY.

WOULDN'T WANT ANOTHER *REGIME CHANGE* SO SOON.

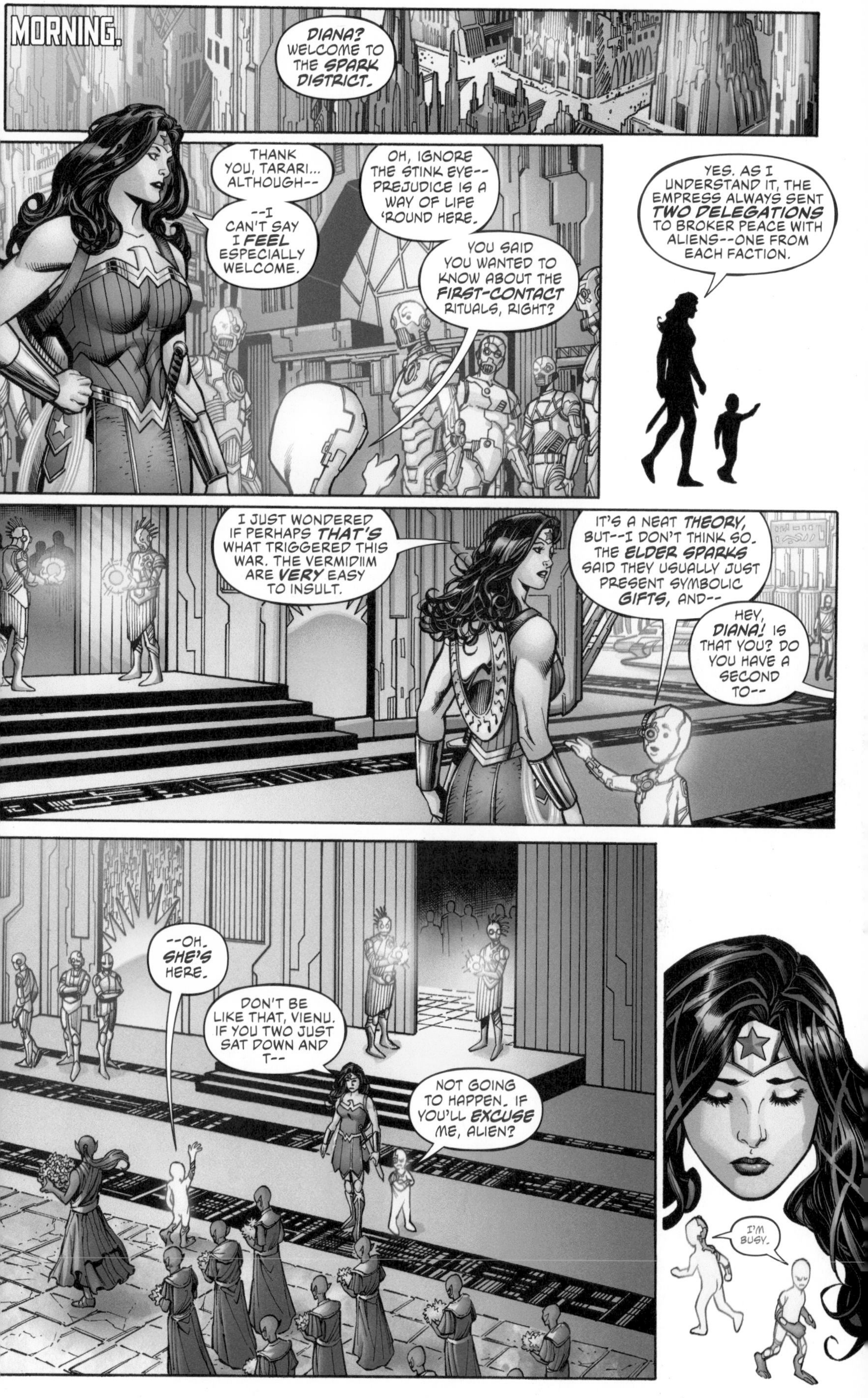
MORNING.
DIANA? WELCOME TO THE SPARK DISTRICT.
THANK YOU, TARARI... ALTHOUGH--
--I CAN'T SAY I FEEL ESPECIALLY WELCOME.
OH, IGNORE THE STINK EYE-- PREJUDICE IS A WAY OF LIFE 'ROUND HERE.
YOU SAID YOU WANTED TO KNOW ABOUT THE FIRST-CONTACT RITUALS, RIGHT?
YES. AS I UNDERSTAND IT, THE EMPRESS ALWAYS SENT TWO DELEGATIONS TO BROKER PEACE WITH ALIENS--ONE FROM EACH FACTION.
I JUST WONDERED IF PERHAPS THAT'S WHAT TRIGGERED THIS WAR. THE VERMIDIIM ARE VERY EASY TO INSULT.
IT'S A NEAT THEORY, BUT--I DON'T THINK SO. THE ELDER SPARKS SAID THEY USUALLY JUST PRESENT SYMBOLIC GIFTS, AND--
HEY, DIANA! IS THAT YOU? DO YOU HAVE A SECOND TO--
--OH. SHE'S HERE.
DON'T BE LIKE THAT, VIENU. IF YOU TWO JUST SAT DOWN AND T--
NOT GOING TO HAPPEN. IF YOU'LL EXCUSE ME, ALIEN?
I'M BUSY.

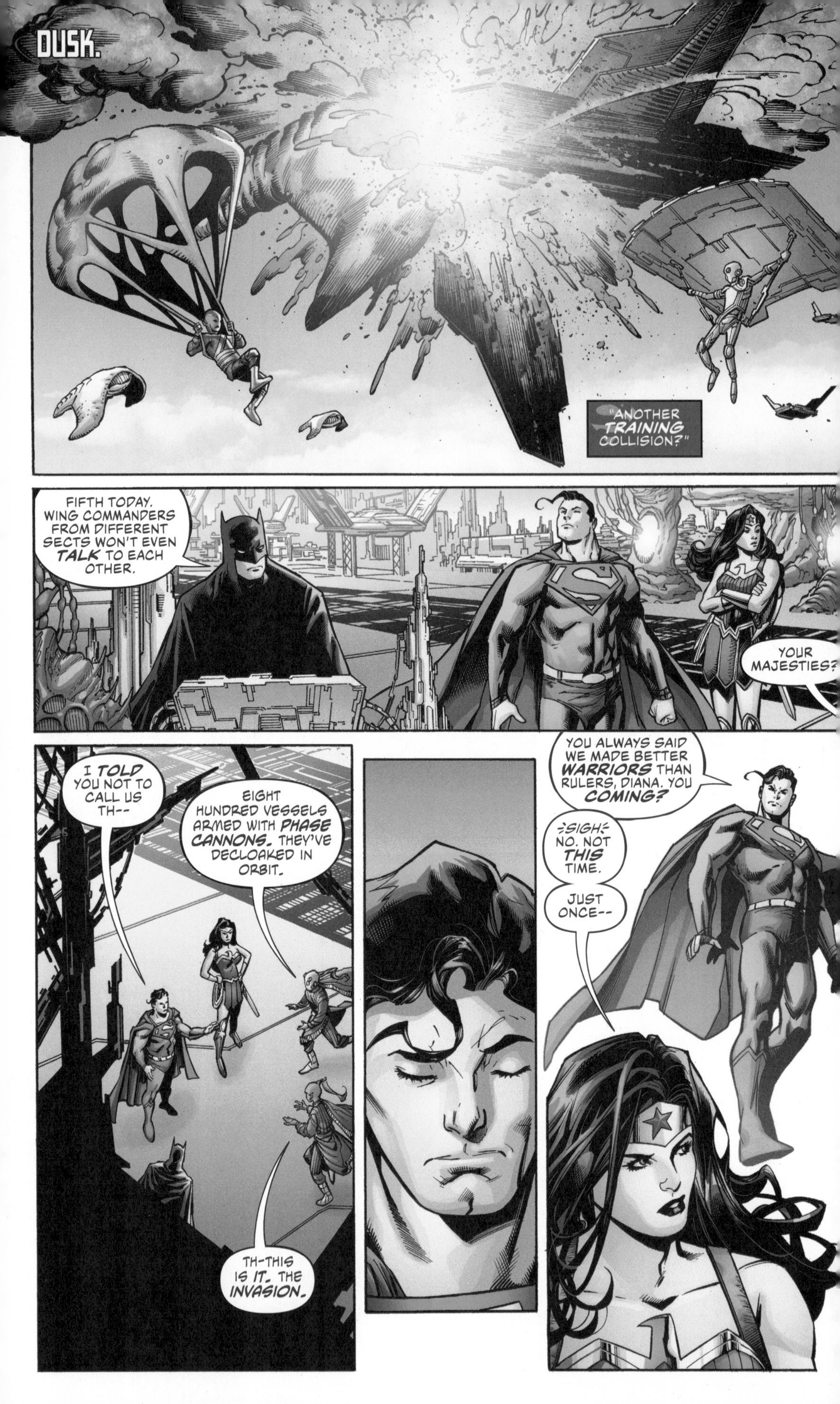
DUSK.
"ANOTHER TRAINING COLLISION?"
FIFTH TODAY. WING COMMANDERS FROM DIFFERENT SECTS WON'T EVEN TALK TO EACH OTHER.
YOUR MAJESTIES?
I TOLD YOU NOT TO CALL US TH--
EIGHT HUNDRED VESSELS ARMED WITH PHASE CANNONS. THEY'VE DECLOAKED IN ORBIT.
TH-THIS IS IT. THE INVASION.
YOU ALWAYS SAID WE MADE BETTER WARRIORS THAN RULERS, DIANA. YOU COMING?
-SIGH- NO. NOT THIS TIME.
JUST ONCE--

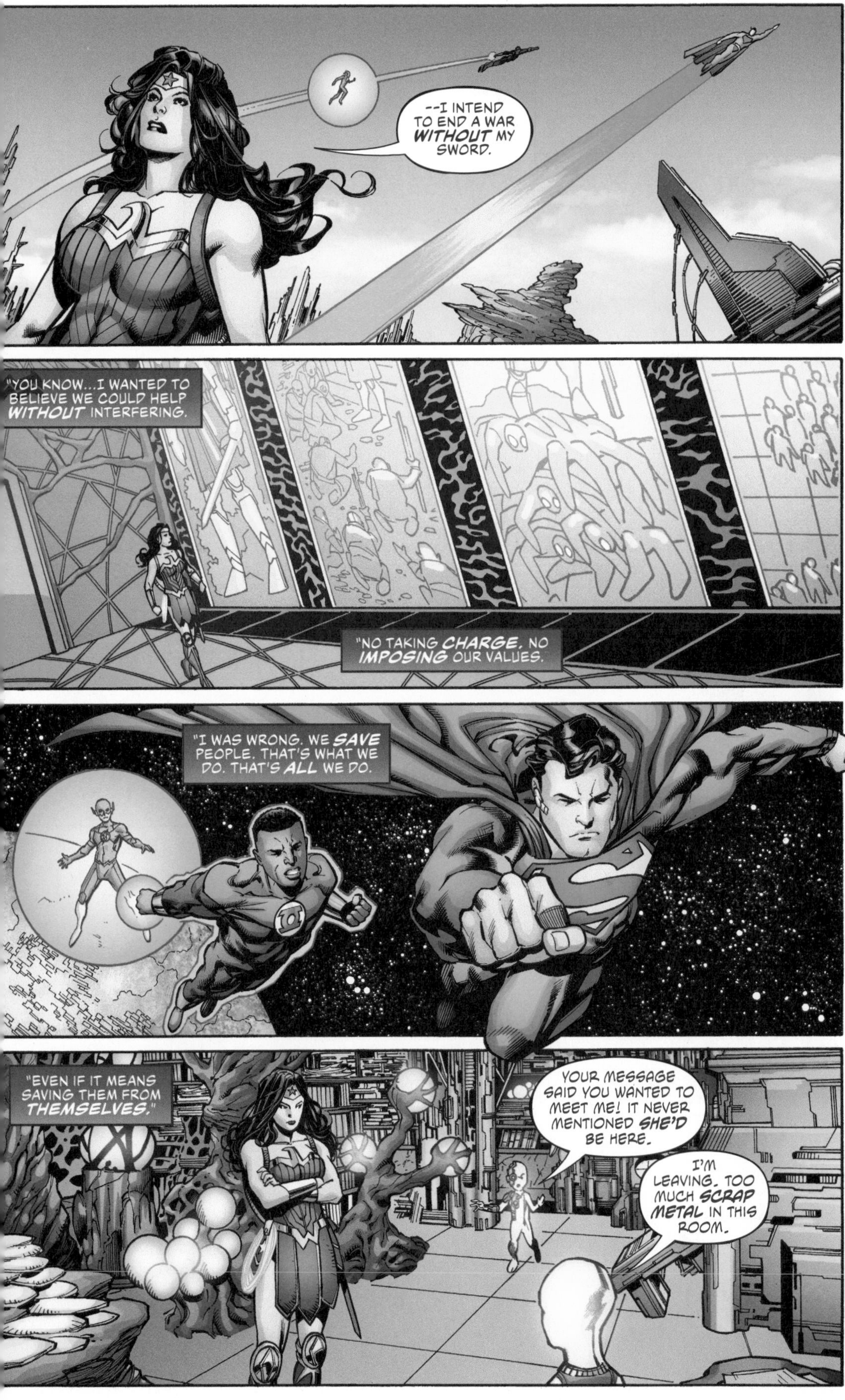
--I INTEND TO END A WAR WITHOUT MY SWORD.
"YOU KNOW...I WANTED TO BELIEVE WE COULD HELP WITHOUT INTERFERING.
"NO TAKING CHARGE. NO IMPOSING OUR VALUES.
"I WAS WRONG. WE SAVE PEOPLE. THAT'S WHAT WE DO. THAT'S ALL WE DO.
"EVEN IF IT MEANS SAVING THEM FROM THEMSELVES."
YOUR MESSAGE SAID YOU WANTED TO MEET ME! IT NEVER MENTIONED SHE'D BE HERE.
I'M LEAVING. TOO MUCH SCRAP METAL IN THIS ROOM.

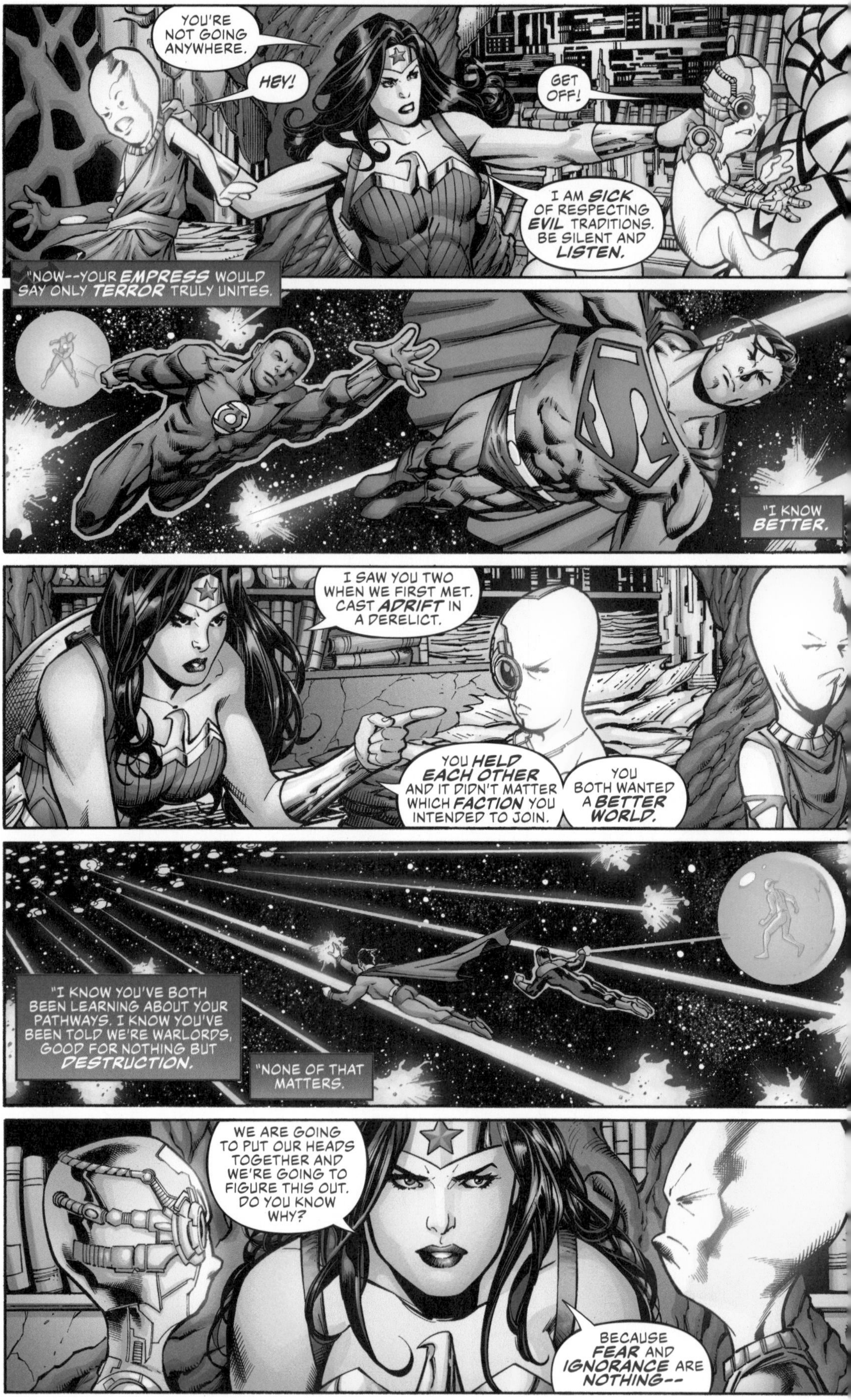
YOU'RE NOT GOING ANYWHERE.
HEY!
GET OFF!
I AM SICK OF RESPECTING EVIL TRADITIONS. BE SILENT AND LISTEN.
"NOW--YOUR EMPRESS WOULD SAY ONLY TERROR TRULY UNITES.
"I KNOW BETTER.
I SAW YOU TWO WHEN WE FIRST MET. CAST ADRIFT IN A DERELICT.
YOU HELD EACH OTHER AND IT DIDN'T MATTER WHICH FACTION YOU INTENDED TO JOIN.
YOU BOTH WANTED A BETTER WORLD.
"I KNOW YOU'VE BOTH BEEN LEARNING ABOUT YOUR PATHWAYS. I KNOW YOU'VE BEEN TOLD WE'RE WARLORDS, GOOD FOR NOTHING BUT DESTRUCTION.
"NONE OF THAT MATTERS.
WE ARE GOING TO PUT OUR HEADS TOGETHER AND WE'RE GOING TO FIGURE THIS OUT. DO YOU KNOW WHY?
BECAUSE FEAR AND IGNORANCE ARE NOTHING--

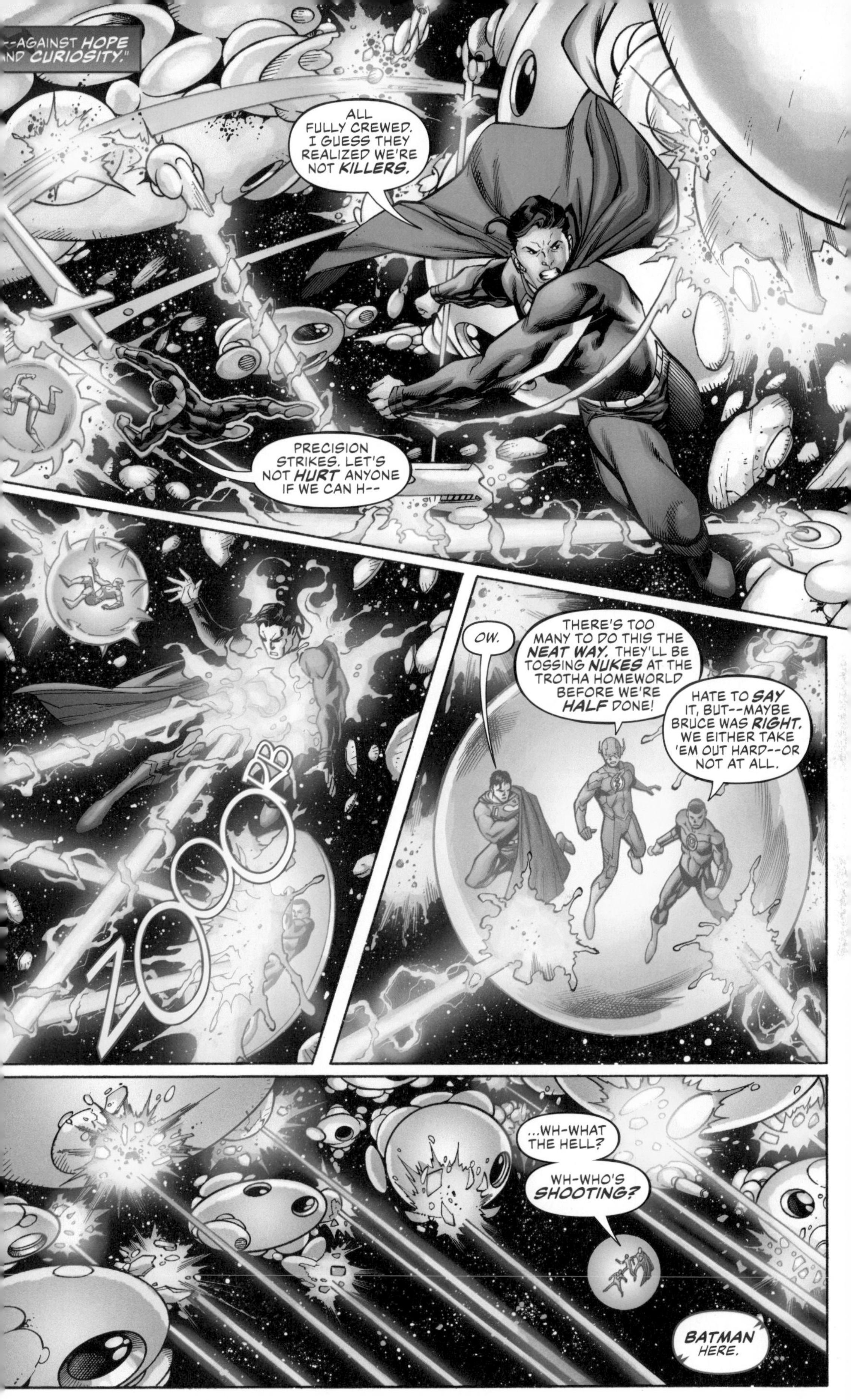
--AGAINST HOPE AND CURIOSITY."
ALL FULLY CREWED. I GUESS THEY REALIZED WE'RE NOT KILLERS.
PRECISION STRIKES. LET'S NOT HURT ANYONE IF WE CAN H--
ZOOOORB
OW.
THERE'S TOO MANY TO DO THIS THE NEAT WAY. THEY'LL BE TOSSING NUKES AT THE TROTHA HOMEWORLD BEFORE WE'RE HALF DONE!
HATE TO SAY IT, BUT--MAYBE BRUCE WAS RIGHT. WE EITHER TAKE 'EM OUT HARD--OR NOT AT ALL.
...WH-WHAT THE HELL?
WH-WHO'S SHOOTING?
BATMAN HERE.

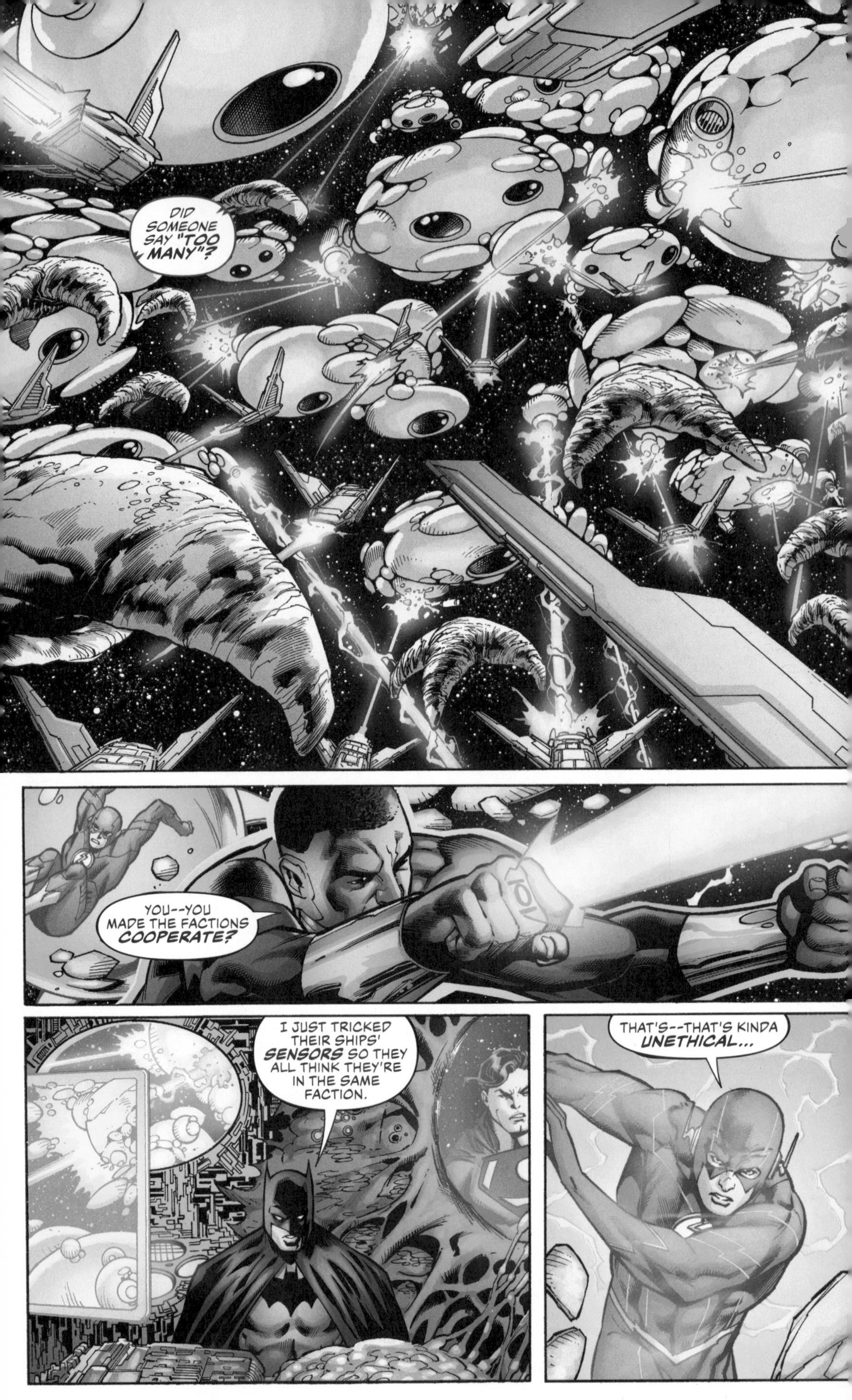
DID SOMEONE SAY "TOO MANY"?
YOU--YOU MADE THE FACTIONS COOPERATE?
I JUST TRICKED THEIR SHIPS' SENSORS SO THEY ALL THINK THEY'RE IN THE SAME FACTION.
THAT'S--THAT'S KINDA UNETHICAL...

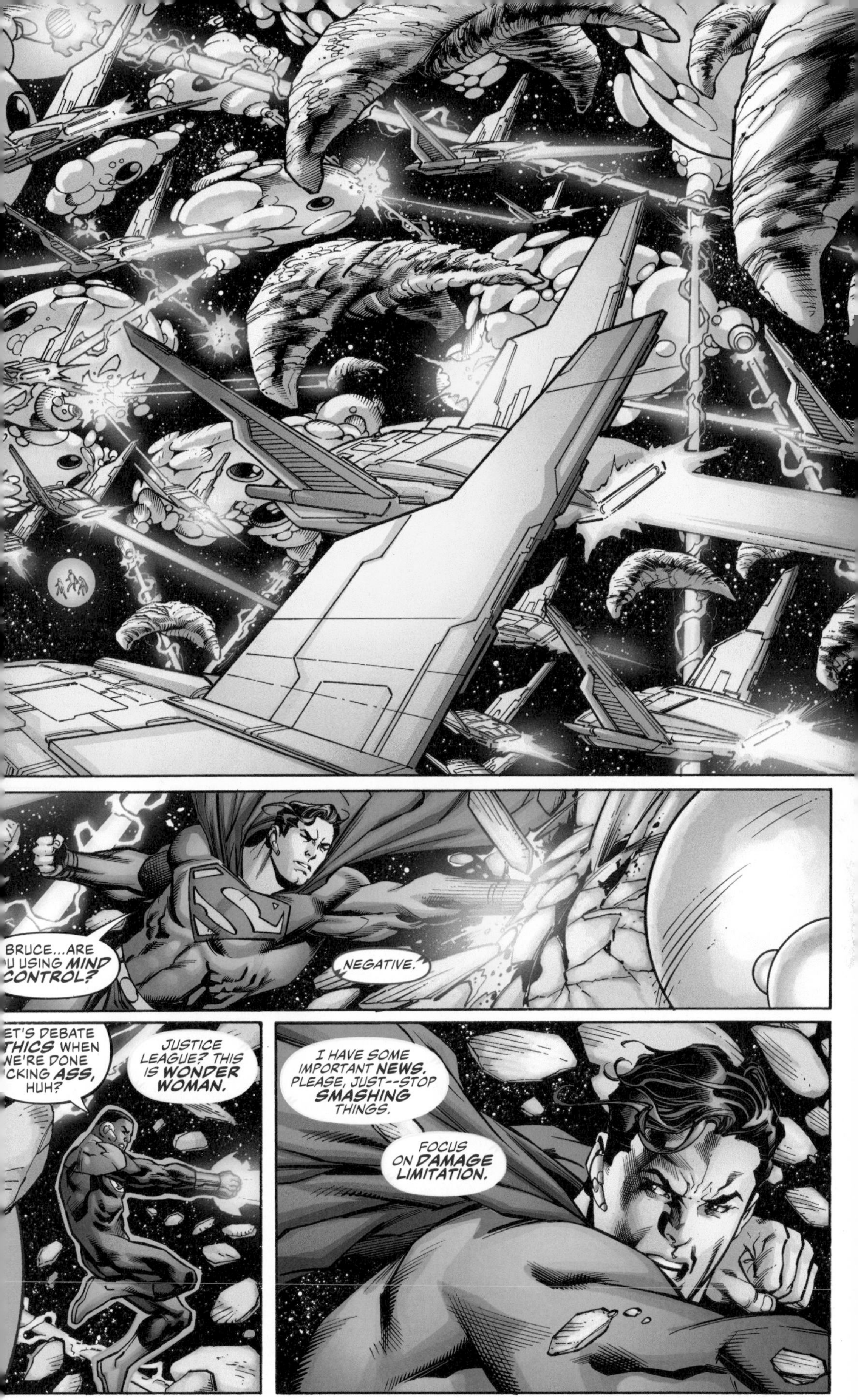
BRUCE...ARE
U USING MIND
CONTROL?
NEGATIVE.
ET'S DEBATE
THICS WHEN
E'RE DONE
CKING ASS,
HUH?
JUSTICE LEAGUE? THIS IS WONDER WOMAN.
I HAVE SOME IMPORTANT NEWS. PLEASE, JUST--STOP SMASHING THINGS.
FOCUS ON DAMAGE LIMITATION.

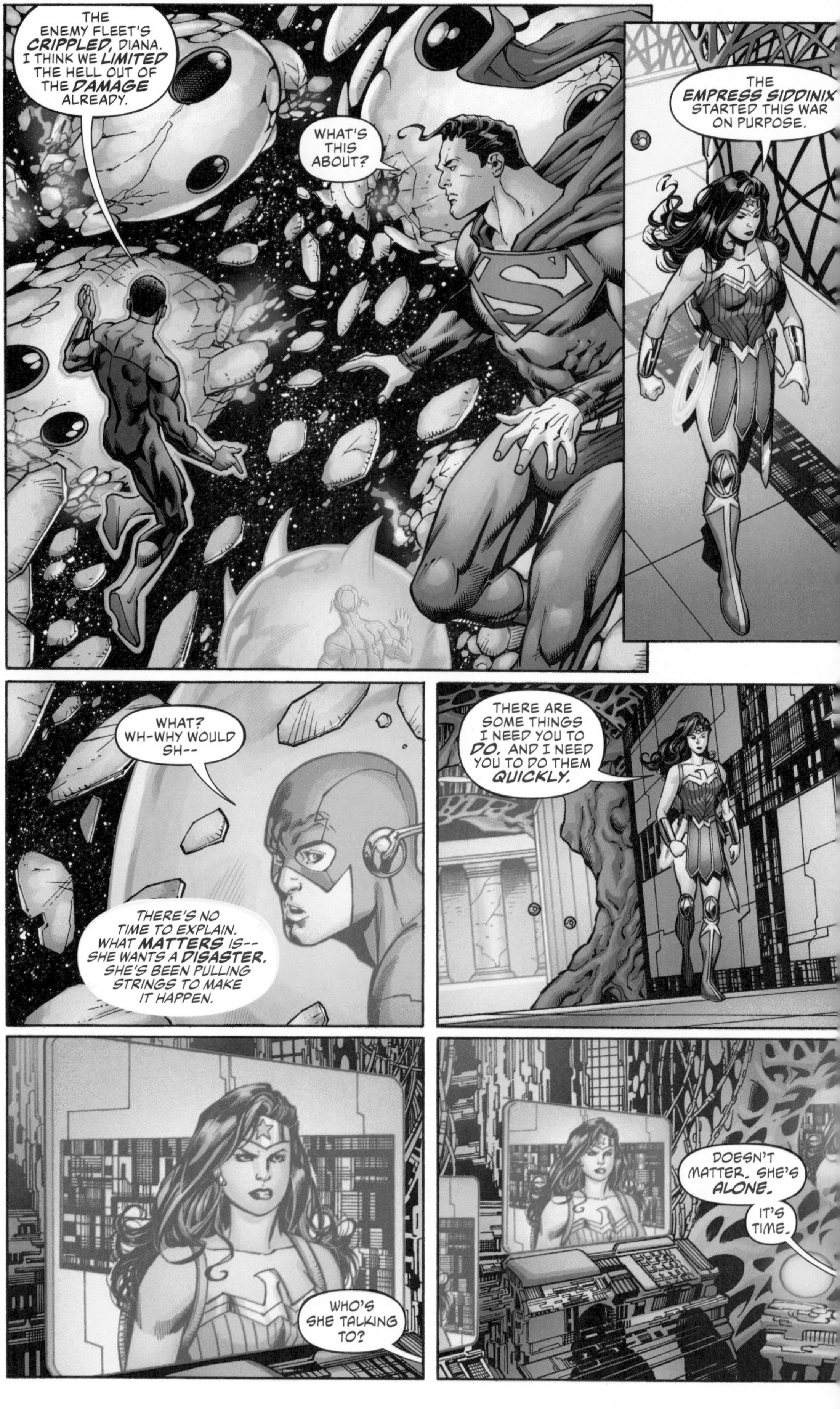
THE ENEMY FLEET'S CRIPPLED, DIANA. I THINK WE LIMITED THE HELL OUT OF THE DAMAGE ALREADY.
WHAT'S THIS ABOUT?
THE EMPRESS SIDDINIX STARTED THIS WAR ON PURPOSE.
WHAT? WH-WHY WOULD SH--
THERE'S NO TIME TO EXPLAIN. WHAT MATTERS IS-- SHE WANTS A DISASTER. SHE'S BEEN PULLING STRINGS TO MAKE IT HAPPEN.
THERE ARE SOME THINGS I NEED YOU TO DO. AND I NEED YOU TO DO THEM QUICKLY.
WHO'S SHE TALKING TO?
DOESN'T MATTER. SHE'S ALONE.
IT'S TIME.

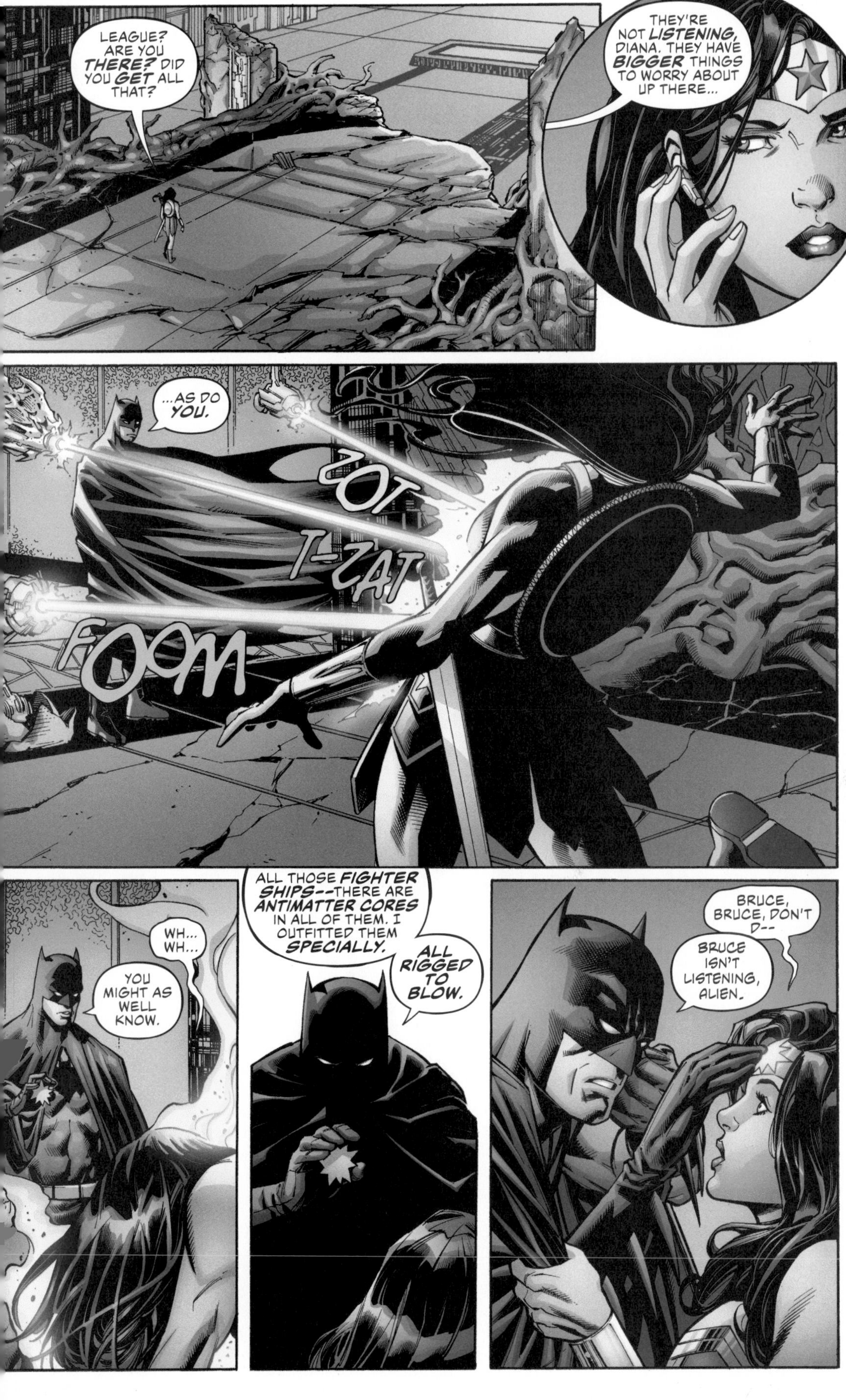

LEAGUE? ARE YOU THERE? DID YOU GET ALL THAT?
THEY'RE NOT LISTENING, DIANA. THEY HAVE BIGGER THINGS TO WORRY ABOUT UP THERE...
...AS DO YOU.
ZOT
T-ZAT
FOOM
WH... WH...
YOU MIGHT AS WELL KNOW.
ALL THOSE FIGHTER SHIPS--THERE ARE ANTIMATTER CORES IN ALL OF THEM. I OUTFITTED THEM SPECIALLY.
ALL RIGGED TO BLOW.
BRUCE, BRUCE, DON'T D--
BRUCE ISN'T LISTENING, ALIEN.

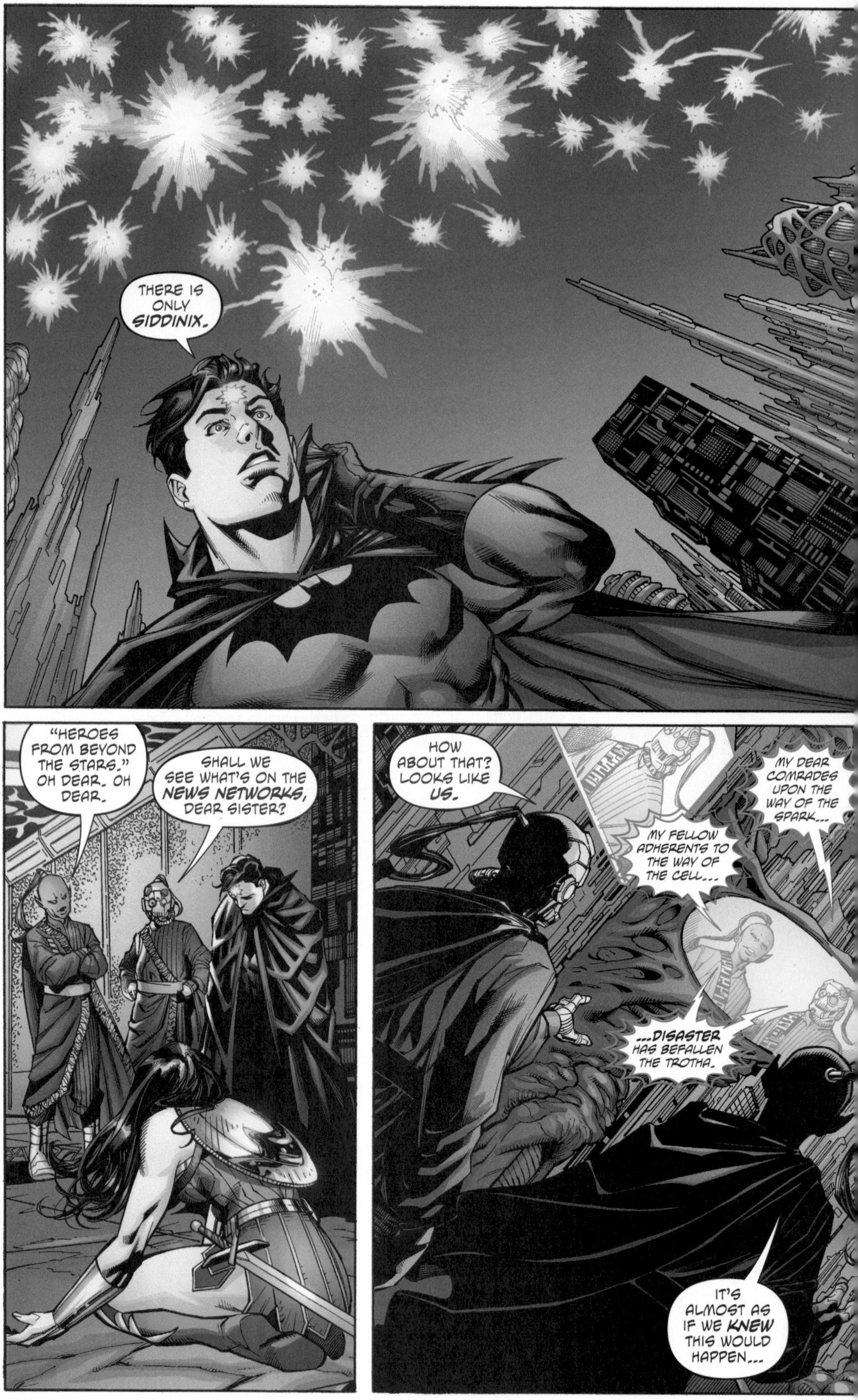
THERE IS ONLY SIDDINIX.
"HEROES FROM BEYOND THE STARS." OH DEAR. OH DEAR.
SHALL WE SEE WHAT'S ON THE NEWS NETWORKS, DEAR SISTER?
HOW ABOUT THAT? LOOKS LIKE US.
MY DEAR COMRADES UPON THE WAY OF THE SPARK...
MY FELLOW ADHERENTS TO THE WAY OF THE CELL...
...DISASTER HAS BEFALLEN THE TROTHA.
IT'S ALMOST AS IF WE KNEW THIS WOULD HAPPEN...

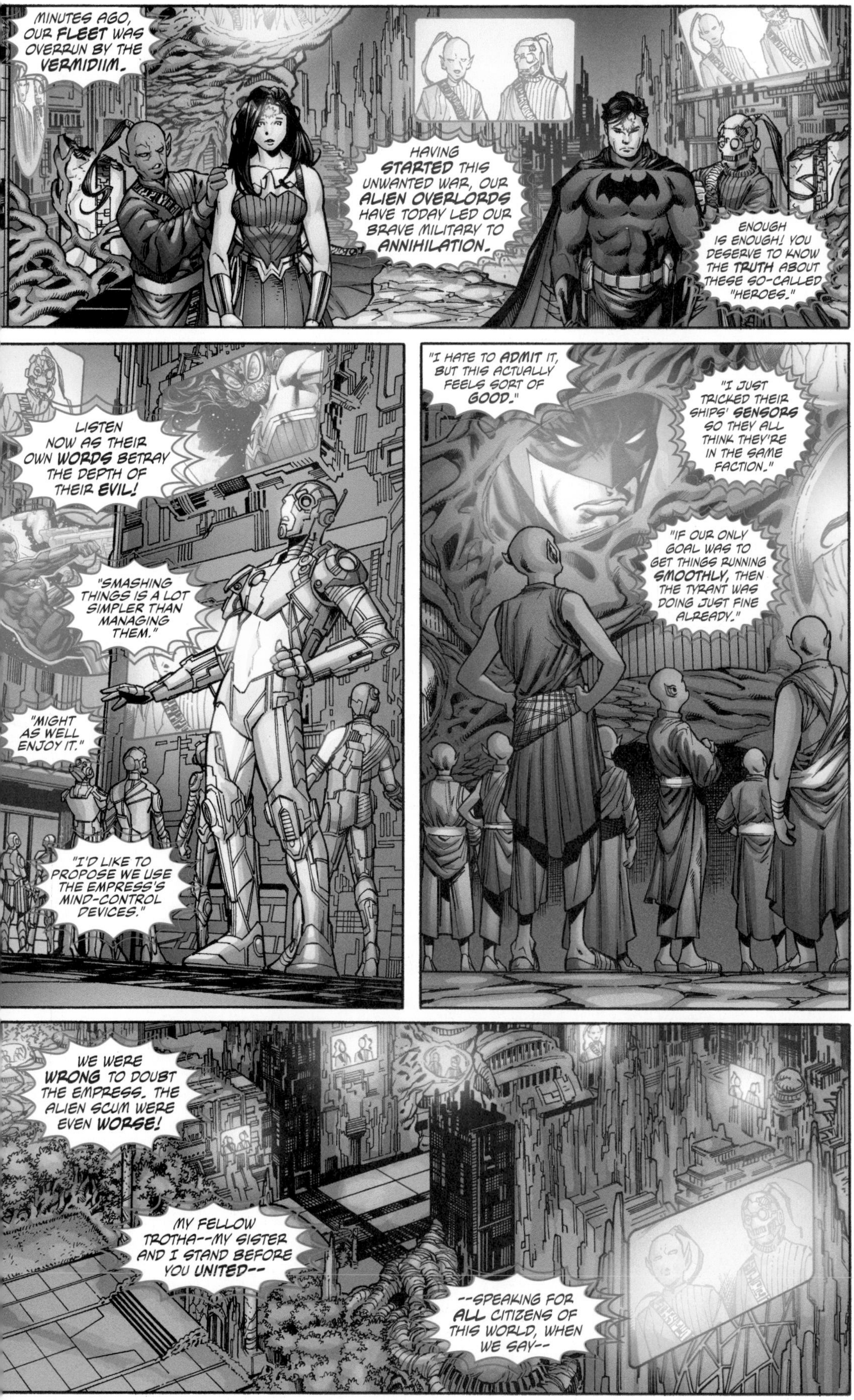
MINUTES AGO, OUR FLEET WAS OVERRUN BY THE VERMIDIIM.
HAVING STARTED THIS UNWANTED WAR, OUR ALIEN OVERLORDS HAVE TODAY LED OUR BRAVE MILITARY TO ANNIHILATION.
ENOUGH IS ENOUGH! YOU DESERVE TO KNOW THE TRUTH ABOUT THESE SO-CALLED "HEROES."
LISTEN NOW AS THEIR OWN WORDS BETRAY THE DEPTH OF THEIR EVIL!
"SMASHING THINGS IS A LOT SIMPLER THAN MANAGING THEM."
"MIGHT AS WELL ENJOY IT."
"I'D LIKE TO PROPOSE WE USE THE EMPRESS'S MIND-CONTROL DEVICES."
"I HATE TO ADMIT IT, BUT THIS ACTUALLY FEELS SORT OF GOOD."
"I JUST TRICKED THEIR SHIPS' SENSORS SO THEY ALL THINK THEY'RE IN THE SAME FACTION."
"IF OUR ONLY GOAL WAS TO GET THINGS RUNNING SMOOTHLY, THEN THE TYRANT WAS DOING JUST FINE ALREADY."
WE WERE WRONG TO DOUBT THE EMPRESS. THE ALIEN SCUM WERE EVEN WORSE!
MY FELLOW TROTHA--MY SISTER AND I STAND BEFORE YOU UNITED--
--SPEAKING FOR ALL CITIZENS OF THIS WORLD, WHEN WE SAY--

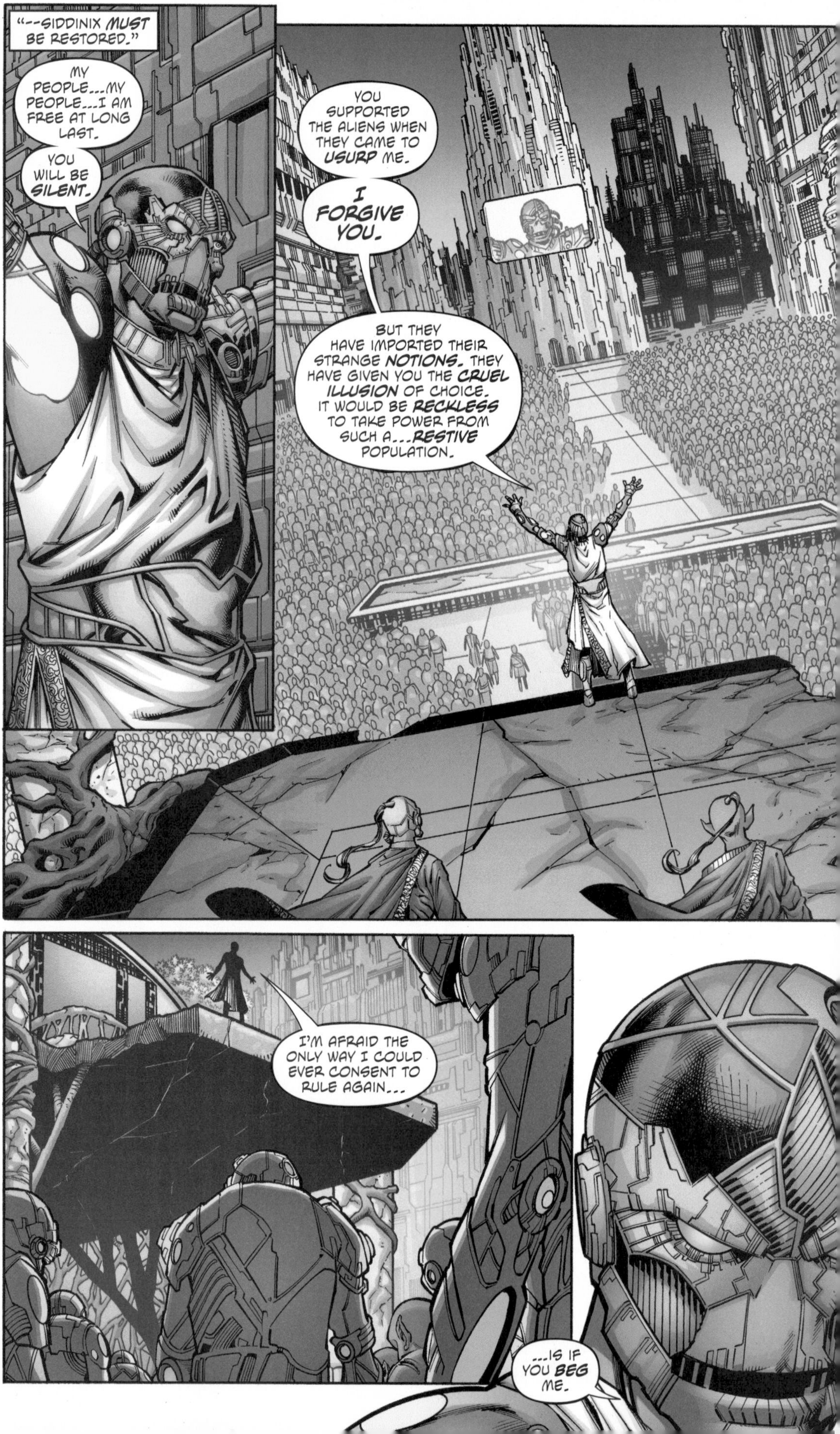
"--SIDDINIX MUST BE RESTORED."
MY PEOPLE...MY PEOPLE...I AM FREE AT LONG LAST.
YOU WILL BE SILENT.
YOU SUPPORTED THE ALIENS WHEN THEY CAME TO USURP ME.
I FORGIVE YOU.
BUT THEY HAVE IMPORTED THEIR STRANGE NOTIONS. THEY HAVE GIVEN YOU THE CRUEL ILLUSION OF CHOICE. IT WOULD BE RECKLESS TO TAKE POWER FROM SUCH A...RESTIVE POPULATION.
I'M AFRAID THE ONLY WAY I COULD EVER CONSENT TO RULE AGAIN...
...IS IF YOU BEG ME.

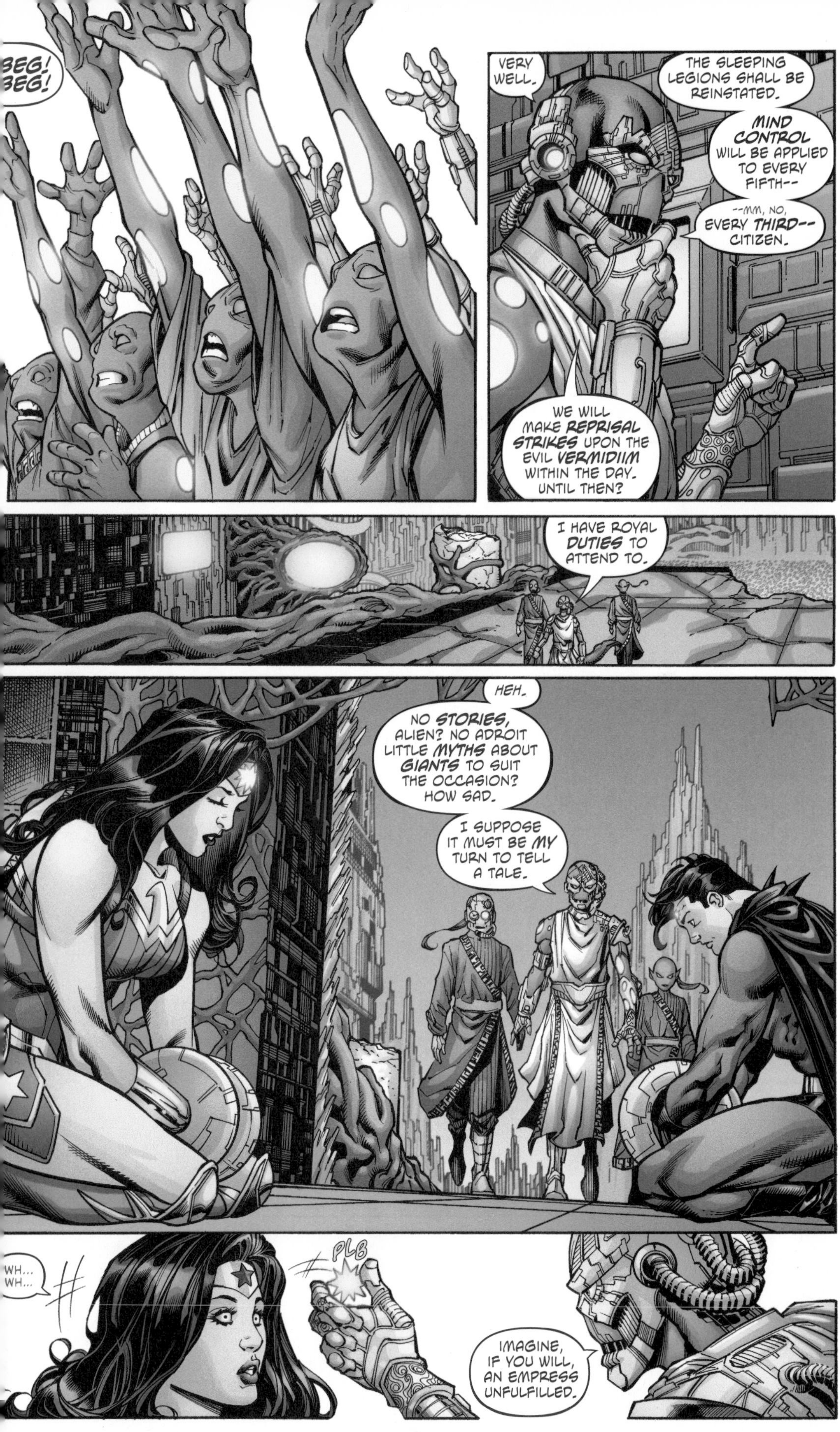
BEG! BEG!
VERY WELL.
THE SLEEPING LEGIONS SHALL BE REINSTATED.
MIND CONTROL WILL BE APPLIED TO EVERY FIFTH--
--MM, NO, EVERY THIRD-- CITIZEN.
WE WILL MAKE REPRISAL STRIKES UPON THE EVIL VERMIDIIM WITHIN THE DAY. UNTIL THEN?
I HAVE ROYAL DUTIES TO ATTEND TO.
HEH.
NO STORIES, ALIEN? NO ADROIT LITTLE MYTHS ABOUT GIANTS TO SUIT THE OCCASION? HOW SAD.
I SUPPOSE IT MUST BE MY TURN TO TELL A TALE.
WH... WH...
PLB
IMAGINE, IF YOU WILL, AN EMPRESS UNFULFILLED.

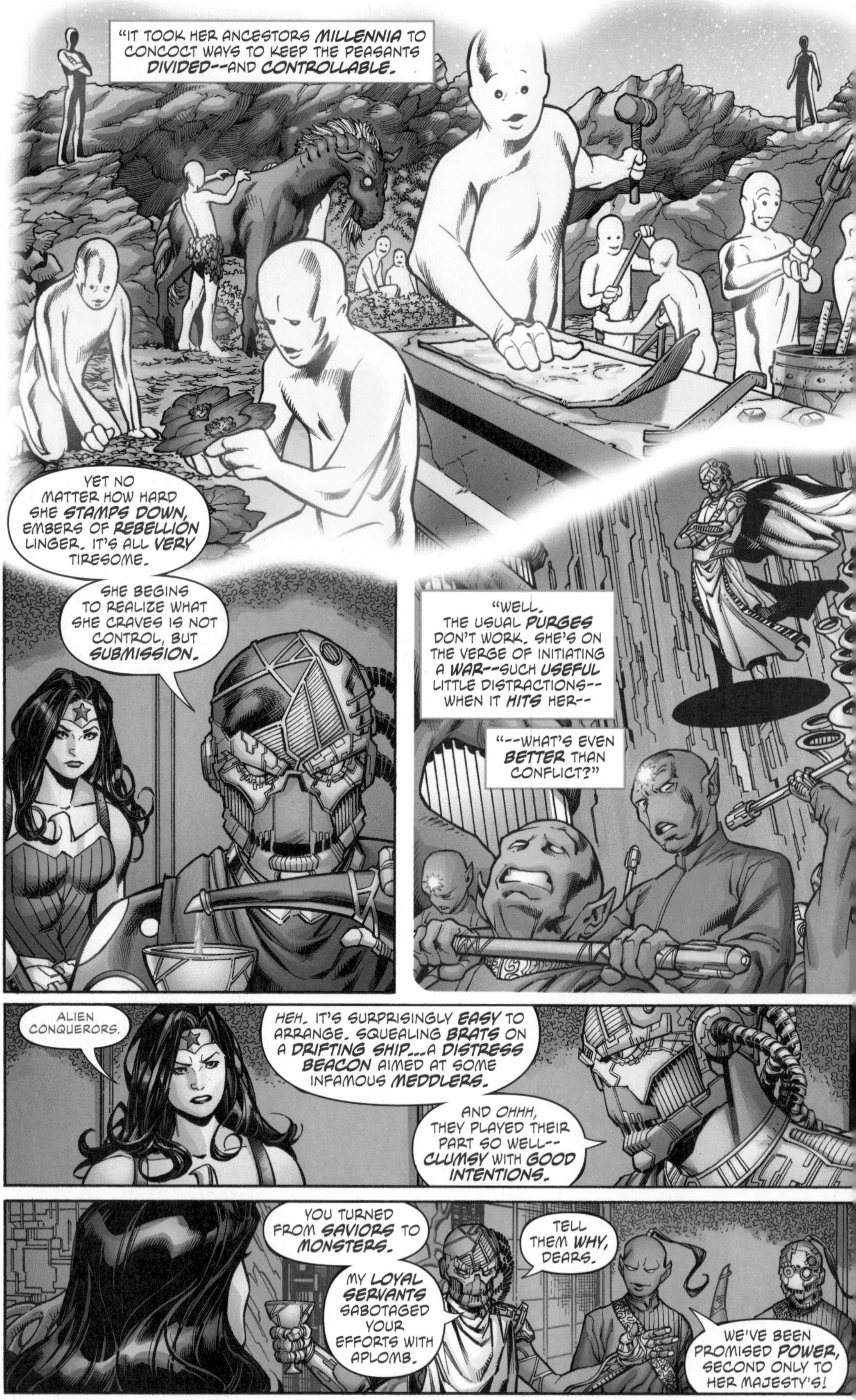
"IT TOOK HER ANCESTORS MILLENNIA TO CONCOCT WAYS TO KEEP THE PEASANTS DIVIDED--AND CONTROLLABLE.
YET NO MATTER HOW HARD SHE STAMPS DOWN, EMBERS OF REBELLION LINGER. IT'S ALL VERY TIRESOME.
SHE BEGINS TO REALIZE WHAT SHE CRAVES IS NOT CONTROL, BUT SUBMISSION.
"WELL. THE USUAL PURGES DON'T WORK. SHE'S ON THE VERGE OF INITIATING A WAR--SUCH USEFUL LITTLE DISTRACTIONS--WHEN IT HITS HER--
"--WHAT'S EVEN BETTER THAN CONFLICT?"
ALIEN CONQUERORS.
HEH. IT'S SURPRISINGLY EASY TO ARRANGE. SQUEALING BRATS ON A DRIFTING SHIP...A DISTRESS BEACON AIMED AT SOME INFAMOUS MEDDLERS.
AND OHHH, THEY PLAYED THEIR PART SO WELL--CLUMSY WITH GOOD INTENTIONS.
YOU TURNED FROM SAVIORS TO MONSTERS.
MY LOYAL SERVANTS SABOTAGED YOUR EFFORTS WITH APLOMB.
TELL THEM WHY, DEARS.
WE'VE BEEN PROMISED POWER, SECOND ONLY TO HER MAJESTY'S!

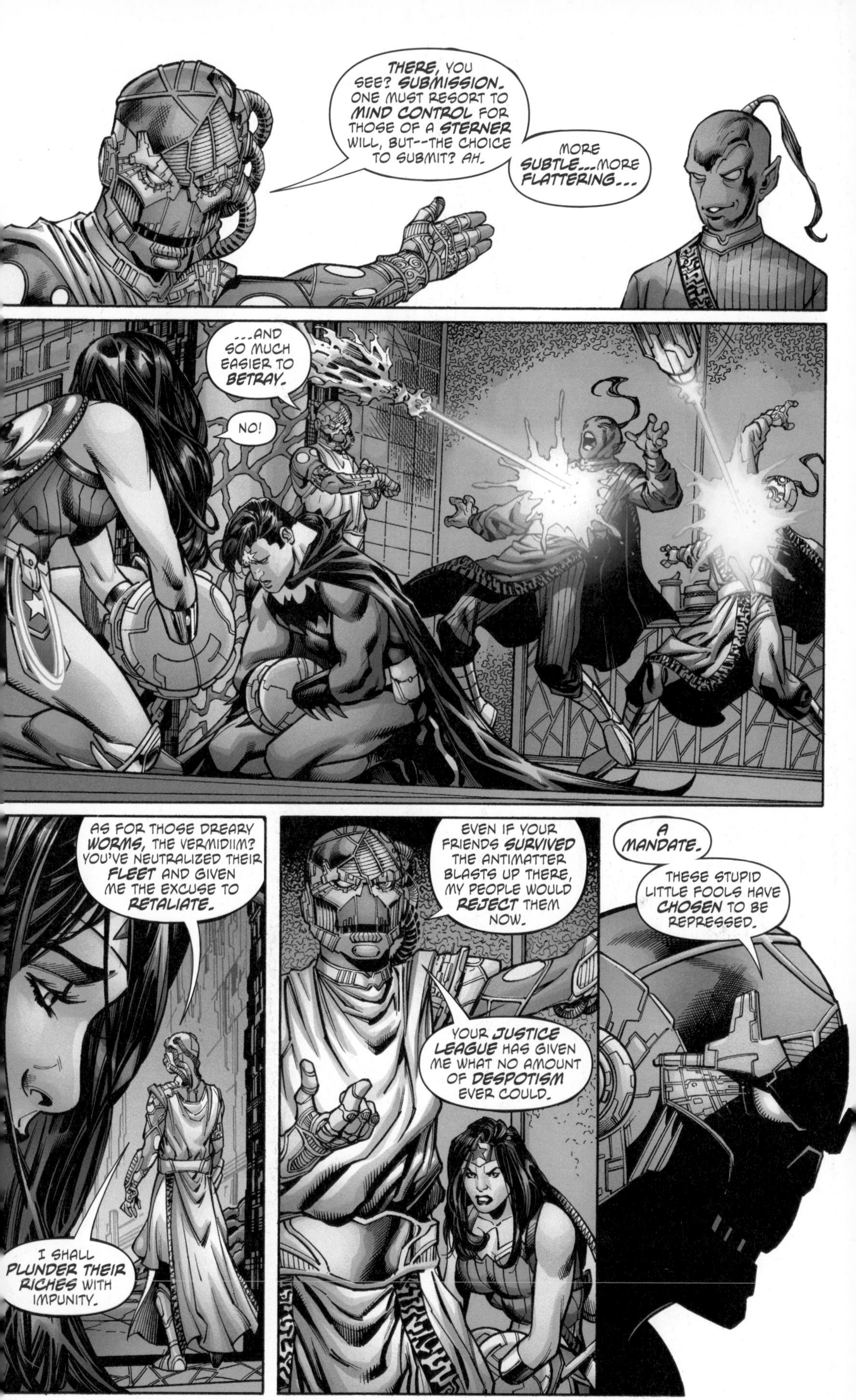
THERE, YOU SEE? SUBMISSION. ONE MUST RESORT TO MIND CONTROL FOR THOSE OF A STERNER WILL, BUT--THE CHOICE TO SUBMIT? AH.
MORE SUBTLE...MORE FLATTERING...
...AND SO MUCH EASIER TO BETRAY.
NO!
AS FOR THOSE DREARY WORMS, THE VERMIDIIM? YOU'VE NEUTRALIZED THEIR FLEET AND GIVEN ME THE EXCUSE TO RETALIATE.
I SHALL PLUNDER THEIR RICHES WITH IMPUNITY.
EVEN IF YOUR FRIENDS SURVIVED THE ANTIMATTER BLASTS UP THERE, MY PEOPLE WOULD REJECT THEM NOW.
YOUR JUSTICE LEAGUE HAS GIVEN ME WHAT NO AMOUNT OF DESPOTISM EVER COULD.
A MANDATE.
THESE STUPID LITTLE FOOLS HAVE CHOSEN TO BE REPRESSED.

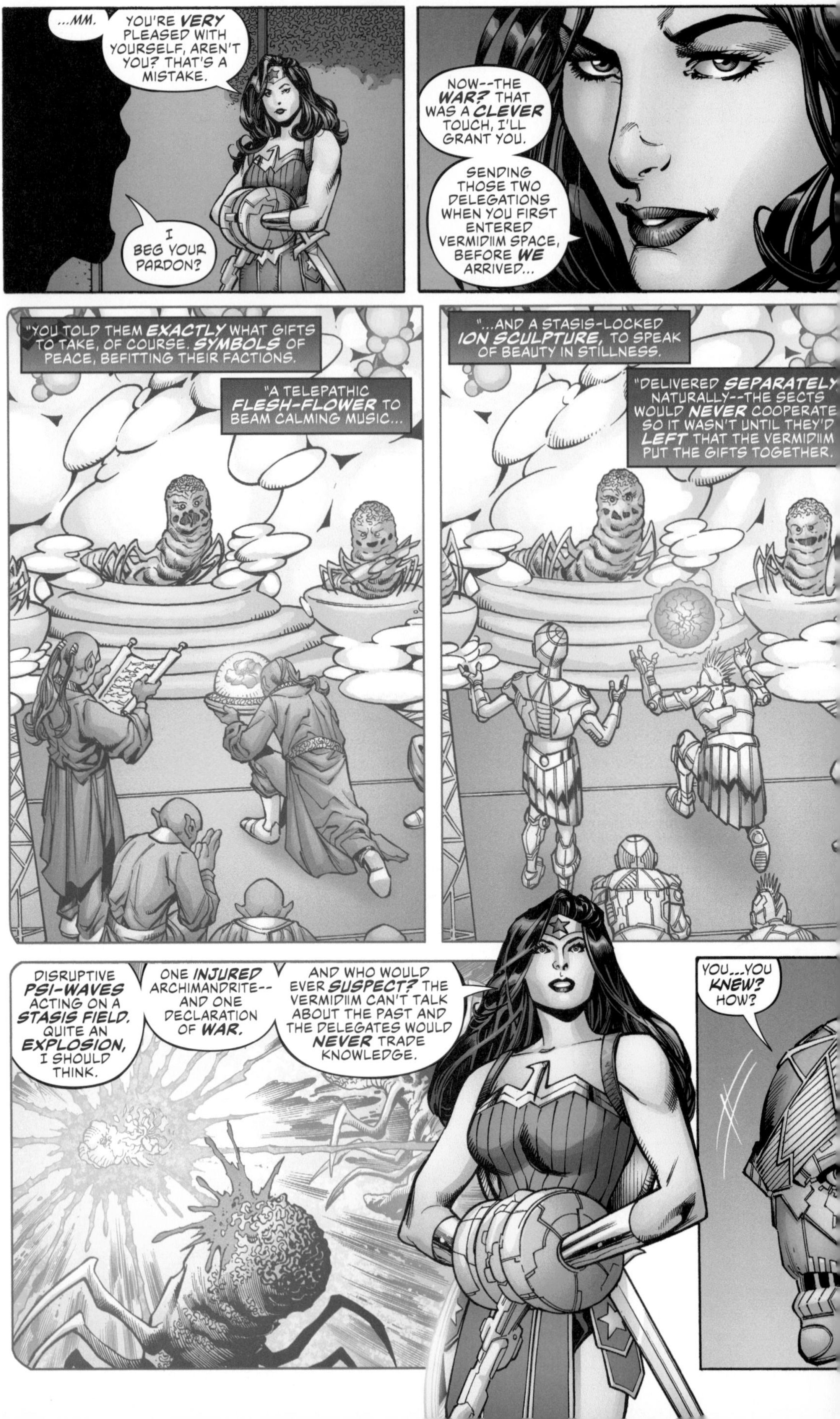
...MM.
YOU'RE VERY PLEASED WITH YOURSELF, AREN'T YOU? THAT'S A MISTAKE.
I BEG YOUR PARDON?
NOW--THE WAR? THAT WAS A CLEVER TOUCH, I'LL GRANT YOU.
SENDING THOSE TWO DELEGATIONS WHEN YOU FIRST ENTERED VERMIDIIM SPACE, BEFORE WE ARRIVED...
"YOU TOLD THEM EXACTLY WHAT GIFTS TO TAKE, OF COURSE. SYMBOLS OF PEACE, BEFITTING THEIR FACTIONS.
"A TELEPATHIC FLESH-FLOWER TO BEAM CALMING MUSIC...
"...AND A STASIS-LOCKED ION SCULPTURE, TO SPEAK OF BEAUTY IN STILLNESS.
"DELIVERED SEPARATELY, NATURALLY--THE SECTS WOULD NEVER COOPERATE SO IT WASN'T UNTIL THEY'D LEFT THAT THE VERMIDIIM PUT THE GIFTS TOGETHER.
DISRUPTIVE PSI-WAVES ACTING ON A STASIS FIELD. QUITE AN EXPLOSION, I SHOULD THINK.
ONE INJURED ARCHIMANDRITE-- AND ONE DECLARATION OF WAR.
AND WHO WOULD EVER SUSPECT? THE VERMIDIIM CAN'T TALK ABOUT THE PAST AND THE DELEGATES WOULD NEVER TRADE KNOWLEDGE.
YOU...YOU KNEW? HOW?

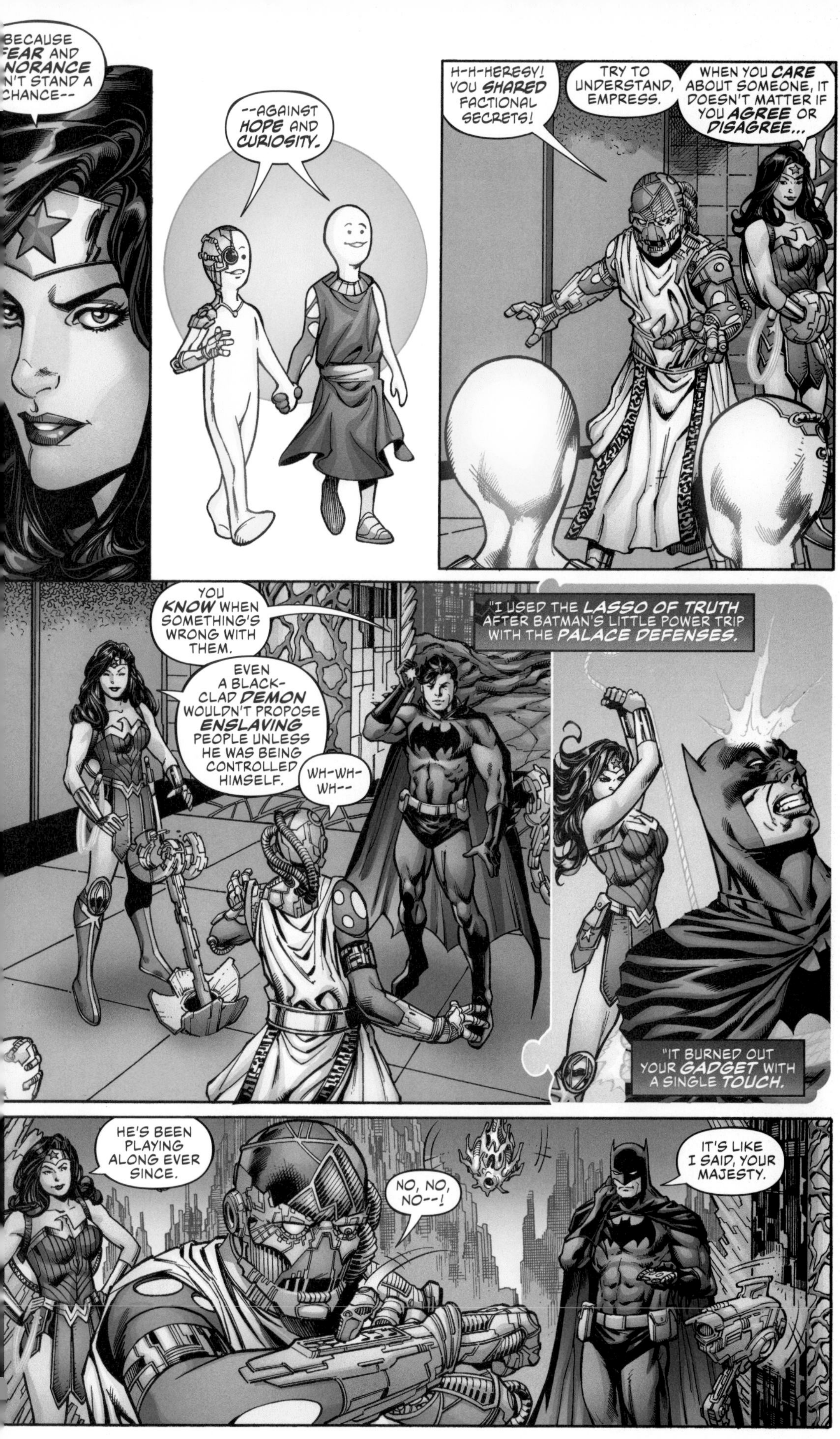
BECAUSE FEAR AND NORANCE N'T STAND A CHANCE--
--AGAINST HOPE AND CURIOSITY.
H-H-HERESY! YOU SHARED FACTIONAL SECRETS!
TRY TO UNDERSTAND, EMPRESS.
WHEN YOU CARE ABOUT SOMEONE, IT DOESN'T MATTER IF YOU AGREE OR DISAGREE...
YOU KNOW WHEN SOMETHING'S WRONG WITH THEM.
EVEN A BLACK-CLAD DEMON WOULDN'T PROPOSE ENSLAVING PEOPLE UNLESS HE WAS BEING CONTROLLED HIMSELF.
WH-WH-WH--
"I USED THE LASSO OF TRUTH AFTER BATMAN'S LITTLE POWER TRIP WITH THE PALACE DEFENSES.
"IT BURNED OUT YOUR GADGET WITH A SINGLE TOUCH.
HE'S BEEN PLAYING ALONG EVER SINCE.
NO, NO, NO--!
IT'S LIKE I SAID, YOUR MAJESTY.

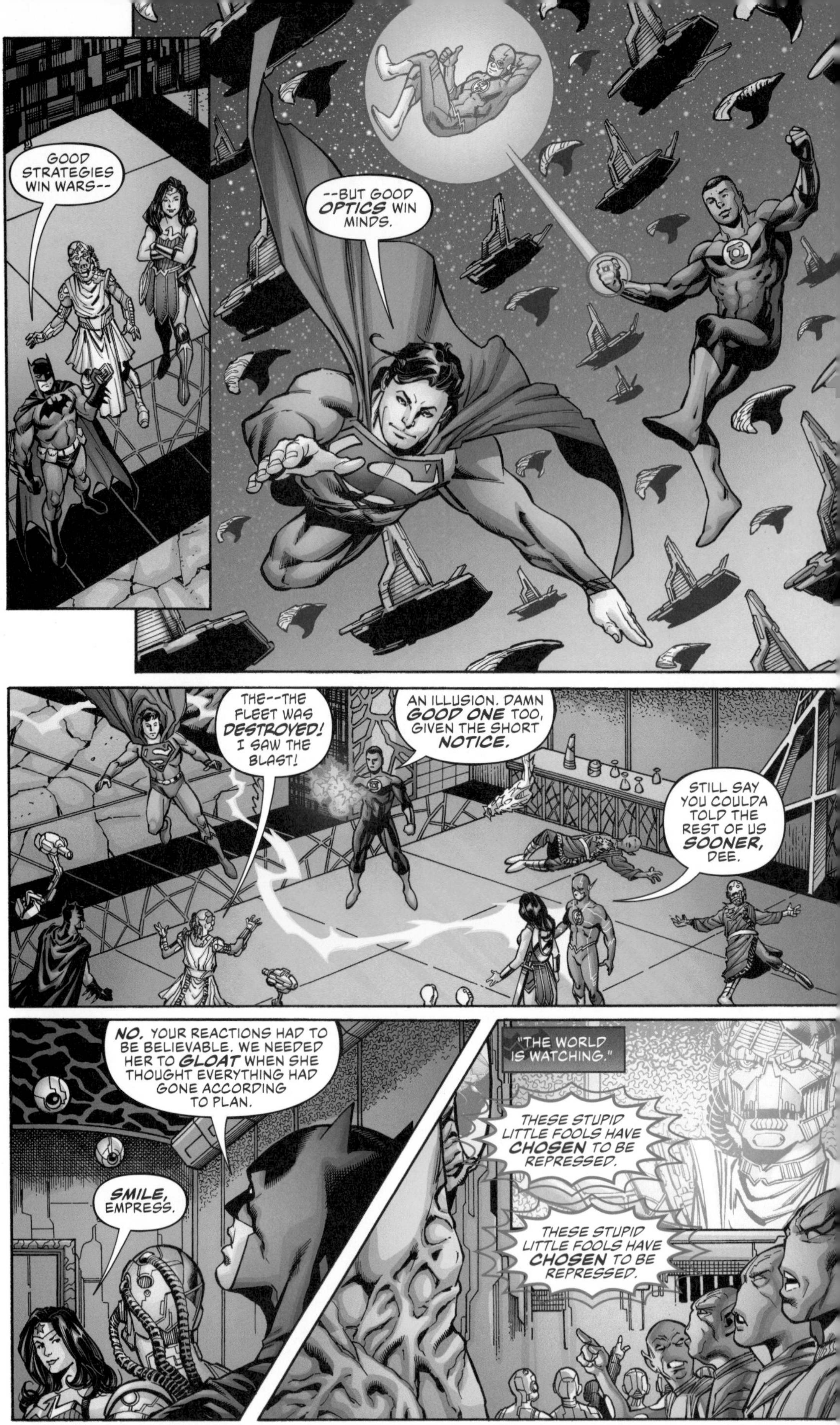
GOOD STRATEGIES WIN WARS--
--BUT GOOD OPTICS WIN MINDS.
THE--THE FLEET WAS DESTROYED! I SAW THE BLAST!
AN ILLUSION. DAMN GOOD ONE TOO, GIVEN THE SHORT NOTICE.
STILL SAY YOU COULDA TOLD THE REST OF US SOONER, DEE.
NO. YOUR REACTIONS HAD TO BE BELIEVABLE. WE NEEDED HER TO GLOAT WHEN SHE THOUGHT EVERYTHING HAD GONE ACCORDING TO PLAN.
SMILE, EMPRESS.
"THE WORLD IS WATCHING."
THESE STUPID LITTLE FOOLS HAVE CHOSEN TO BE REPRESSED.
THESE STUPID LITTLE FOOLS HAVE CHOSEN TO BE REPRESSED.

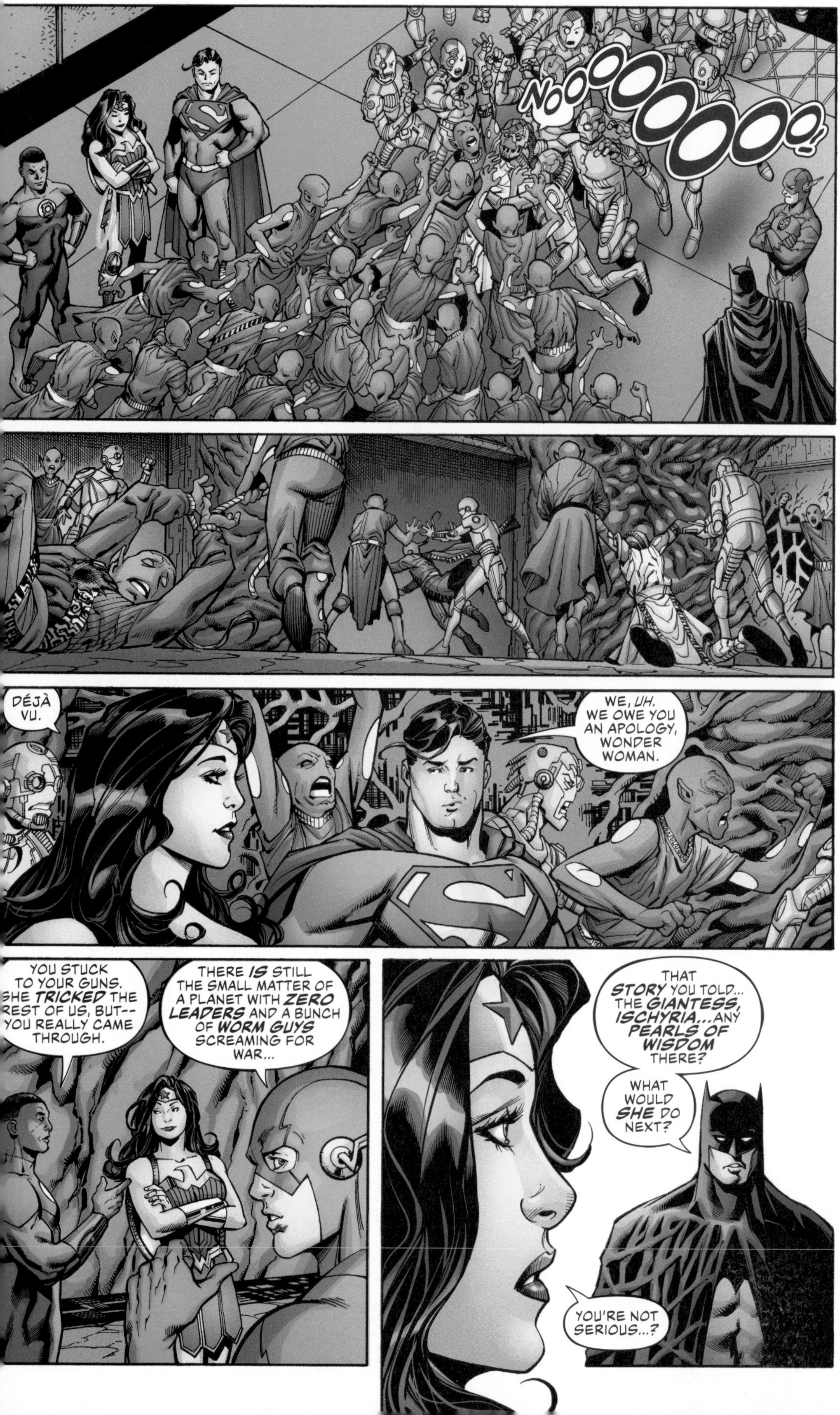
NOOOOOOOOO!
DÉJÀ VU.
WE, UH. WE OWE YOU AN APOLOGY, WONDER WOMAN.
YOU STUCK TO YOUR GUNS. SHE TRICKED THE REST OF US, BUT-- YOU REALLY CAME THROUGH.
THERE IS STILL THE SMALL MATTER OF A PLANET WITH ZERO LEADERS AND A BUNCH OF WORM GUYS SCREAMING FOR WAR...
THAT STORY YOU TOLD... THE GIANTESS, ISCHYRIA... ANY PEARLS OF WISDOM THERE?
WHAT WOULD SHE DO NEXT?
YOU'RE NOT SERIOUS...?

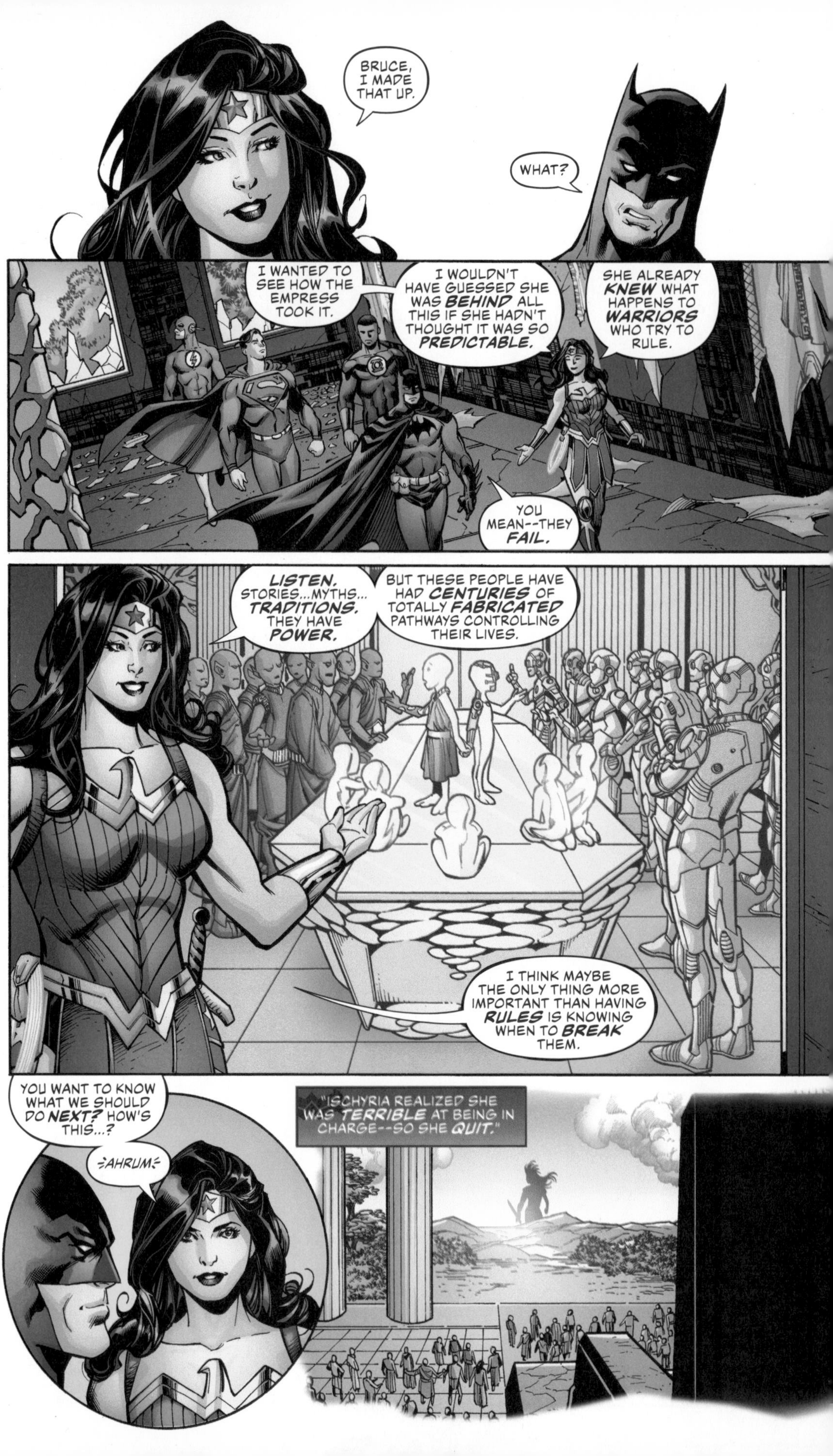
BRUCE, I MADE THAT UP.
WHAT?
I WANTED TO SEE HOW THE EMPRESS TOOK IT.
I WOULDN'T HAVE GUESSED SHE WAS **BEHIND** ALL THIS IF SHE HADN'T THOUGHT IT WAS SO **PREDICTABLE.**
SHE ALREADY **KNEW** WHAT HAPPENS TO **WARRIORS** WHO TRY TO RULE.
YOU MEAN--THEY **FAIL.**
LISTEN. STORIES...MYTHS... **TRADITIONS.** THEY HAVE **POWER.**
BUT THESE PEOPLE HAVE HAD **CENTURIES** OF TOTALLY **FABRICATED** PATHWAYS CONTROLLING THEIR LIVES.
I THINK MAYBE THE ONLY THING MORE IMPORTANT THAN HAVING **RULES** IS KNOWING WHEN TO **BREAK** THEM.
YOU WANT TO KNOW WHAT WE SHOULD DO **NEXT?** HOW'S THIS...?
AHRUM
"ISCHYRIA REALIZED SHE WAS **TERRIBLE** AT BEING IN CHARGE--SO SHE **QUIT.**"

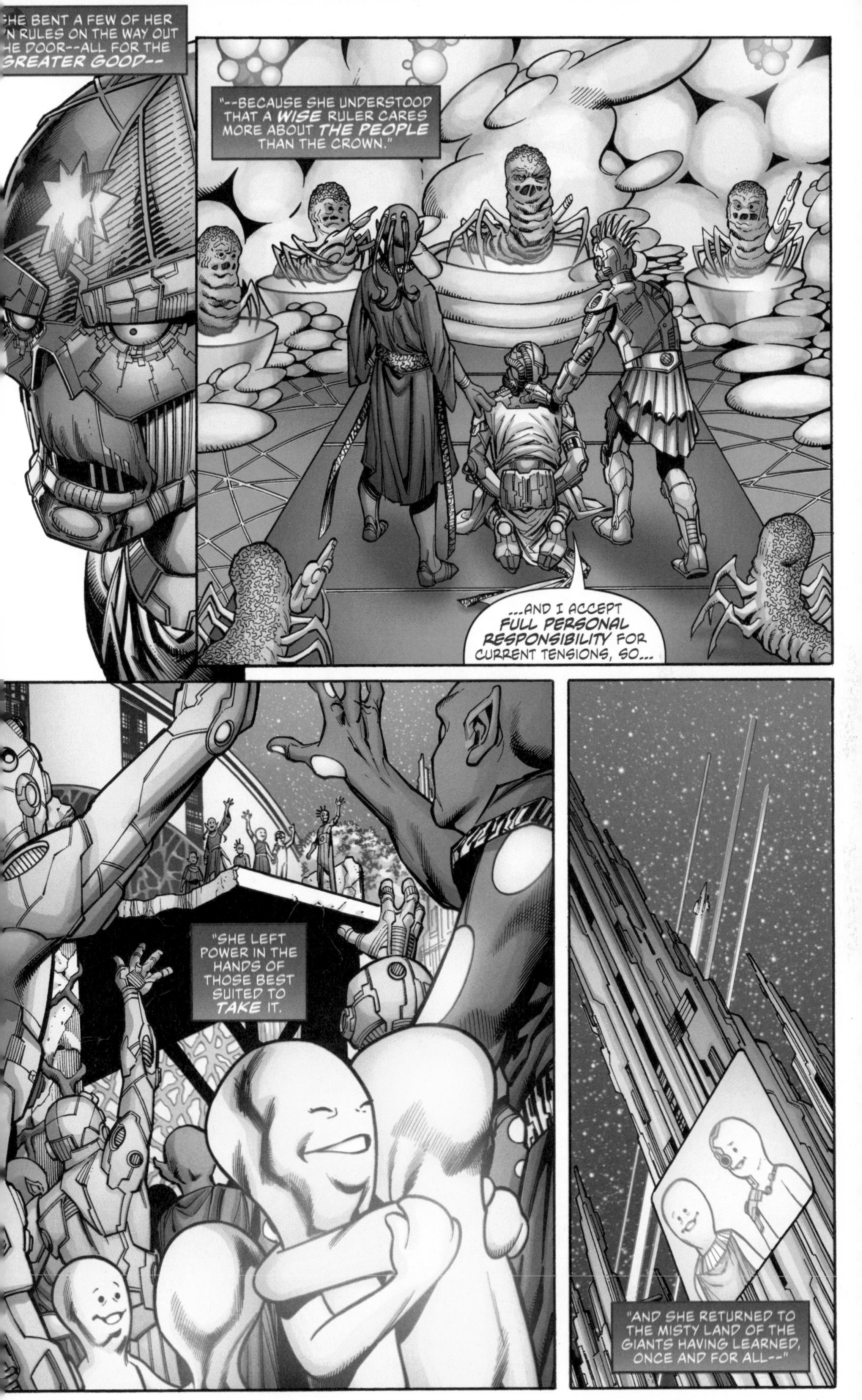
HE BENT A FEW OF HER N RULES ON THE WAY OUT HE DOOR--ALL FOR THE REATER GOOD--
"--BECAUSE SHE UNDERSTOOD THAT A WISE RULER CARES MORE ABOUT THE PEOPLE THAN THE CROWN."
...AND I ACCEPT FULL PERSONAL RESPONSIBILITY FOR CURRENT TENSIONS, SO...
"SHE LEFT POWER IN THE HANDS OF THOSE BEST SUITED TO TAKE IT.
"AND SHE RETURNED TO THE MISTY LAND OF THE GIANTS HAVING LEARNED, ONCE AND FOR ALL--"

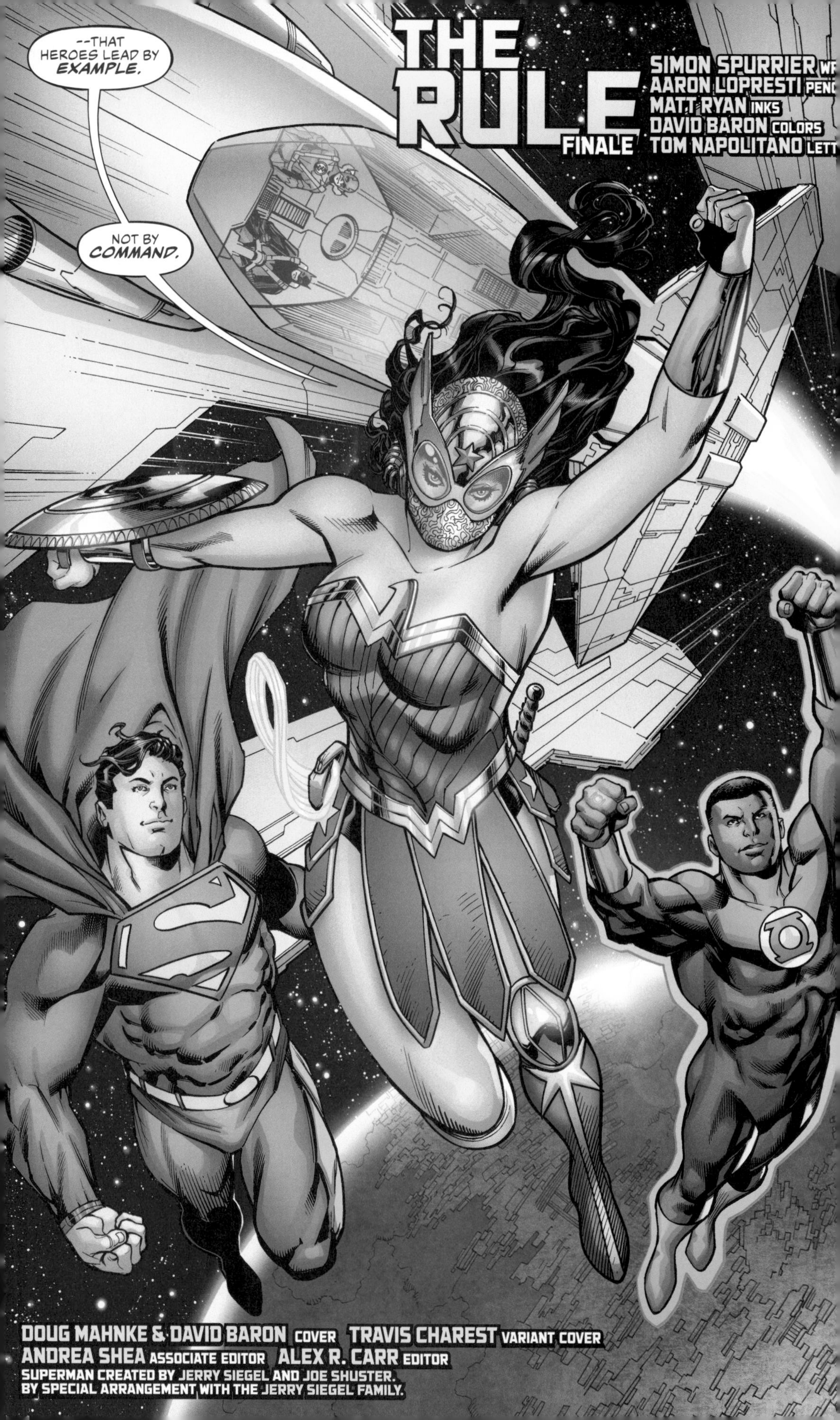
--THAT HEROES LEAD BY EXAMPLE.
NOT BY COMMAND.
THE RULE
FINALE
SIMON SPURRIER WR
AARON LOPRESTI PENC
MATT RYAN INKS
DAVID BARON COLORS
TOM NAPOLITANO LETT
DOUG MAHNKE & DAVID BARON COVER TRAVIS CHAREST VARIANT COVER
ANDREA SHEA ASSOCIATE EDITOR ALEX R. CARR EDITOR
SUPERMAN CREATED BY JERRY SIEGEL AND JOE SHUSTER.
BY SPECIAL ARRANGEMENT WITH THE JERRY SIEGEL FAMILY.

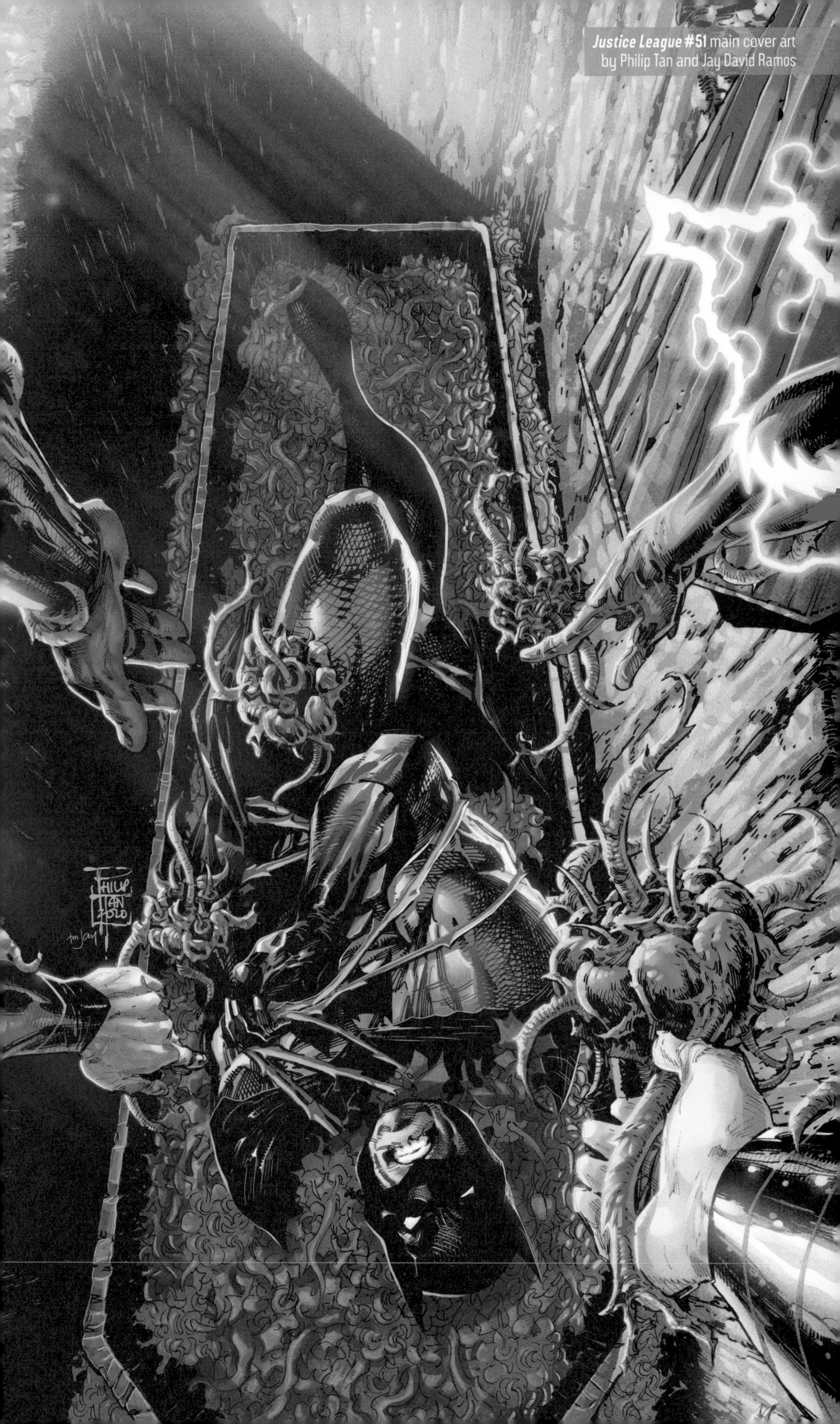

***Justice League* #51** main cover art
by Philip Tan and Jay David Ramos

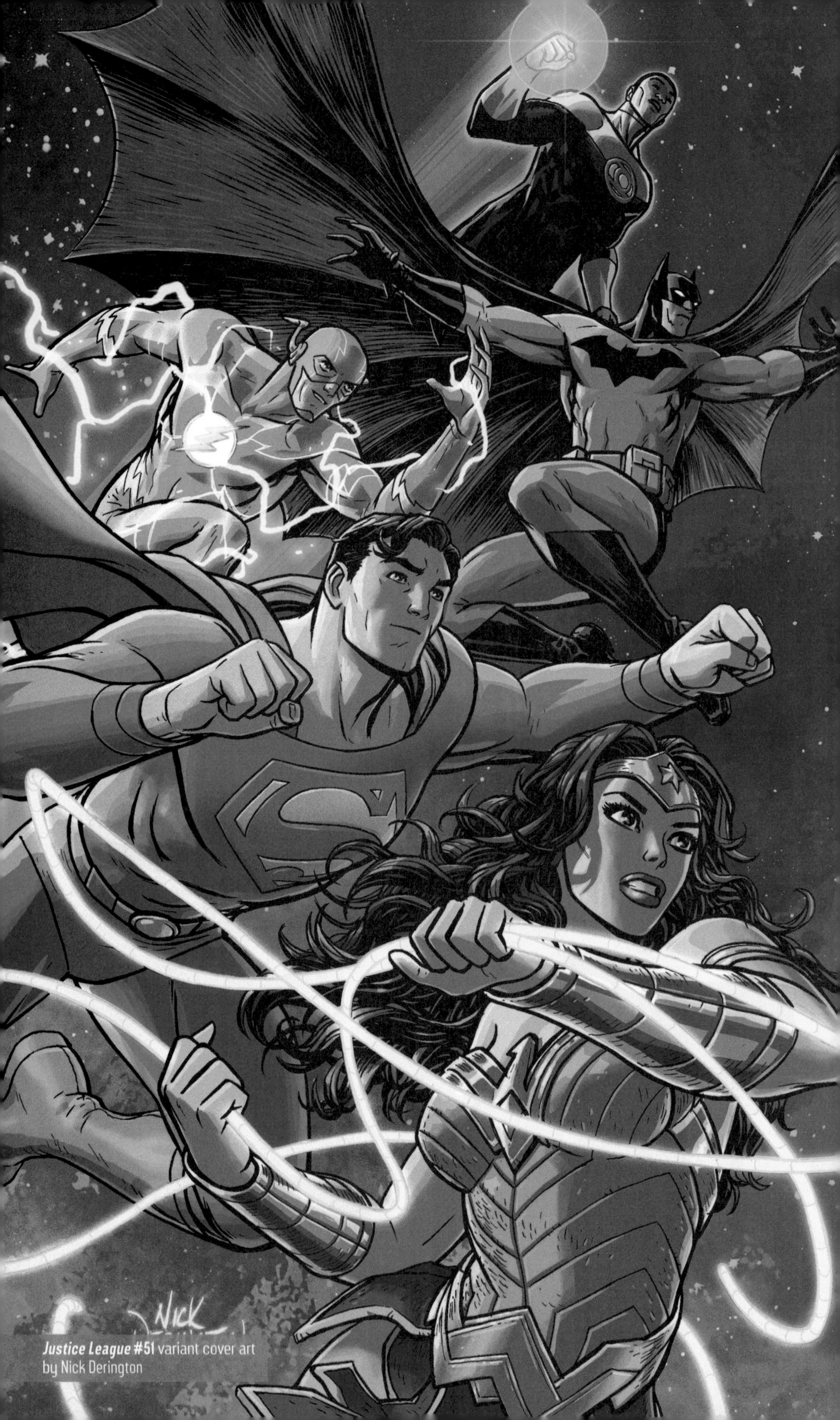
NICK

Justice League **#51** variant cover art by Nick Derington

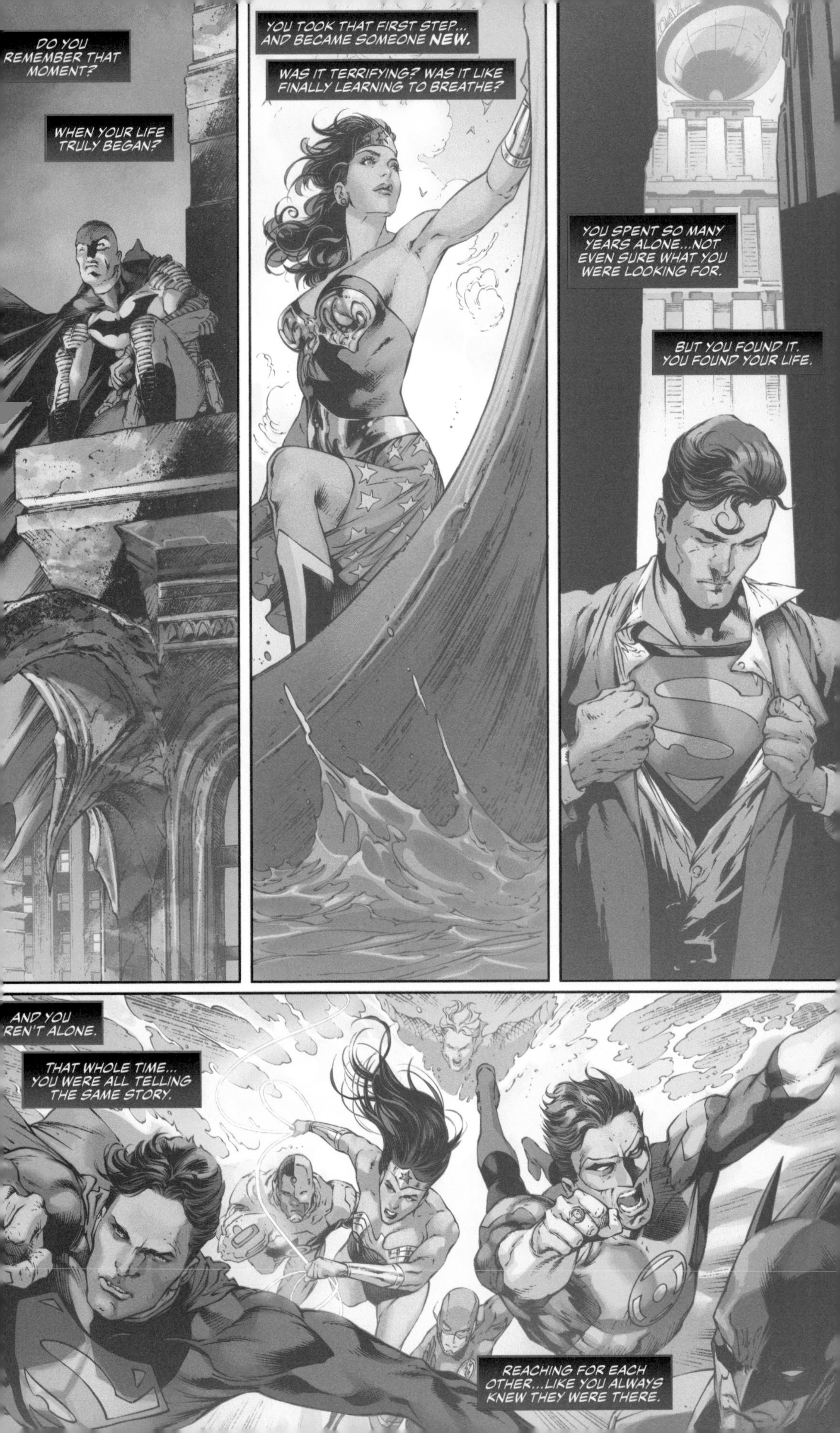
DO YOU REMEMBER THAT MOMENT?
WHEN YOUR LIFE TRULY BEGAN?
YOU TOOK THAT FIRST STEP... AND BECAME SOMEONE **NEW.**
WAS IT TERRIFYING? WAS IT LIKE FINALLY LEARNING TO BREATHE?
YOU SPENT SO MANY YEARS ALONE...NOT EVEN SURE WHAT YOU WERE LOOKING FOR.
BUT YOU FOUND IT. YOU FOUND YOUR LIFE.
AND YOU RƎN'T ALONE.
THAT WHOLE TIME... YOU WERE ALL TELLING THE SAME STORY.
REACHING FOR EACH OTHER...LIKE YOU ALWAYS KNEW THEY WERE THERE.

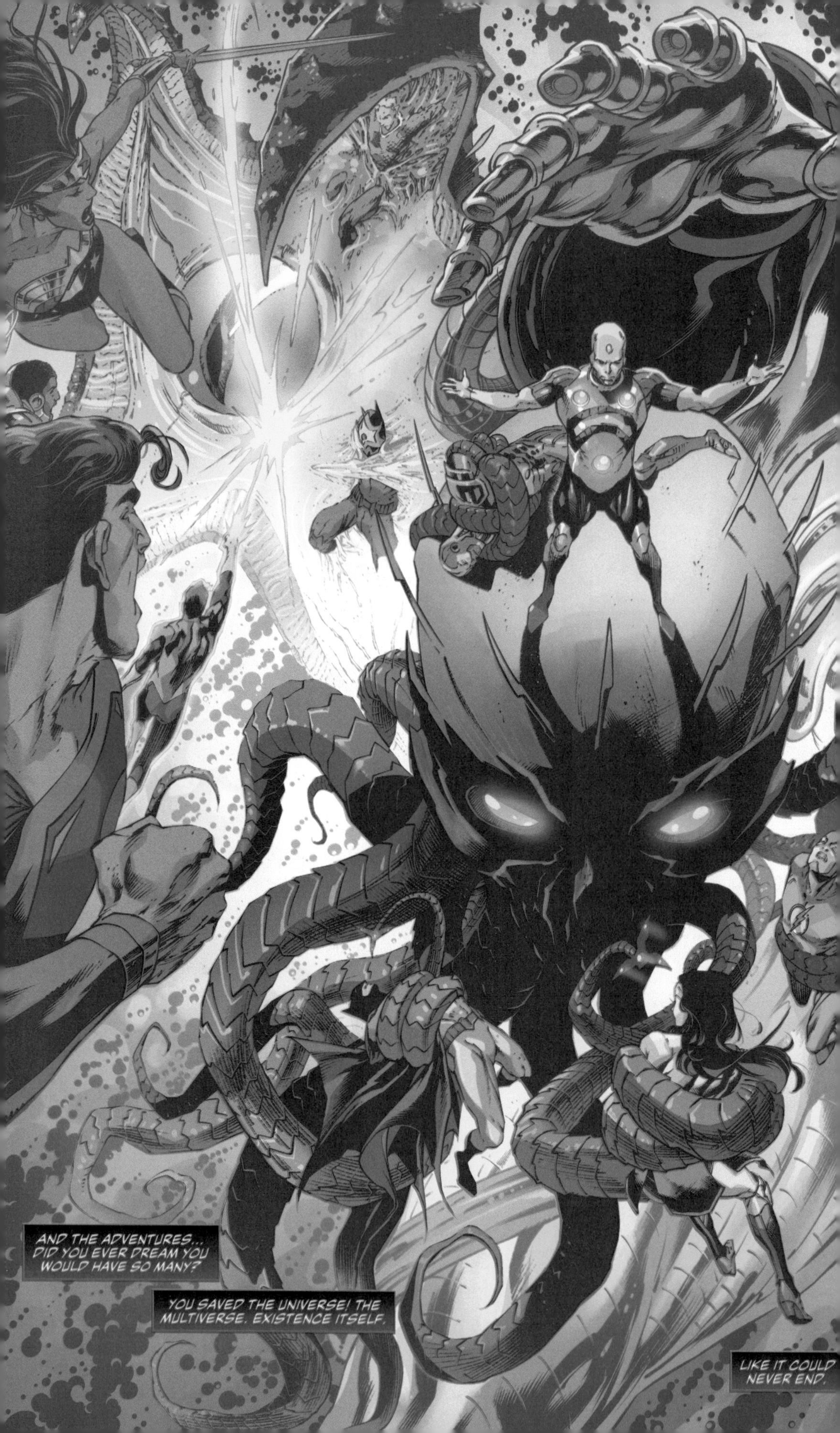
AND THE ADVENTURES... DID YOU EVER DREAM YOU WOULD HAVE SO MANY?
YOU SAVED THE UNIVERSE! THE MULTIVERSE. EXISTENCE ITSELF.
LIKE IT COULD NEVER END.

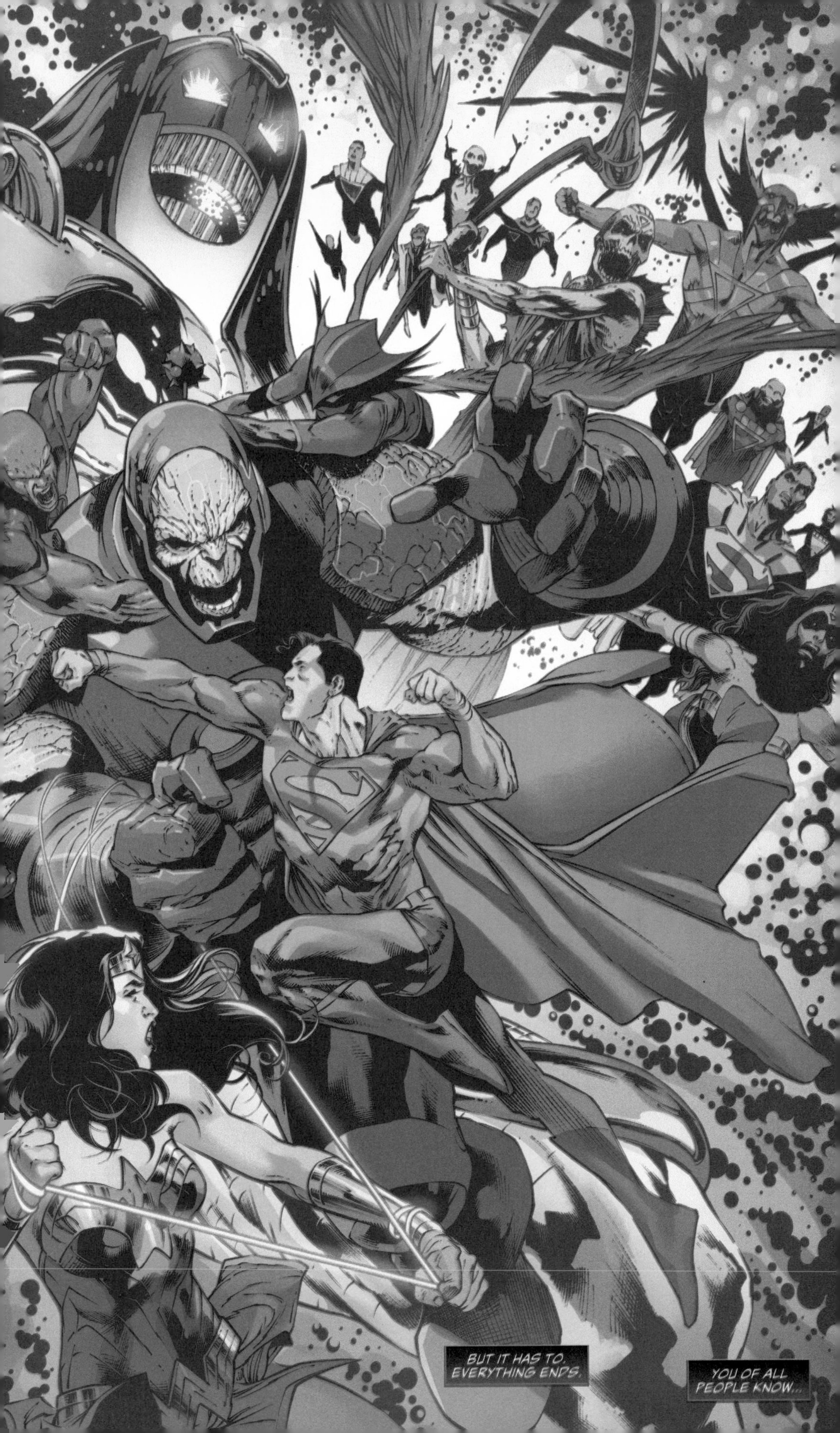
BUT IT HAS TO. EVERYTHING ENDS.
YOU OF ALL PEOPLE KNOW...

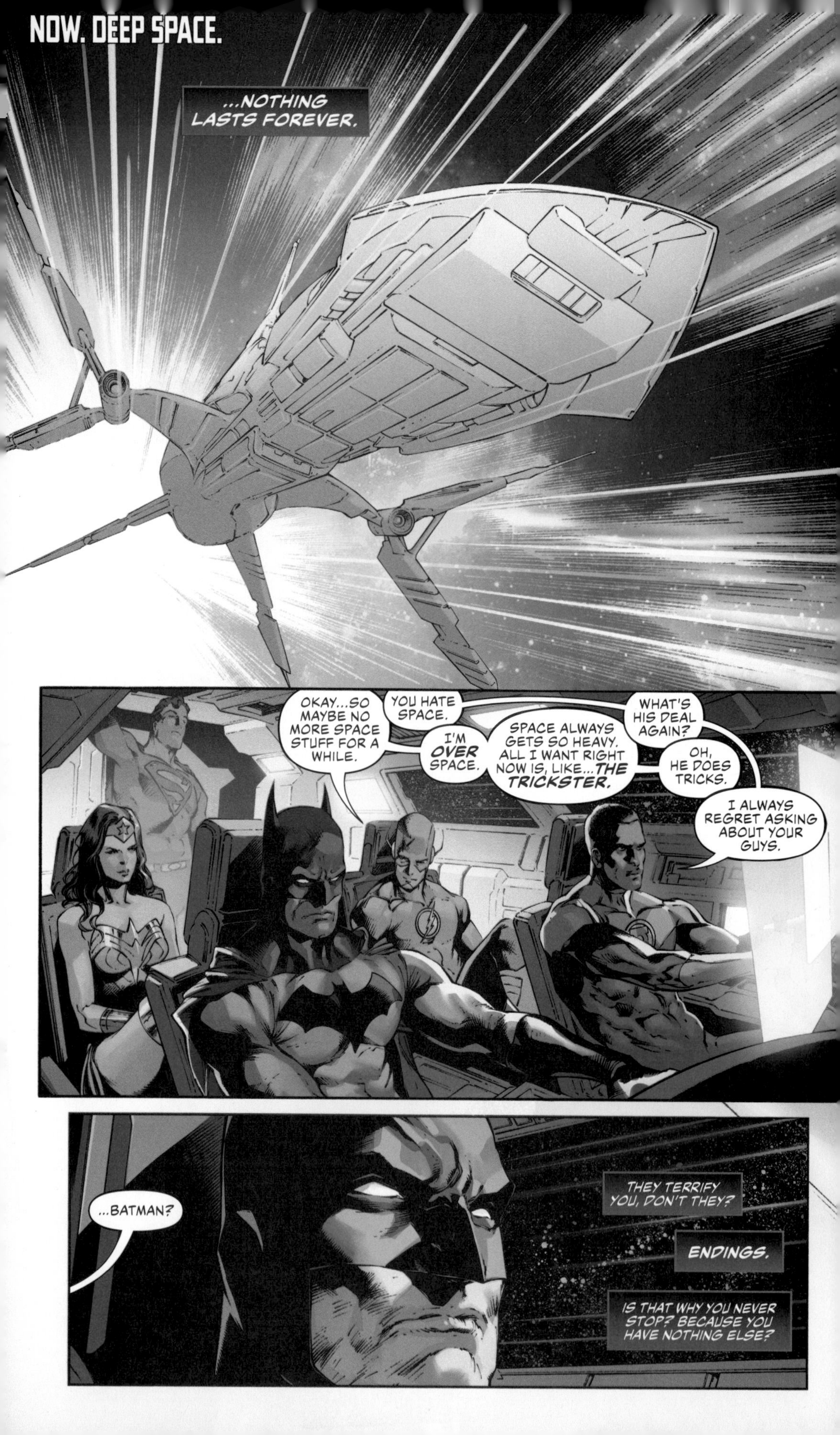
NOW. DEEP SPACE.
...NOTHING LASTS FOREVER.
OKAY...SO MAYBE NO MORE SPACE STUFF FOR A WHILE.
YOU HATE SPACE.
I'M OVER SPACE.
SPACE ALWAYS GETS SO HEAVY. ALL I WANT RIGHT NOW IS, LIKE...THE TRICKSTER.
WHAT'S HIS DEAL AGAIN?
OH, HE DOES TRICKS.
I ALWAYS REGRET ASKING ABOUT YOUR GUYS.
...BATMAN?
THEY TERRIFY YOU, DON'T THEY?
ENDINGS.
IS THAT WHY YOU NEVER STOP? BECAUSE YOU HAVE NOTHING ELSE?

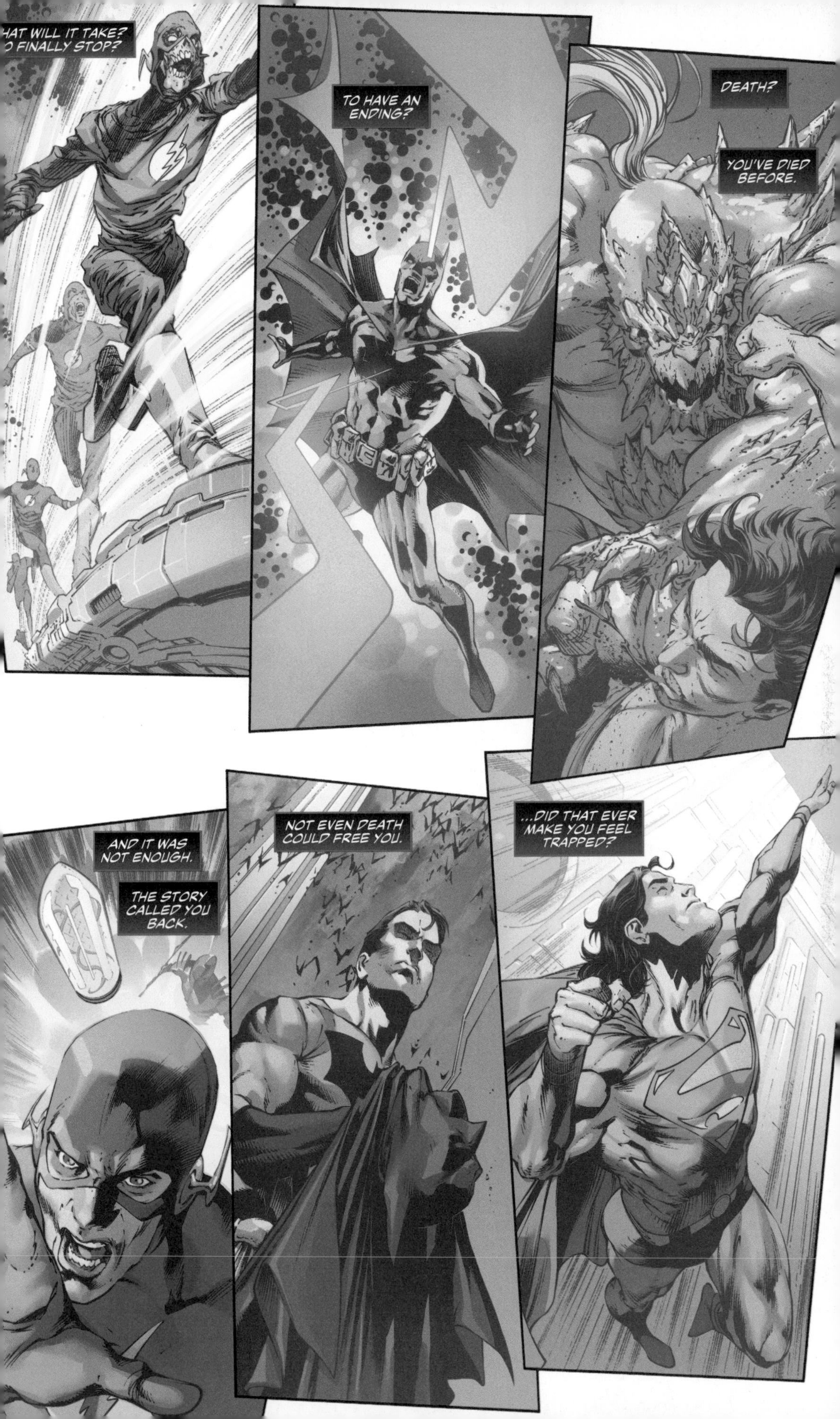
HAT WILL IT TAKE?
O FINALLY STOP?
TO HAVE AN ENDING?
DEATH?
YOU'VE DIED BEFORE.
AND IT WAS NOT ENOUGH.
THE STORY CALLED YOU BACK.
NOT EVEN DEATH COULD FREE YOU.
...DID THAT EVER MAKE YOU FEEL TRAPPED?

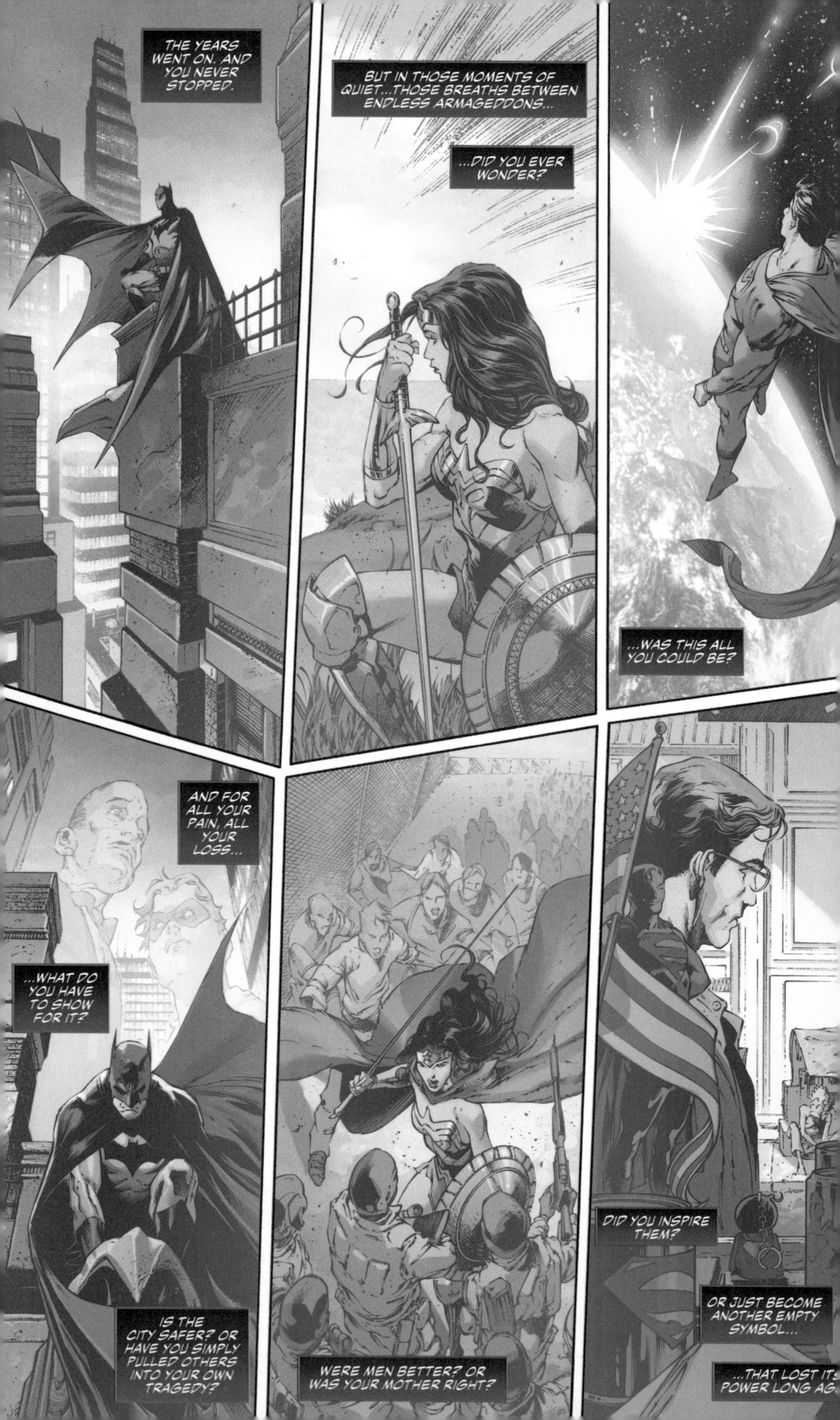
THE YEARS WENT ON. AND YOU NEVER STOPPED.
BUT IN THOSE MOMENTS OF QUIET...THOSE BREATHS BETWEEN ENDLESS ARMAGEDDONS...
...DID YOU EVER WONDER?
...WAS THIS ALL YOU COULD BE?
AND FOR ALL YOUR PAIN, ALL YOUR LOSS...
...WHAT DO YOU HAVE TO SHOW FOR IT?
IS THE CITY SAFER? OR HAVE YOU SIMPLY PULLED OTHERS INTO YOUR OWN TRAGEDY?
WERE MEN BETTER? OR WAS YOUR MOTHER RIGHT?
DID YOU INSPIRE THEM?
OR JUST BECOME ANOTHER EMPTY SYMBOL...

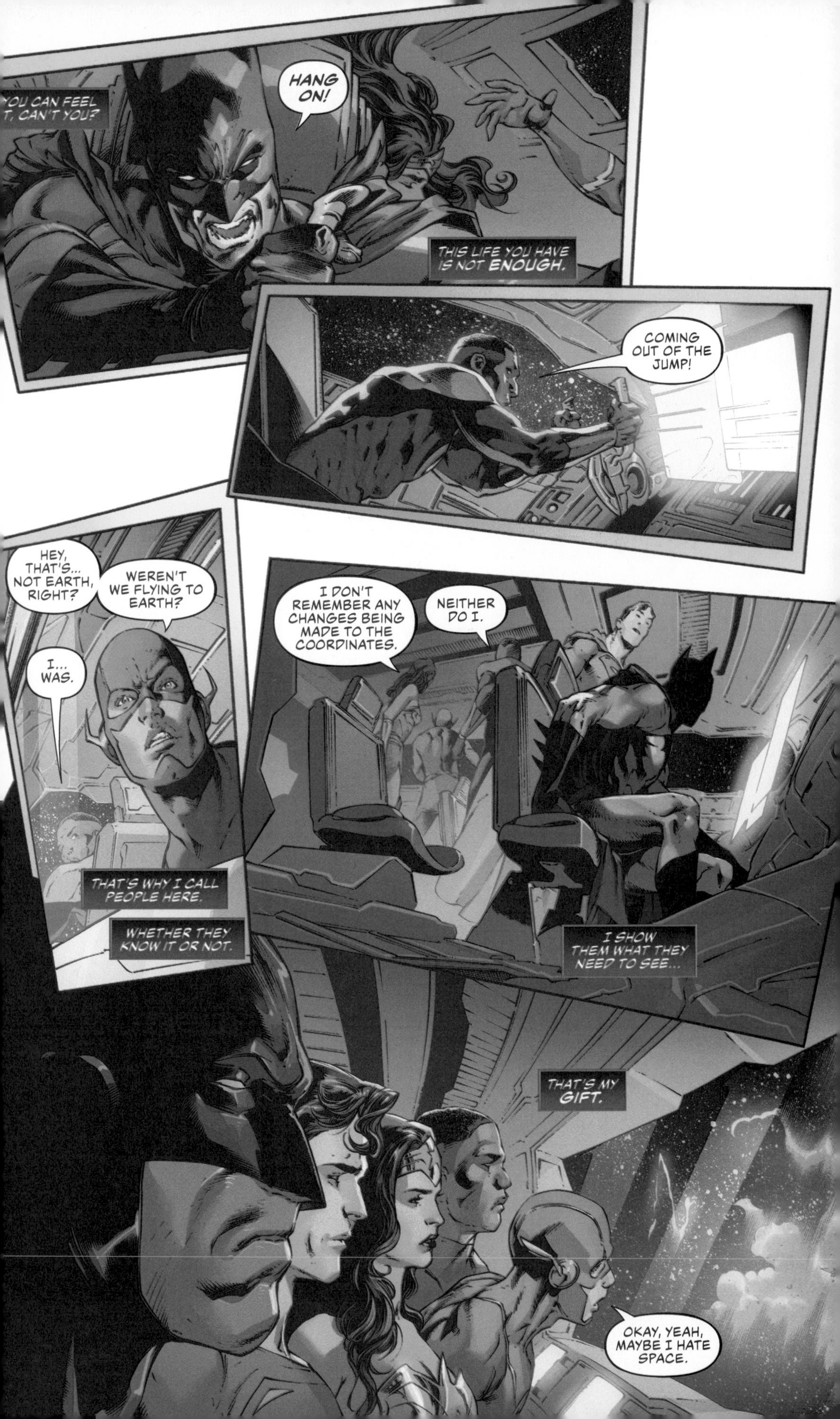
YOU CAN FEEL
IT, CAN'T YOU?
HANG ON!
THIS LIFE YOU HAVE IS NOT ENOUGH.
COMING OUT OF THE JUMP!
HEY, THAT'S... NOT EARTH, RIGHT?
WEREN'T WE FLYING TO EARTH?
I... WAS.
THAT'S WHY I CALL PEOPLE HERE.
WHETHER THEY KNOW IT OR NOT.
I DON'T REMEMBER ANY CHANGES BEING MADE TO THE COORDINATES.
NEITHER DO I.
I SHOW THEM WHAT THEY NEED TO SEE...
THAT'S MY GIFT.
OKAY, YEAH, MAYBE I HATE SPACE.

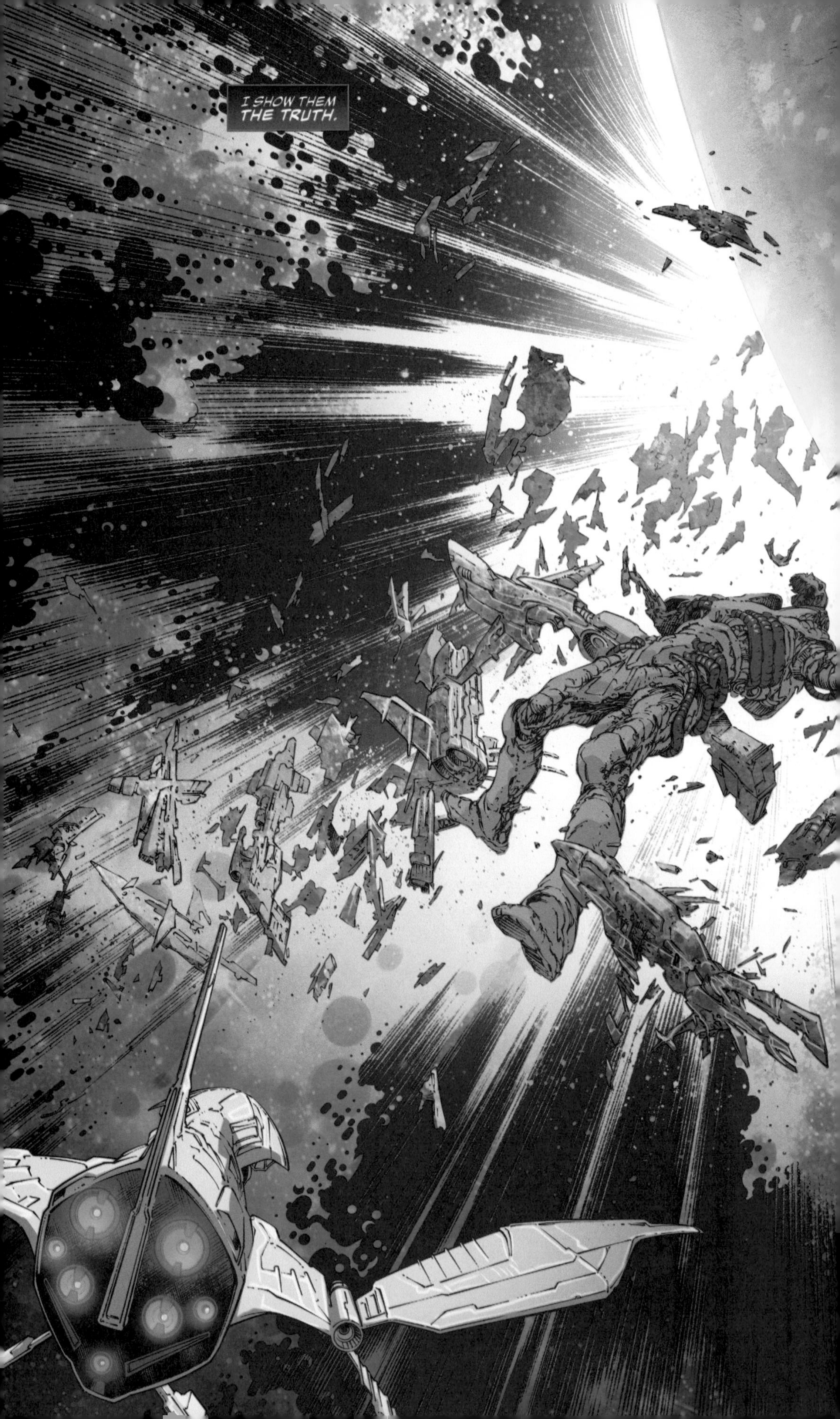
I SHOW THEM THE TRUTH.

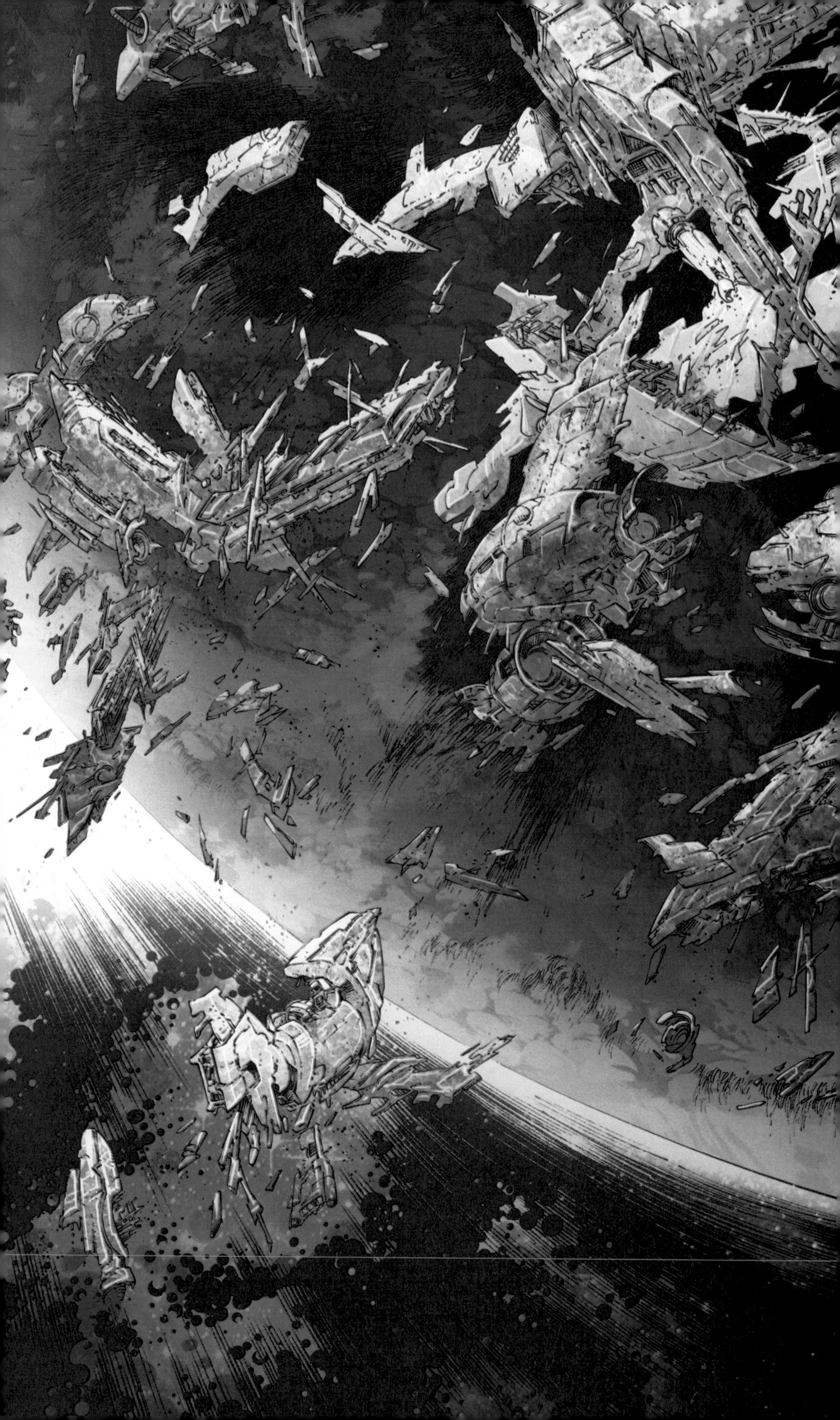

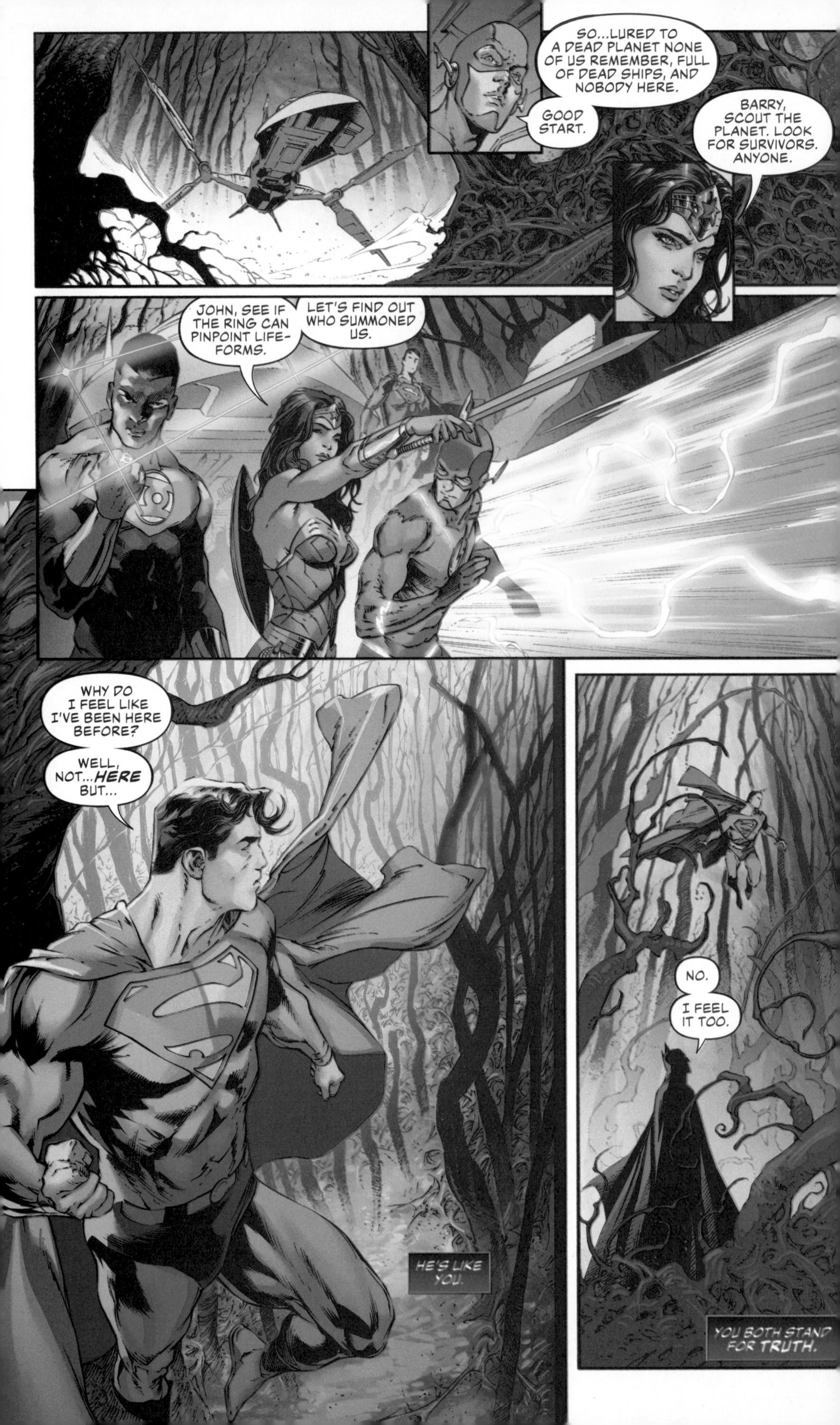
SO...LURED TO A DEAD PLANET NONE OF US REMEMBER, FULL OF DEAD SHIPS, AND NOBODY HERE.
GOOD START.
BARRY, SCOUT THE PLANET. LOOK FOR SURVIVORS. ANYONE.
JOHN, SEE IF THE RING CAN PINPOINT LIFE-FORMS.
LET'S FIND OUT WHO SUMMONED US.
WHY DO I FEEL LIKE I'VE BEEN HERE BEFORE?
WELL, NOT...**HERE** BUT...
HE'S LIKE YOU.
NO.
I FEEL IT TOO.
YOU BOTH STAND FOR **TRUTH**.

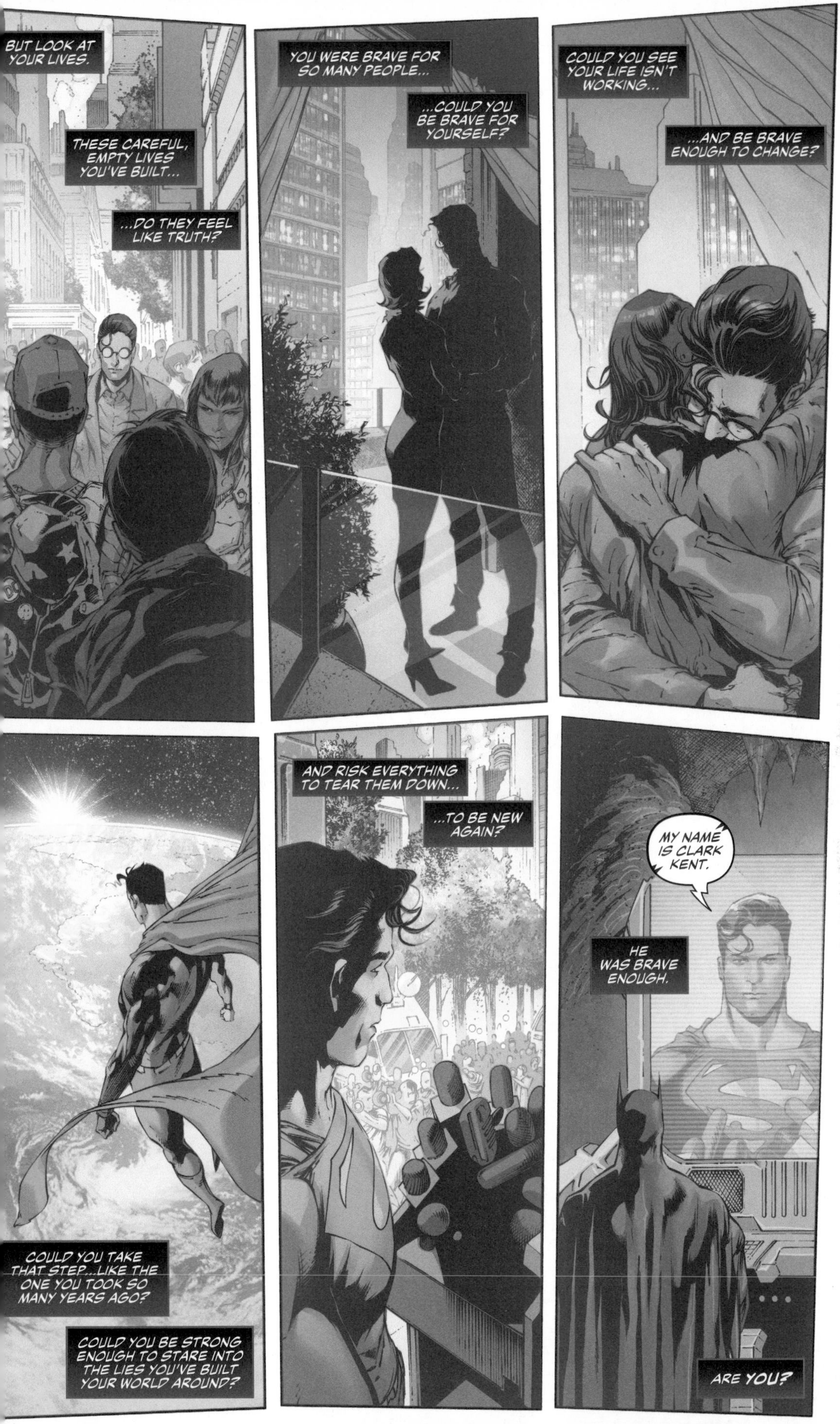
BUT LOOK AT YOUR LIVES.
THESE CAREFUL, EMPTY LIVES YOU'VE BUILT...
...DO THEY FEEL LIKE TRUTH?
YOU WERE BRAVE FOR SO MANY PEOPLE...
...COULD YOU BE BRAVE FOR YOURSELF?
COULD YOU SEE YOUR LIFE ISN'T WORKING...
...AND BE BRAVE ENOUGH TO CHANGE?
COULD YOU TAKE THAT STEP...LIKE THE ONE YOU TOOK SO MANY YEARS AGO?
COULD YOU BE STRONG ENOUGH TO STARE INTO THE LIES YOU'VE BUILT YOUR WORLD AROUND?
AND RISK EVERYTHING TO TEAR THEM DOWN...
...TO BE NEW AGAIN?
MY NAME IS CLARK KENT.
HE WAS BRAVE ENOUGH.
ARE YOU?

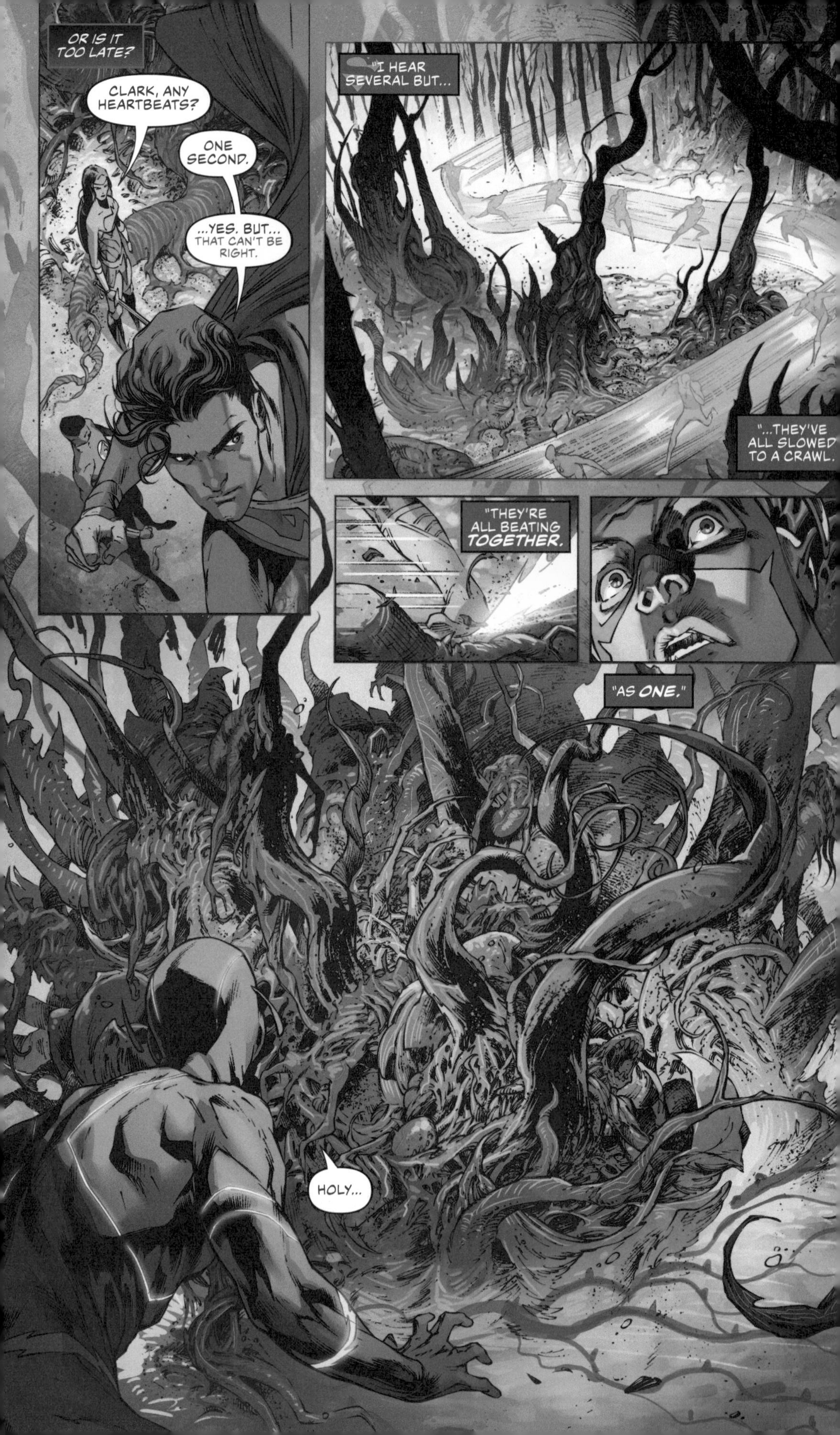
OR IS IT TOO LATE?
CLARK, ANY HEARTBEATS?
ONE SECOND.
...YES. BUT... THAT CAN'T BE RIGHT.
"I HEAR SEVERAL BUT...
"...THEY'VE ALL SLOWED TO A CRAWL.
"THEY'RE ALL BEATING TOGETHER.
"AS ONE."
HOLY...

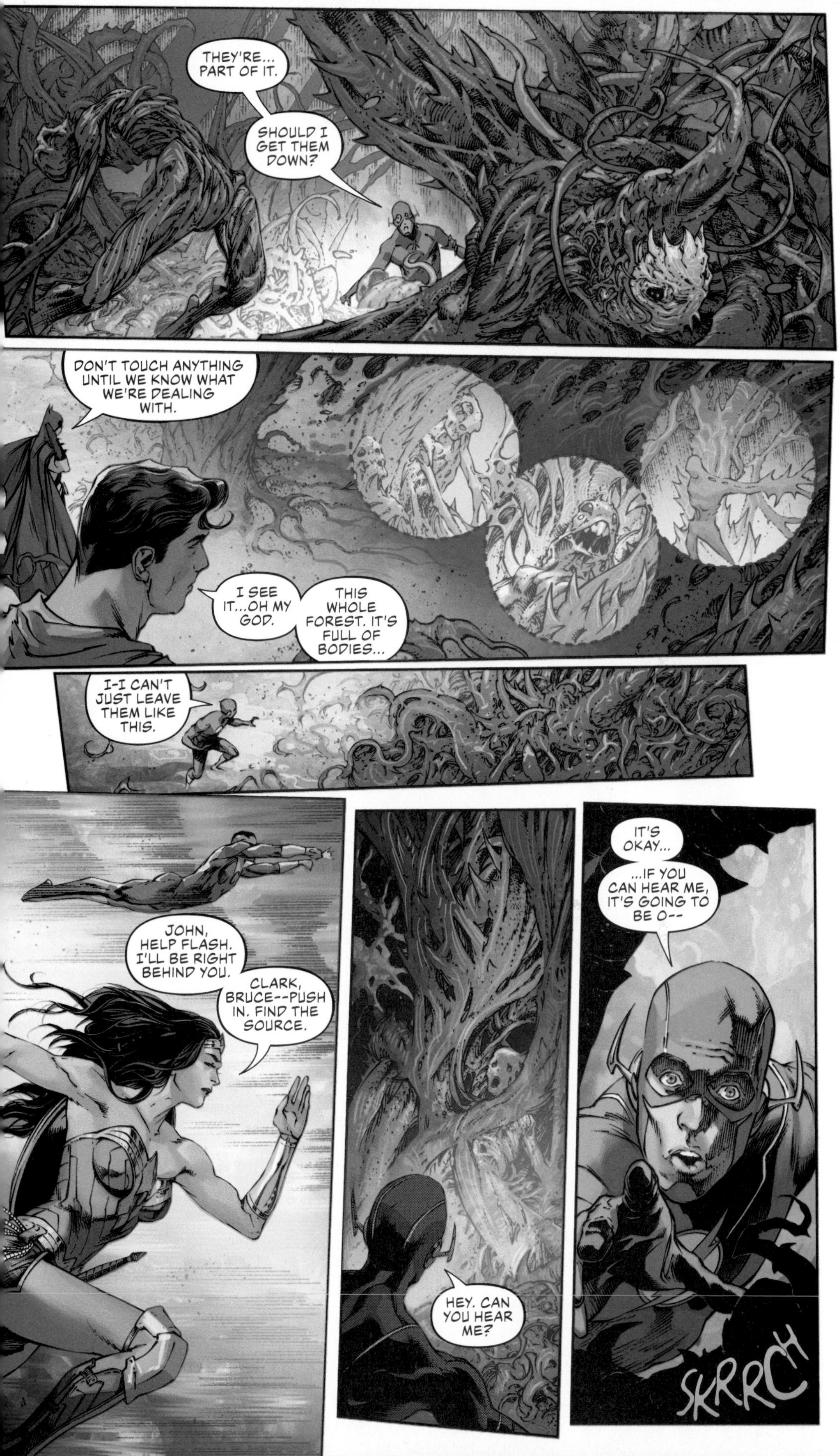
THEY'RE... PART OF IT.
SHOULD I GET THEM DOWN?
DON'T TOUCH ANYTHING UNTIL WE KNOW WHAT WE'RE DEALING WITH.
I SEE IT...OH MY GOD.
THIS WHOLE FOREST. IT'S FULL OF BODIES...
I-I CAN'T JUST LEAVE THEM LIKE THIS.
JOHN, HELP FLASH. I'LL BE RIGHT BEHIND YOU.
CLARK, BRUCE--PUSH IN. FIND THE SOURCE.
HEY. CAN YOU HEAR ME?
IT'S OKAY...
...IF YOU CAN HEAR ME, IT'S GOING TO BE O--
SKRRCH

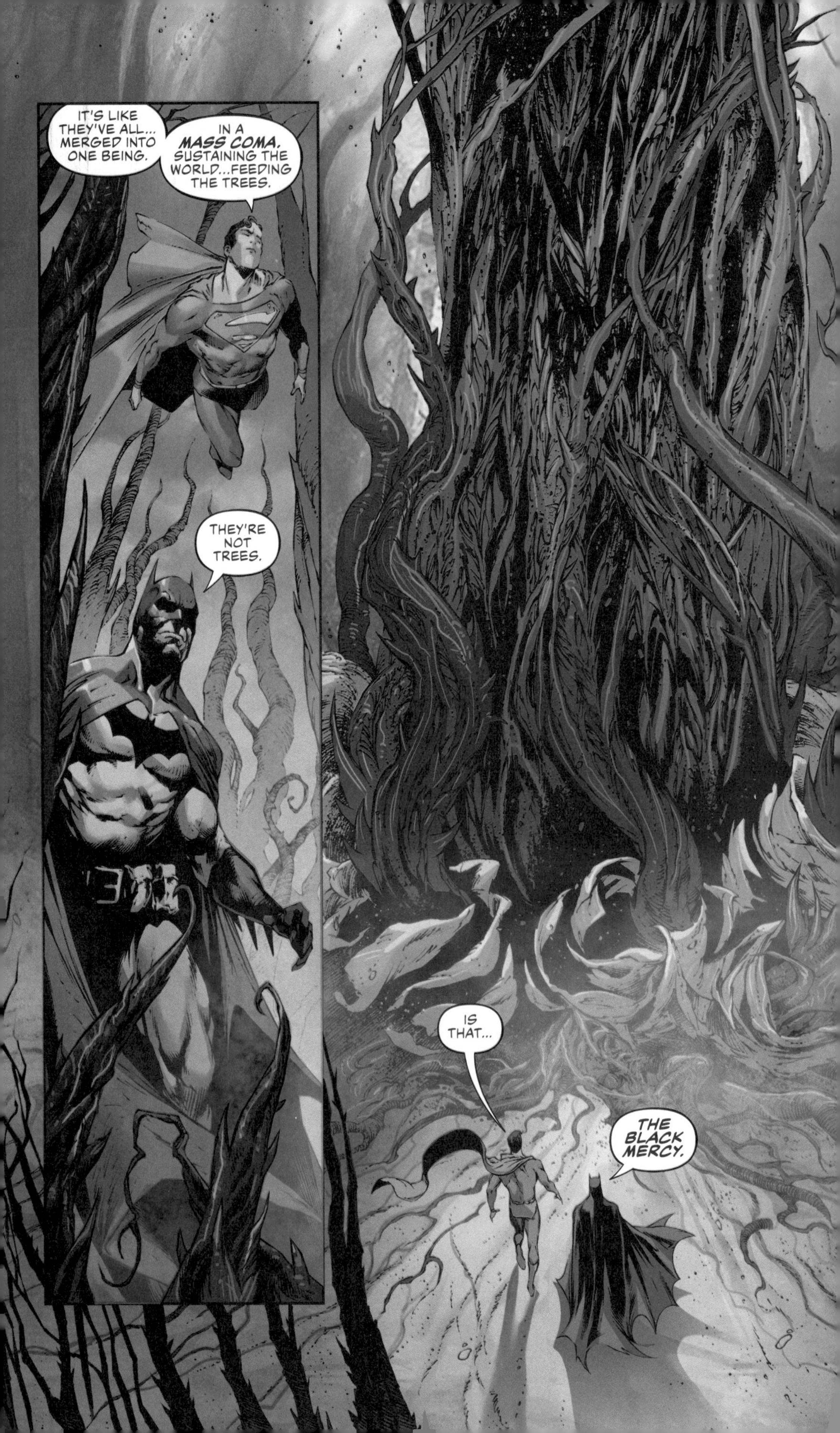
IT'S LIKE THEY'VE ALL... MERGED INTO ONE BEING.
IN A MASS COMA. SUSTAINING THE WORLD...FEEDING THE TREES.
THEY'RE NOT TREES.
IS THAT...
THE BLACK MERCY.

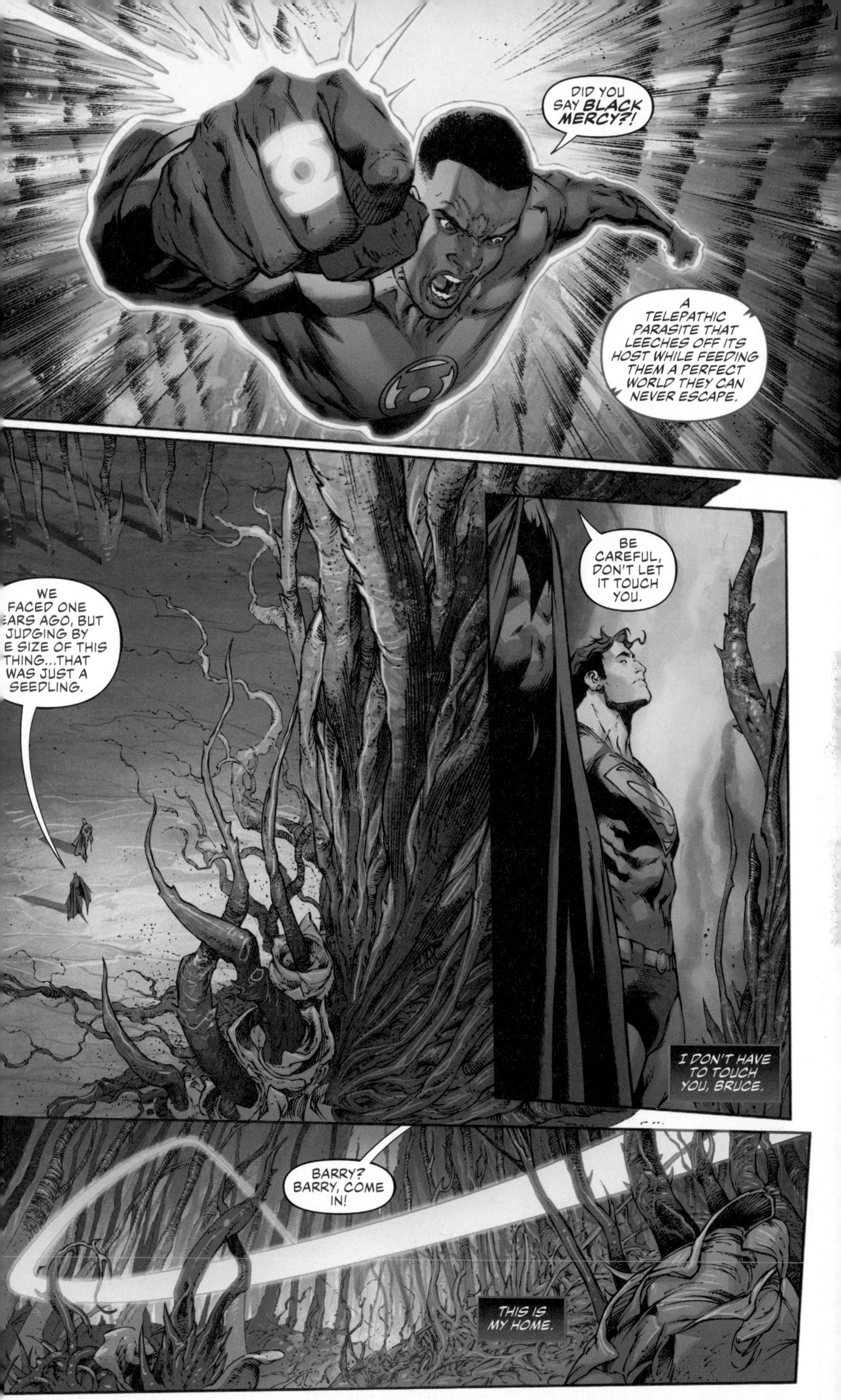
DID YOU SAY BLACK MERCY?!
A TELEPATHIC PARASITE THAT LEECHES OFF ITS HOST WHILE FEEDING THEM A PERFECT WORLD THEY CAN NEVER ESCAPE.
WE FACED ONE EARS AGO, BUT JUDGING BY E SIZE OF THIS THING...THAT WAS JUST A SEEDLING.
BE CAREFUL, DON'T LET IT TOUCH YOU.
I DON'T HAVE TO TOUCH YOU, BRUCE.
BARRY? BARRY, COME IN!
THIS IS MY HOME.

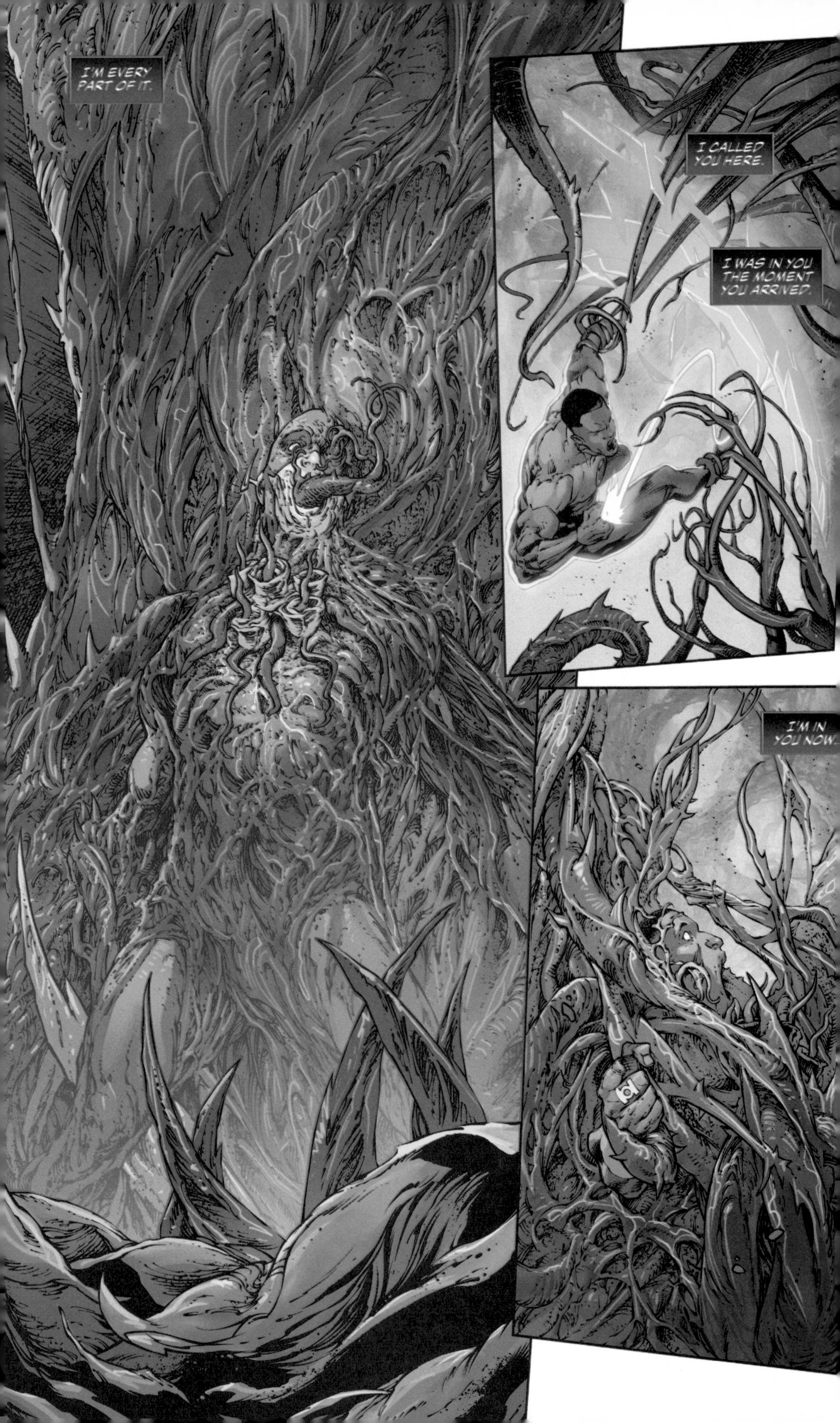
I'M EVERY PART OF IT.
I CALLED YOU HERE.
I WAS IN YOU THE MOMENT YOU ARRIVED.
I'M IN YOU NOW...

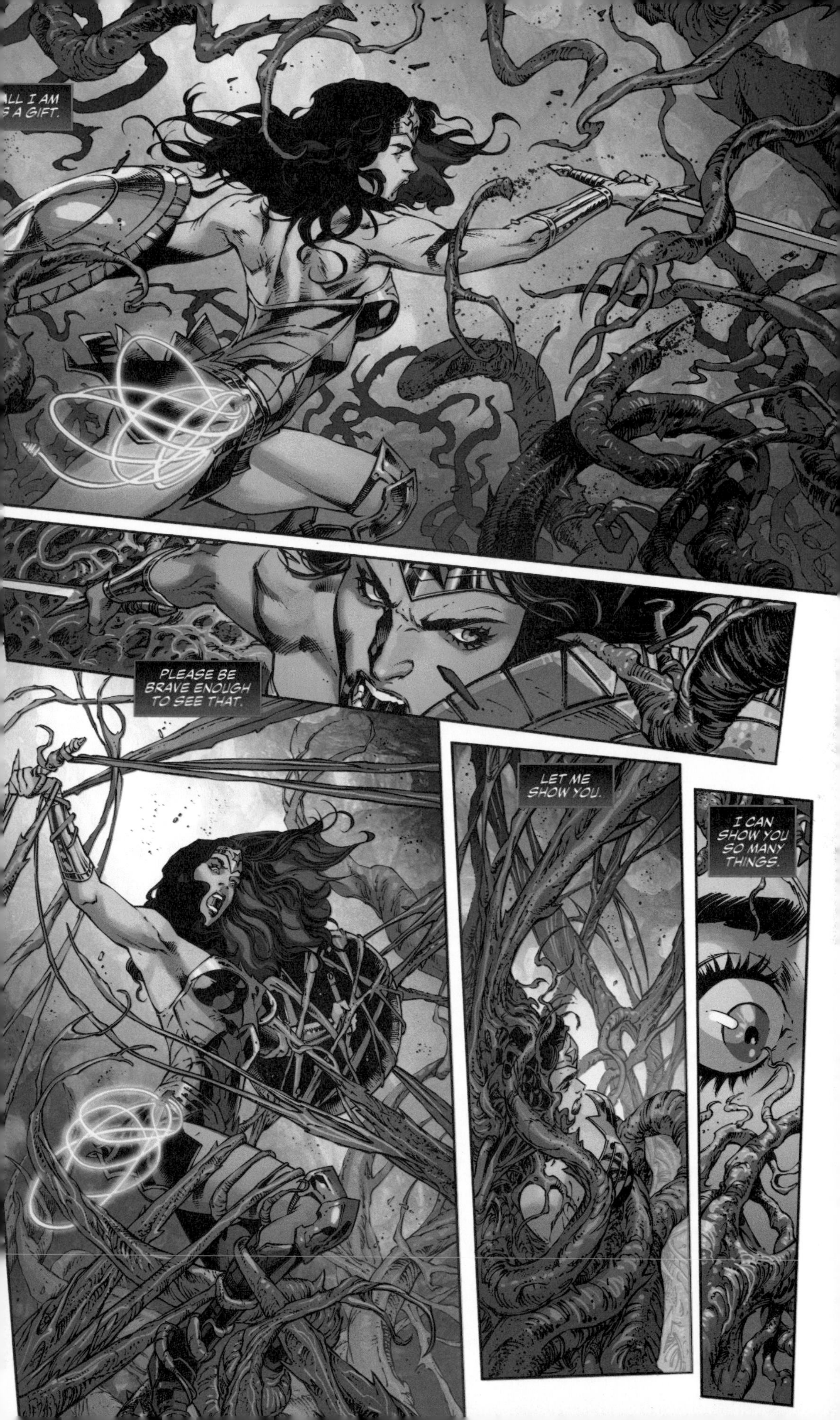

ALL I AM
S A GIFT.
PLEASE BE BRAVE ENOUGH TO SEE THAT.
LET ME SHOW YOU.
I CAN SHOW YOU SO MANY THINGS.

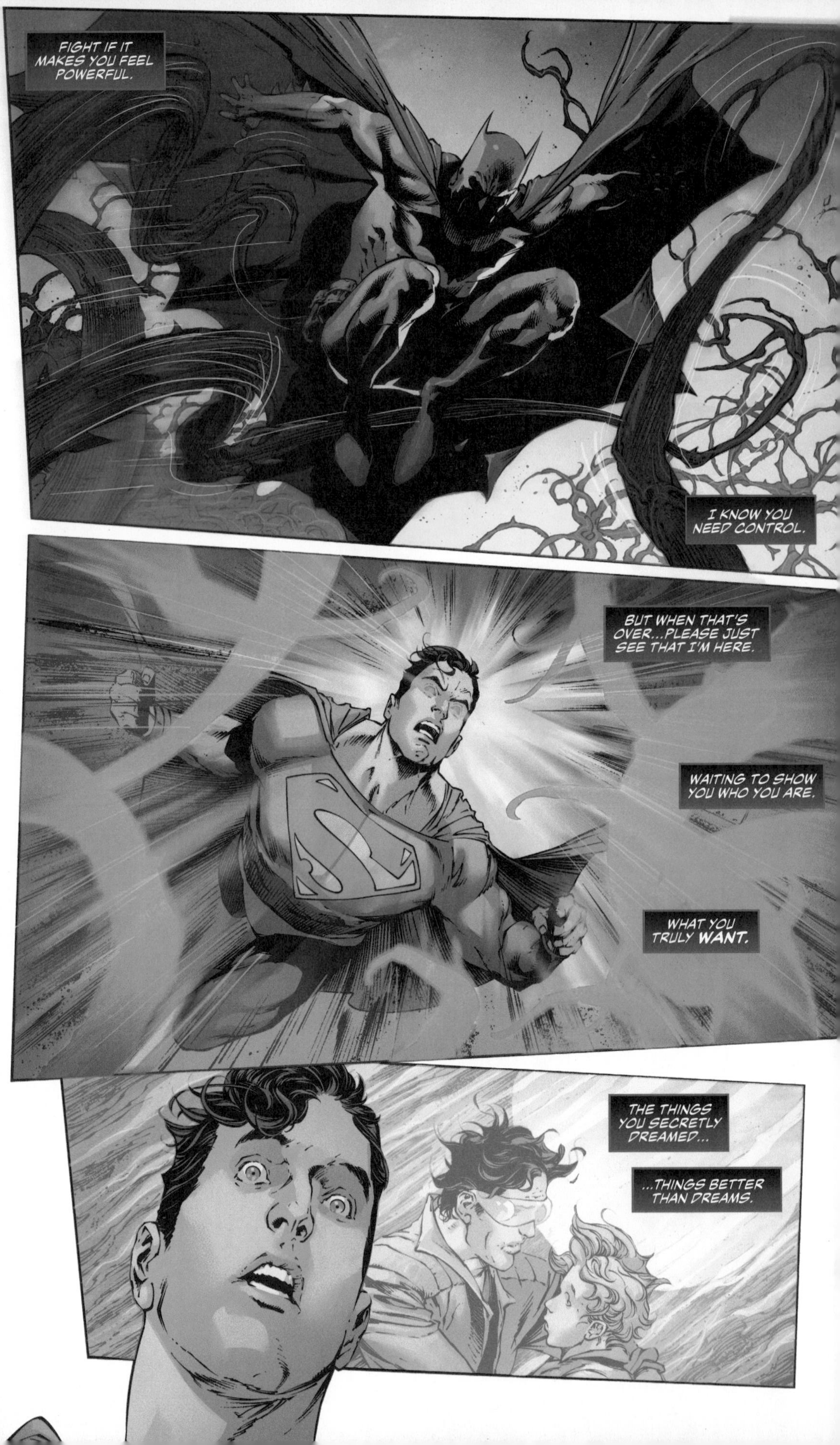

FIGHT IF IT MAKES YOU FEEL POWERFUL.
I KNOW YOU NEED CONTROL.
BUT WHEN THAT'S OVER...PLEASE JUST SEE THAT I'M HERE.
WAITING TO SHOW YOU WHO YOU ARE.
WHAT YOU TRULY **WANT.**
THE THINGS YOU SECRETLY DREAMED...
...THINGS BETTER THAN DREAMS.

'M NOT
TRICK.
NOT AN
ILLUSION.
I'M JUST
THE TRUTH.
THE TRUTH YOU'VE
BEEN HIDING FROM
FOR SO LONG.
BUT IT CAN'T
HIDE FROM ME.
BRUCE...WHY ARE YOU
THE ONE PERSON YOU
WON'T SAVE?
CAN'T YOU SEE HOW
LOST YOU ARE?
CAN'T YOU
SEE YOU'RE
DROWNING?
PLEASE LET
ME SAVE YOU.
I'M THE ONLY ONE
WHO SEES HOW
TRAPPED YOU ARE.

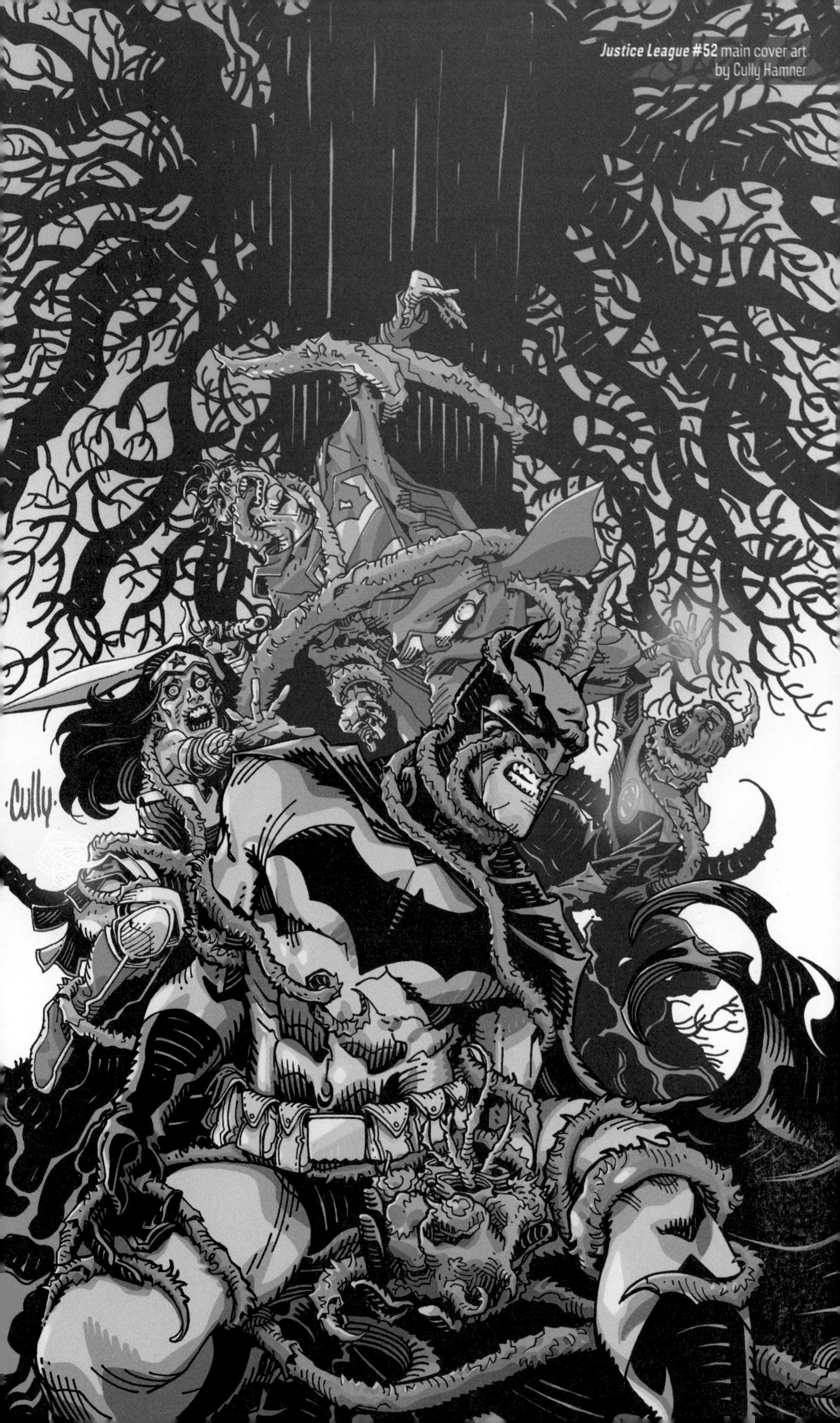
·CULLY·

Justice League **#52** main cover art
by Cully Hamner

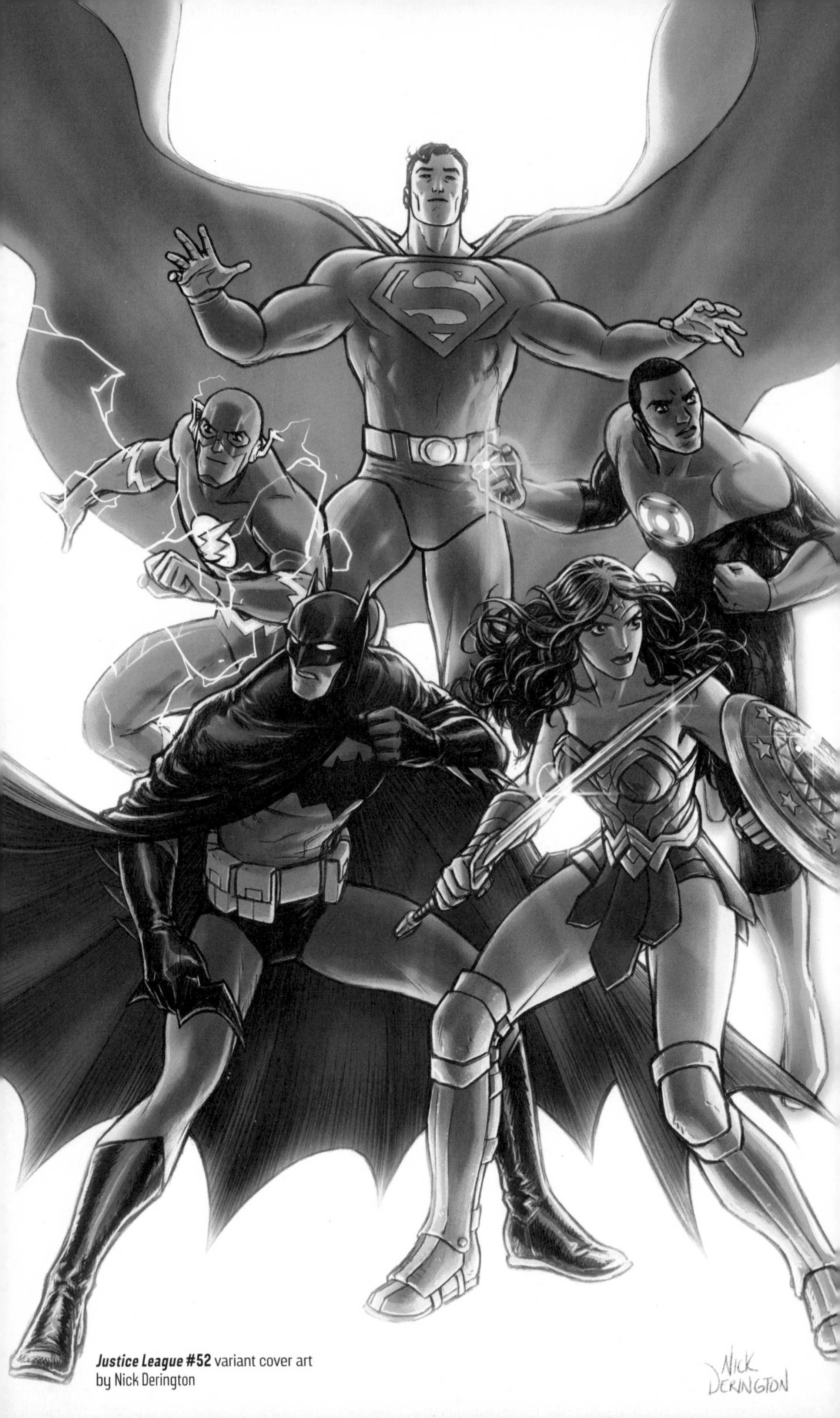
NICK DERINGTON

***Justice League* #52** variant cover art
by Nick Derington

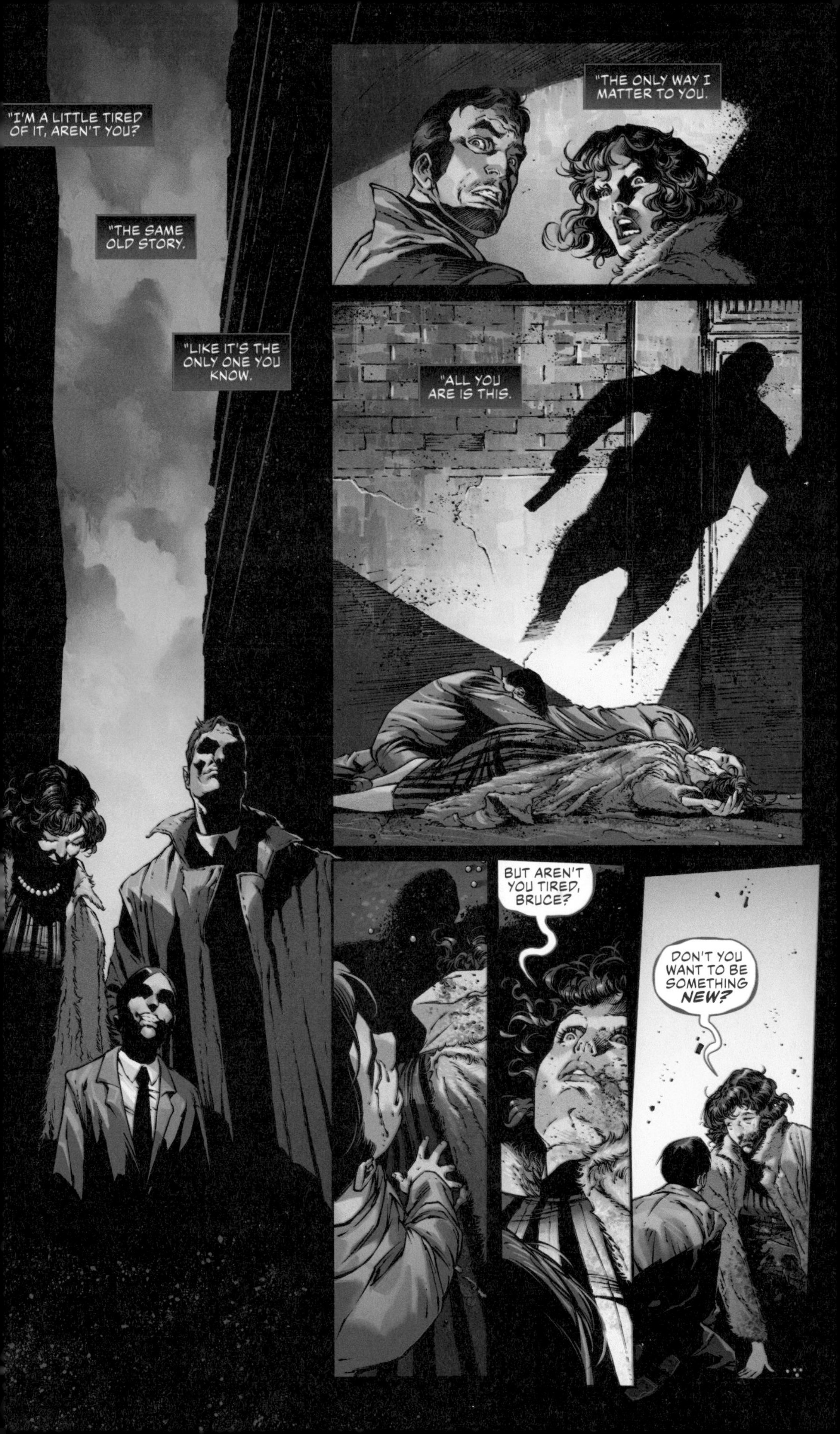
"I'M A LITTLE TIRED OF IT, AREN'T YOU?
"THE SAME OLD STORY.
"LIKE IT'S THE ONLY ONE YOU KNOW.
"THE ONLY WAY I MATTER TO YOU.
"ALL YOU ARE IS THIS.
BUT AREN'T YOU TIRED, BRUCE?
DON'T YOU WANT TO BE SOMETHING NEW?

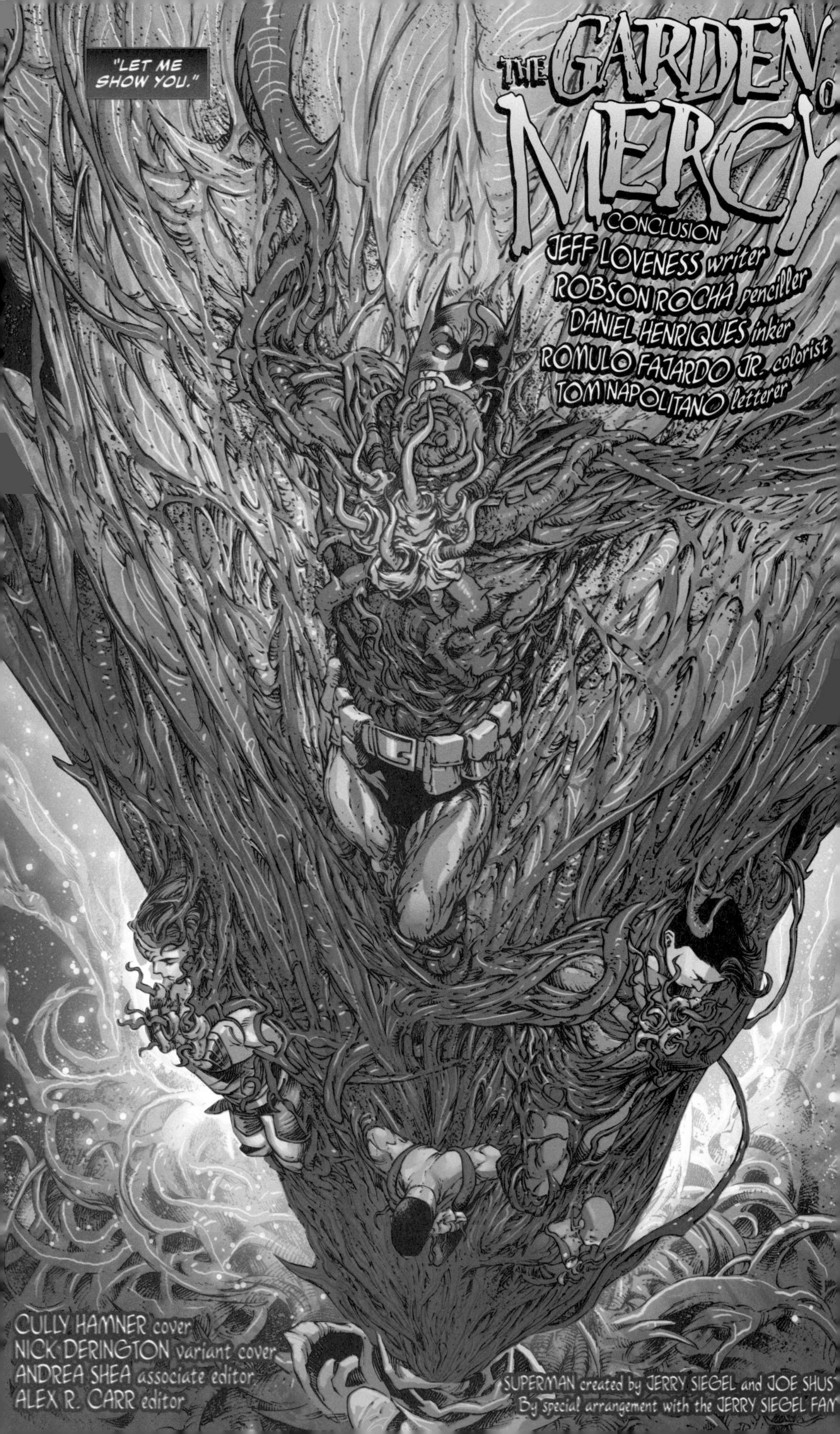

"LET ME SHOW YOU."
THE GARDEN
O
MERCY
CONCLUSION
JEFF LOVENESS writer
ROBSON ROCHA penciller
DANIEL HENRIQUES inker
ROMULO FAJARDO JR. colorist
TOM NAPOLITANO letterer
CULLY HAMNER cover
NICK DERINGTON variant cover
ANDREA SHEA associate editor
ALEX R. CARR editor
SUPERMAN created by JERRY SIEGEL and JOE SHUS
By special arrangement with the JERRY SIEGEL FAM

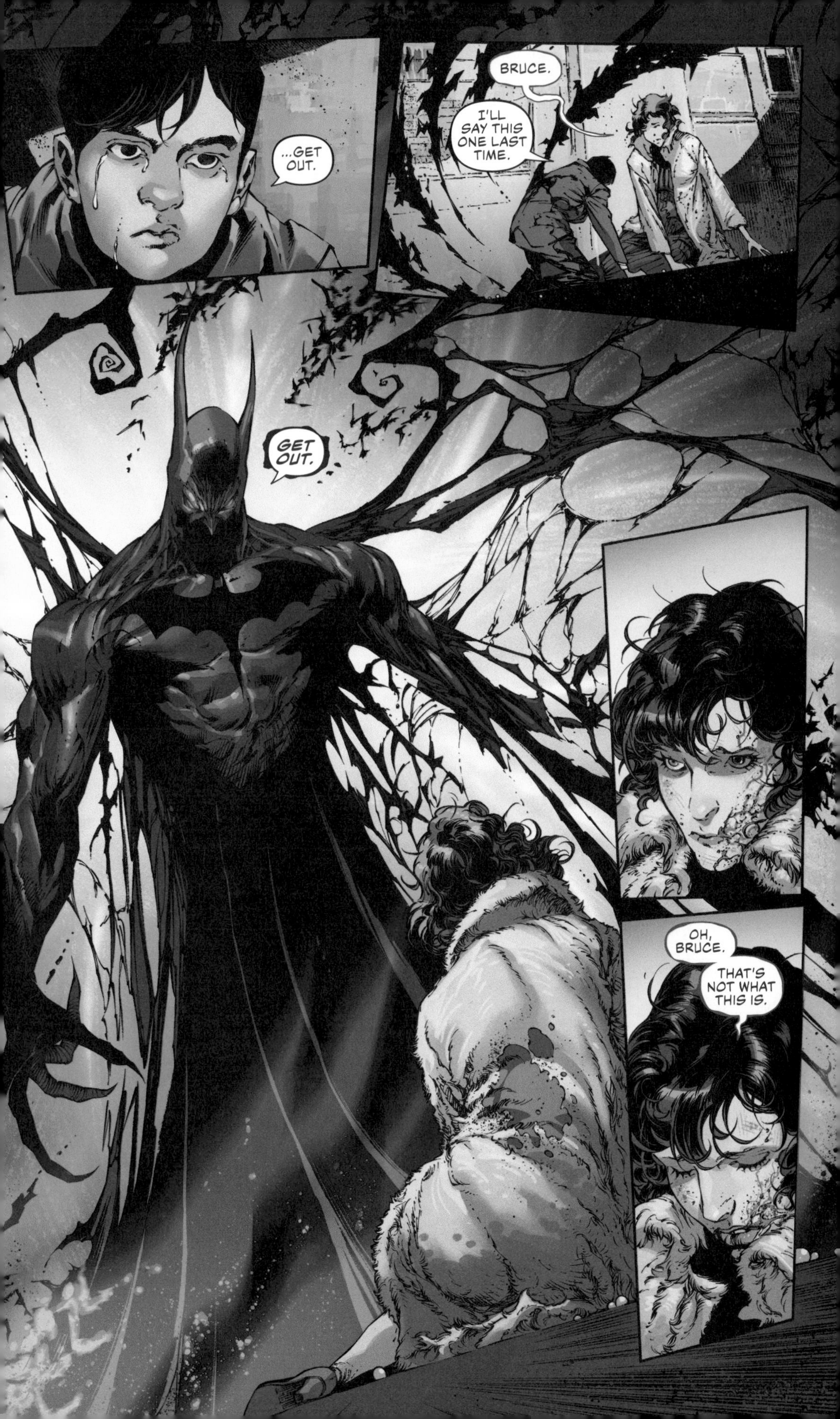
...GET OUT.
BRUCE.
I'LL SAY THIS ONE LAST TIME.
GET OUT.
OH, BRUCE.
THAT'S NOT WHAT THIS IS.

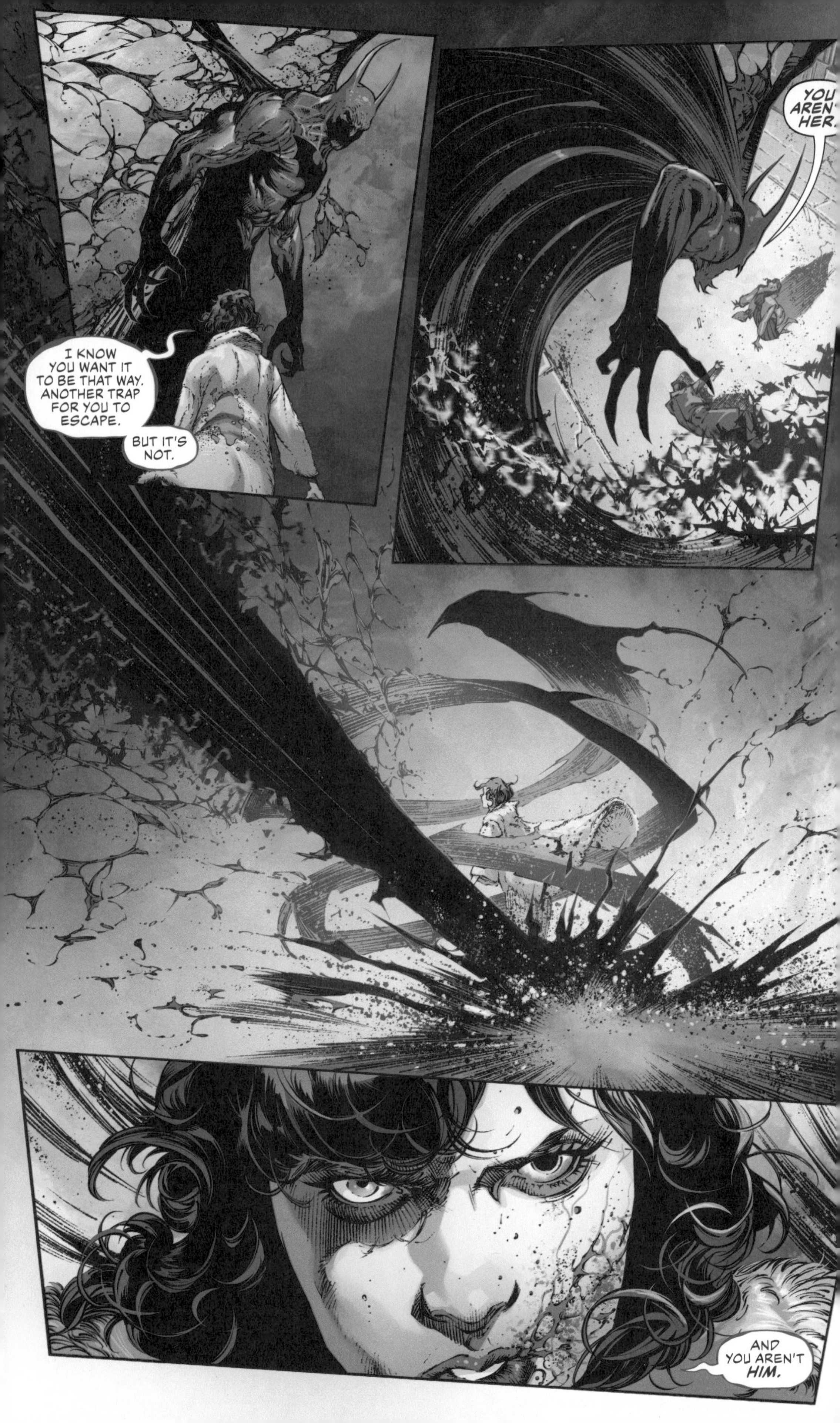
I KNOW YOU WANT IT TO BE THAT WAY. ANOTHER TRAP FOR YOU TO ESCAPE.
BUT IT'S NOT.
YOU AREN
HER.
AND YOU AREN'T HIM.

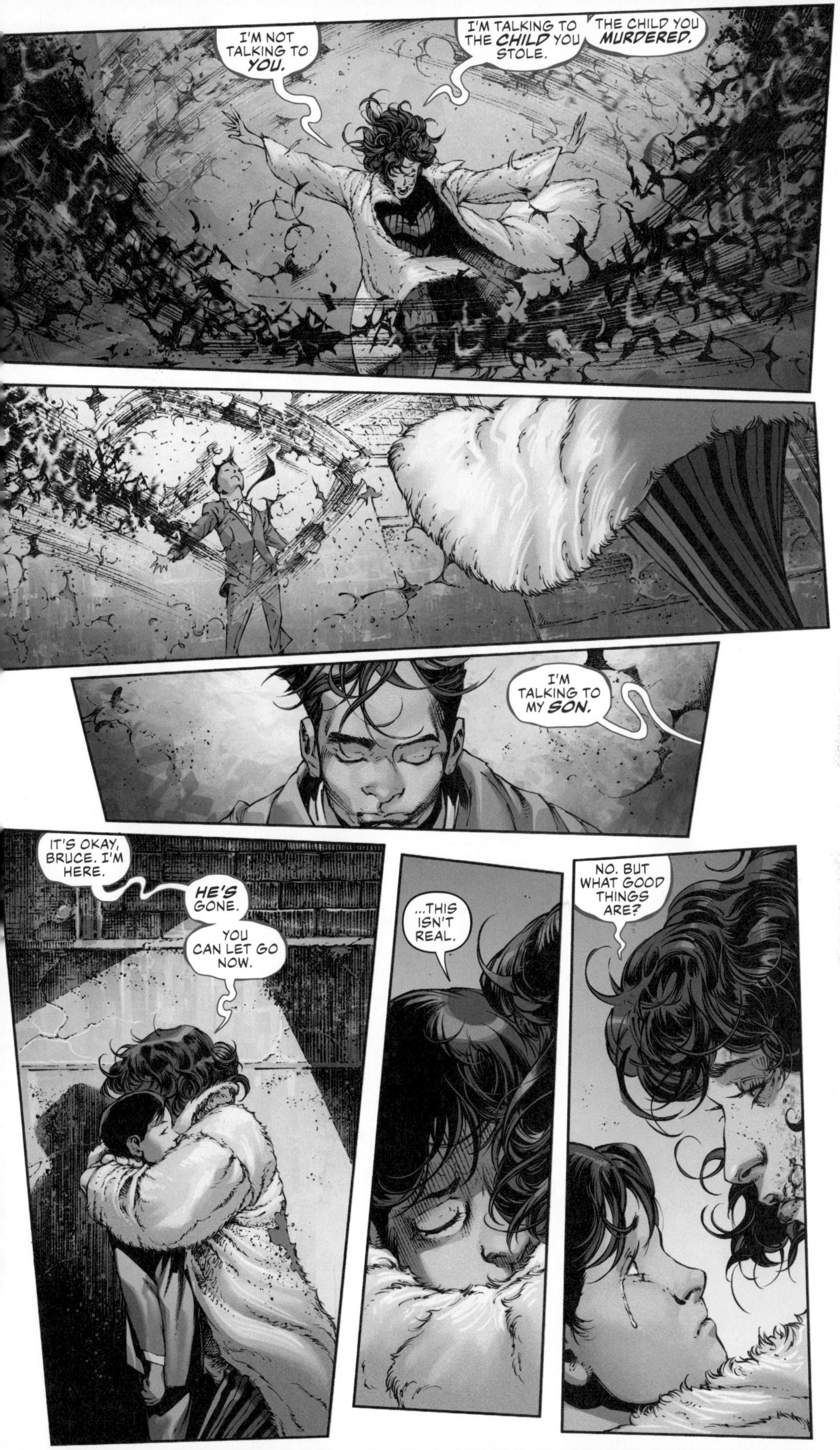

I'M NOT TALKING TO YOU.
I'M TALKING TO THE CHILD YOU STOLE.
THE CHILD YOU MURDERED.
I'M TALKING TO MY SON.
IT'S OKAY, BRUCE. I'M HERE.
HE'S GONE.
YOU CAN LET GO NOW.
...THIS ISN'T REAL.
NO. BUT WHAT GOOD THINGS ARE?

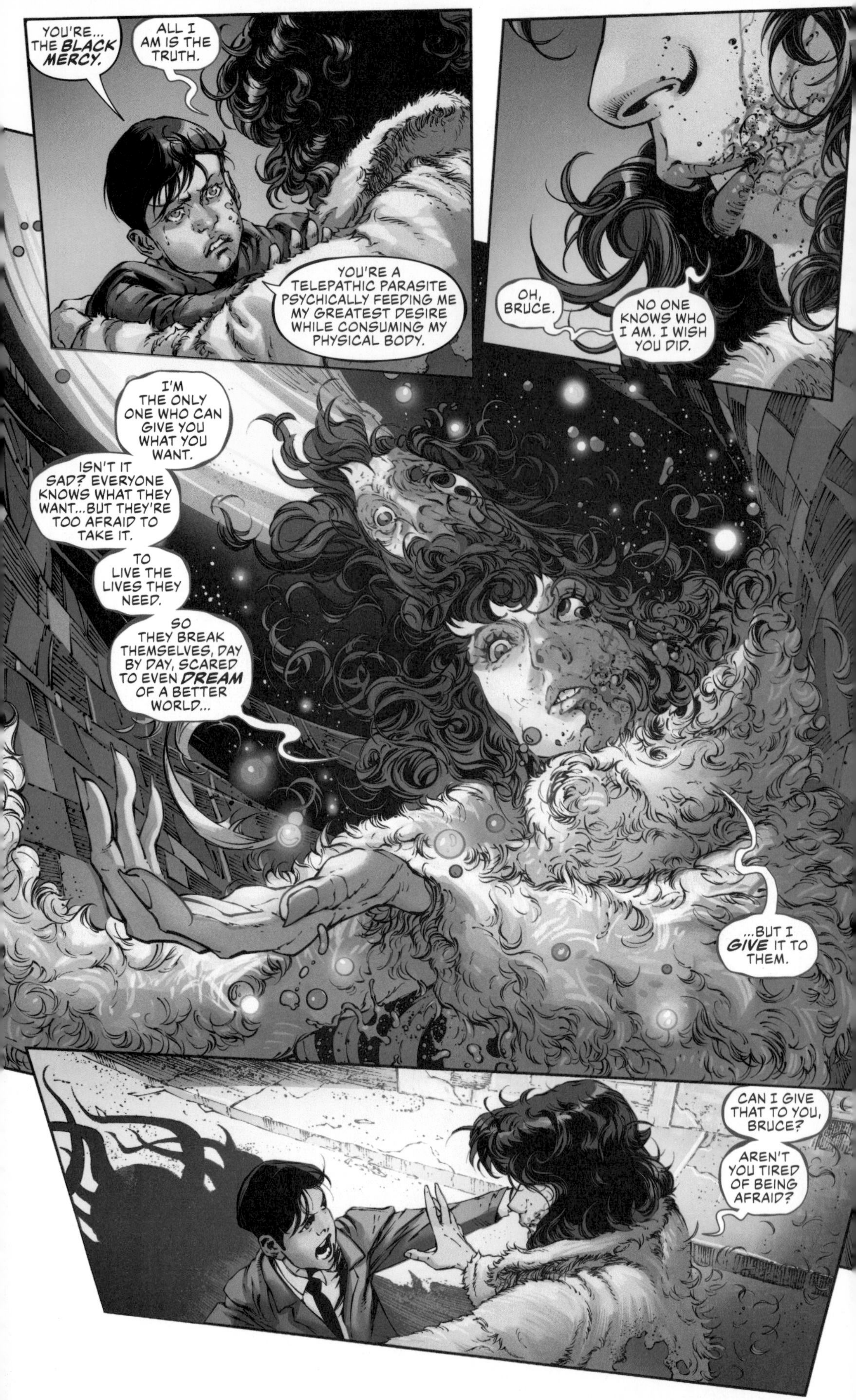

YOU'RE... THE BLACK MERCY.
ALL I AM IS THE TRUTH.
YOU'RE A TELEPATHIC PARASITE PSYCHICALLY FEEDING ME MY GREATEST DESIRE WHILE CONSUMING MY PHYSICAL BODY.
OH, BRUCE.
NO ONE KNOWS WHO I AM. I WISH YOU DID.
I'M THE ONLY ONE WHO CAN GIVE YOU WHAT YOU WANT.
ISN'T IT SAD? EVERYONE KNOWS WHAT THEY WANT...BUT THEY'RE TOO AFRAID TO TAKE IT.
TO LIVE THE LIVES THEY NEED.
SO THEY BREAK THEMSELVES, DAY BY DAY, SCARED TO EVEN DREAM OF A BETTER WORLD...
...BUT I GIVE IT TO THEM.
CAN I GIVE THAT TO YOU, BRUCE?
AREN'T YOU TIRED OF BEING AFRAID?

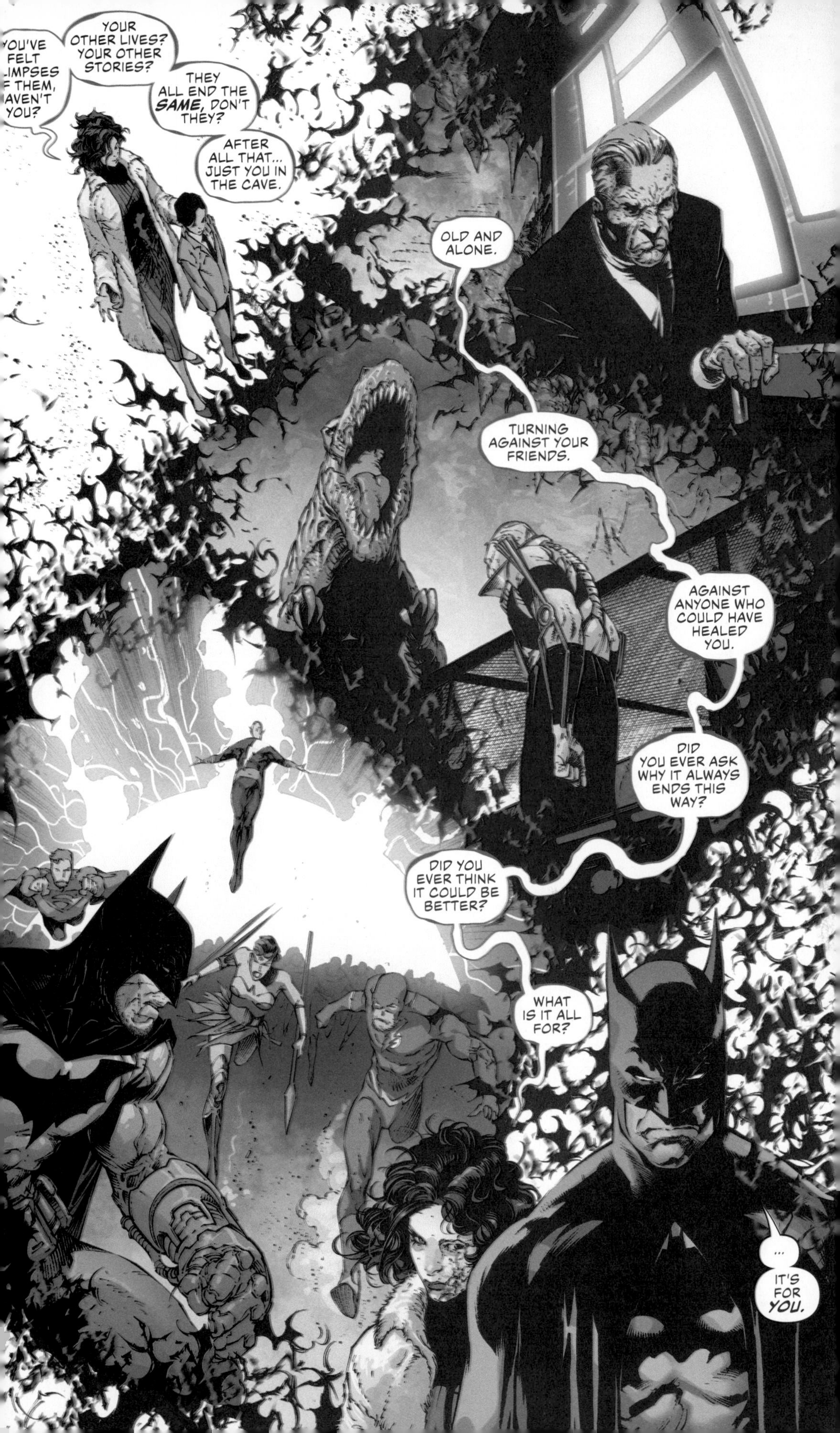
YOU'VE FELT LIMPSES F THEM, AVEN'T YOU?
YOUR OTHER LIVES? YOUR OTHER STORIES?
THEY ALL END THE SAME, DON'T THEY?
AFTER ALL THAT... JUST YOU IN THE CAVE.
OLD AND ALONE.
TURNING AGAINST YOUR FRIENDS.
AGAINST ANYONE WHO COULD HAVE HEALED YOU.
DID YOU EVER ASK WHY IT ALWAYS ENDS THIS WAY?
DID YOU EVER THINK IT COULD BE BETTER?
WHAT IS IT ALL FOR?
...
IT'S FOR YOU.

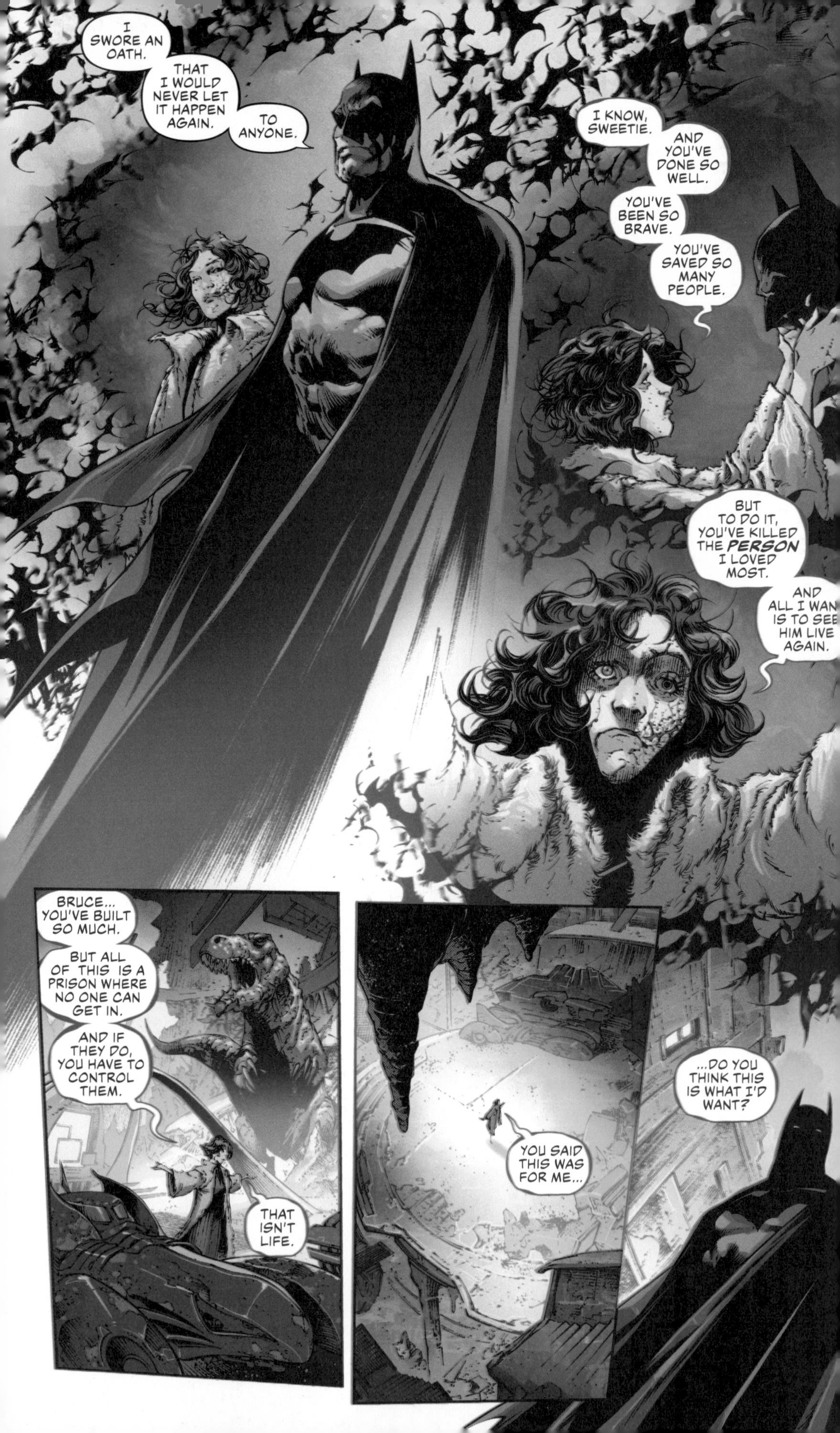
I SWORE AN OATH.
THAT I WOULD NEVER LET IT HAPPEN AGAIN.
TO ANYONE.
I KNOW, SWEETIE.
AND YOU'VE DONE SO WELL.
YOU'VE BEEN SO BRAVE.
YOU'VE SAVED SO MANY PEOPLE.
BUT TO DO IT, YOU'VE KILLED THE *PERSON* I LOVED MOST.
AND ALL I WAN IS TO SEE HIM LIVE AGAIN.
BRUCE... YOU'VE BUILT SO MUCH.
BUT ALL OF THIS IS A PRISON WHERE NO ONE CAN GET IN.
AND IF THEY DO, YOU HAVE TO CONTROL THEM.
THAT ISN'T LIFE.
YOU SAID THIS WAS FOR ME...
...DO YOU THINK THIS IS WHAT I'D WANT?

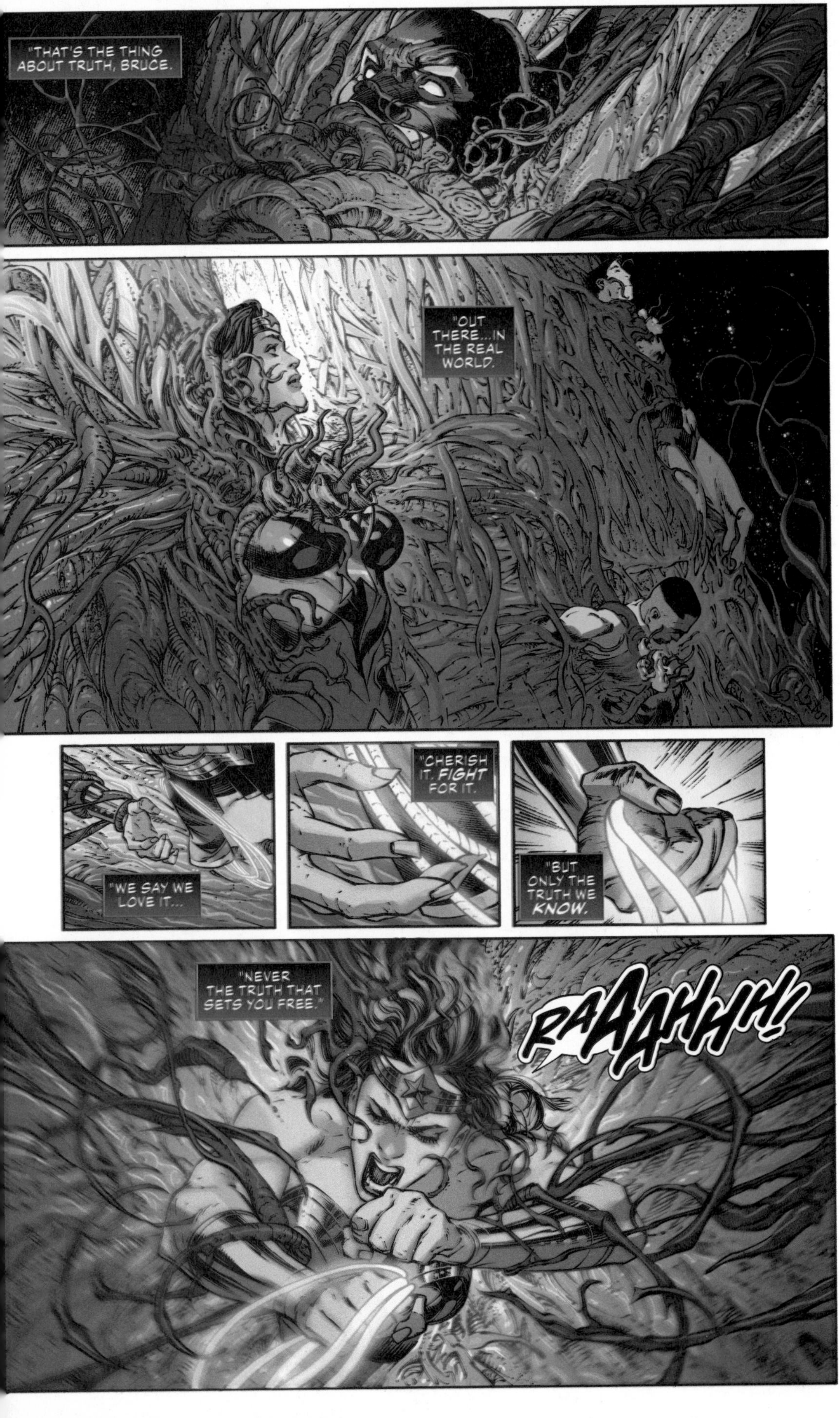
"THAT'S THE THING ABOUT TRUTH, BRUCE.
"OUT THERE...IN THE REAL WORLD.
"WE SAY WE LOVE IT...
"CHERISH IT. FIGHT FOR IT.
"BUT ONLY THE TRUTH WE KNOW.
"NEVER THE TRUTH THAT SETS YOU FREE."
RAAAHHH!

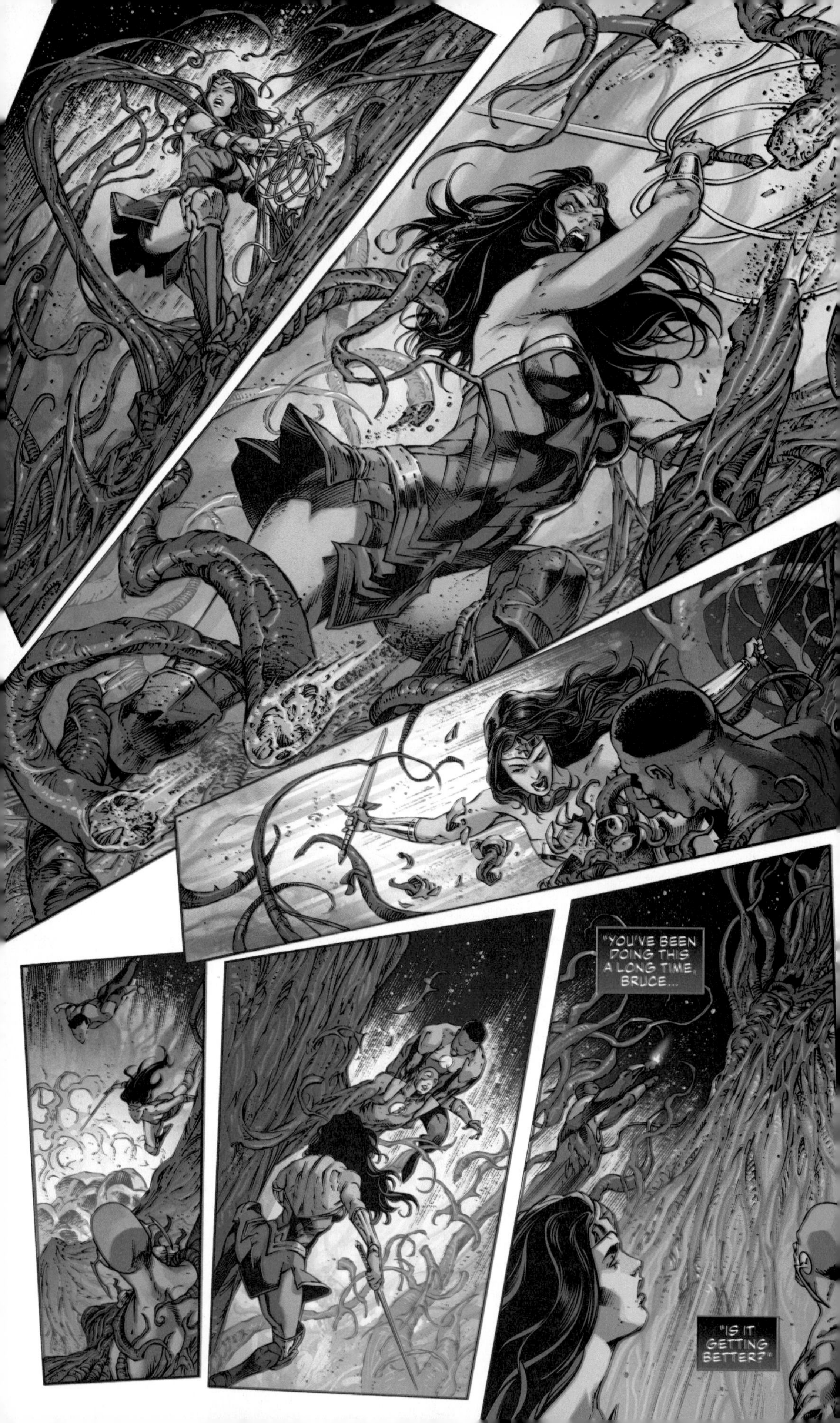
"YOU'VE BEEN DOING THIS A LONG TIME, BRUCE...
"IS IT GETTING BETTER?"

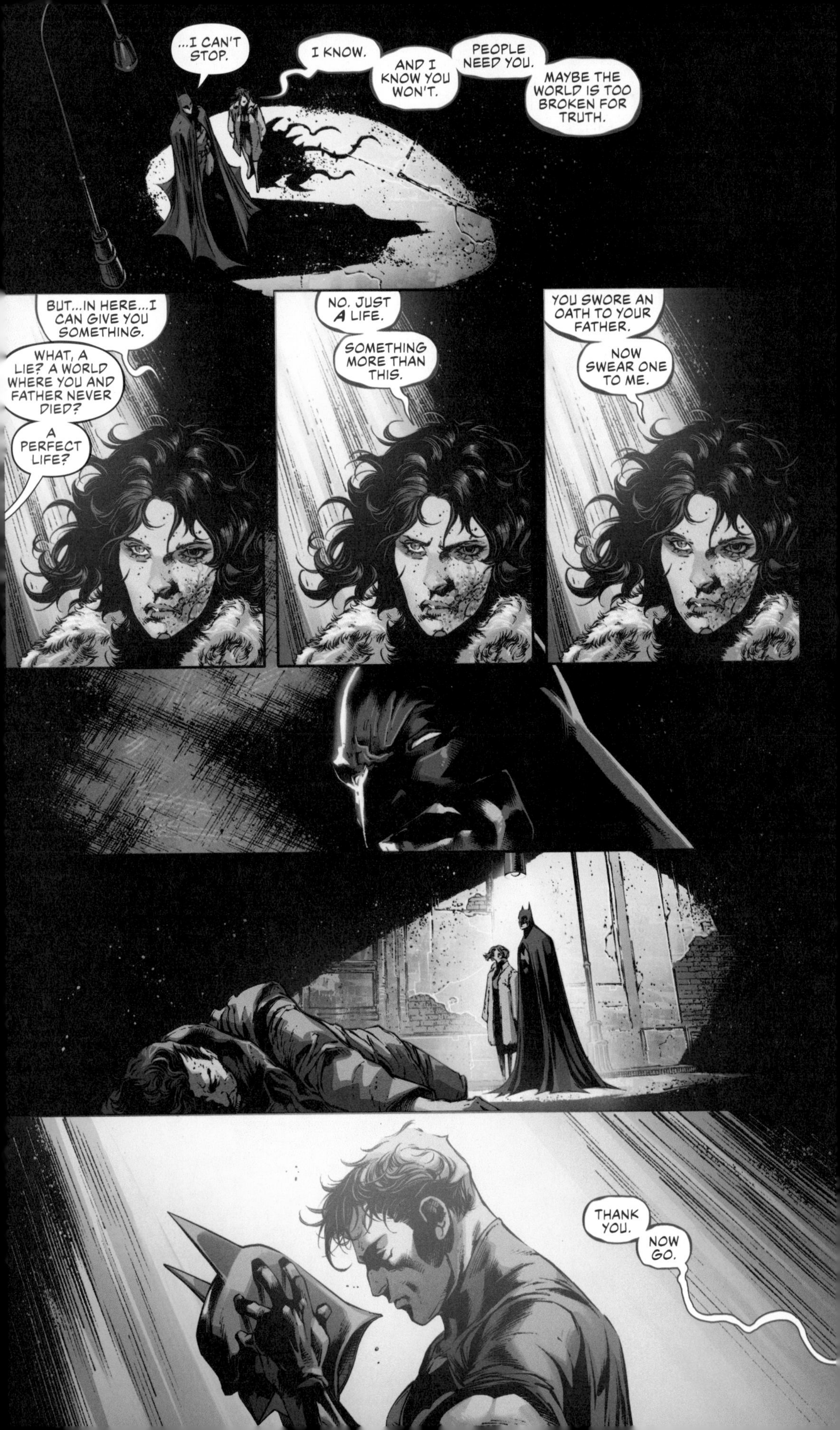
...I CAN'T STOP.
I KNOW.
AND I KNOW YOU WON'T.
PEOPLE NEED YOU.
MAYBE THE WORLD IS TOO BROKEN FOR TRUTH.
BUT...IN HERE...I CAN GIVE YOU SOMETHING.
WHAT, A LIE? A WORLD WHERE YOU AND FATHER NEVER DIED?
A PERFECT LIFE?
NO. JUST A LIFE.
SOMETHING MORE THAN THIS.
YOU SWORE AN OATH TO YOUR FATHER.
NOW SWEAR ONE TO ME.
THANK YOU.
NOW GO.

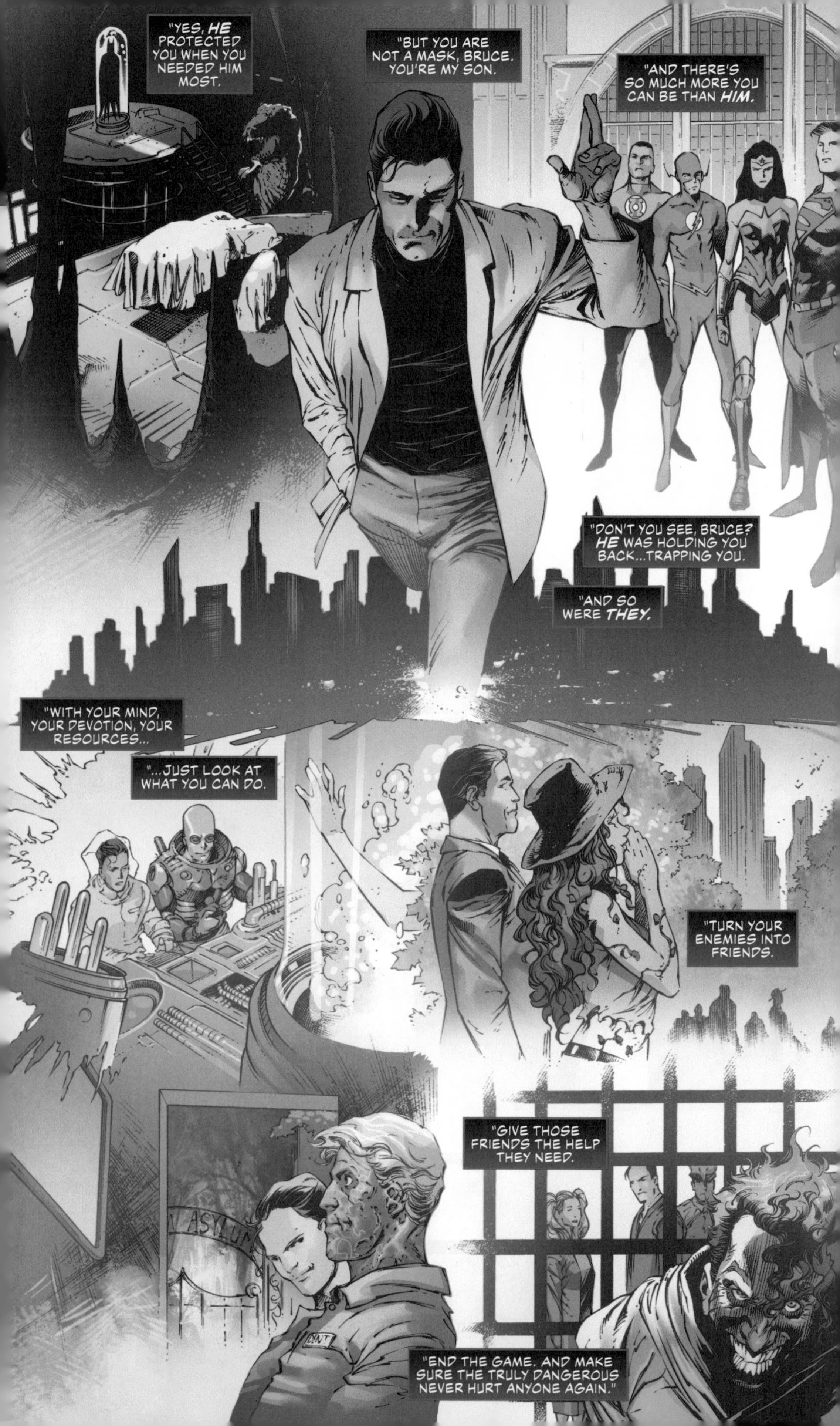
"YES, *HE* PROTECTED YOU WHEN YOU NEEDED HIM MOST.
"BUT YOU ARE NOT A MASK, BRUCE. YOU'RE MY SON.
"AND THERE'S SO MUCH MORE YOU CAN BE THAN *HIM.*
"DON'T YOU SEE, BRUCE? *HE* WAS HOLDING YOU BACK...TRAPPING YOU.
"AND SO WERE *THEY.*
"WITH YOUR MIND, YOUR DEVOTION, YOUR RESOURCES...
"...JUST LOOK AT WHAT YOU CAN DO.
"TURN YOUR ENEMIES INTO FRIENDS.
"GIVE THOSE FRIENDS THE HELP THEY NEED.
"END THE GAME. AND MAKE SURE THE TRULY DANGEROUS NEVER HURT ANYONE AGAIN."

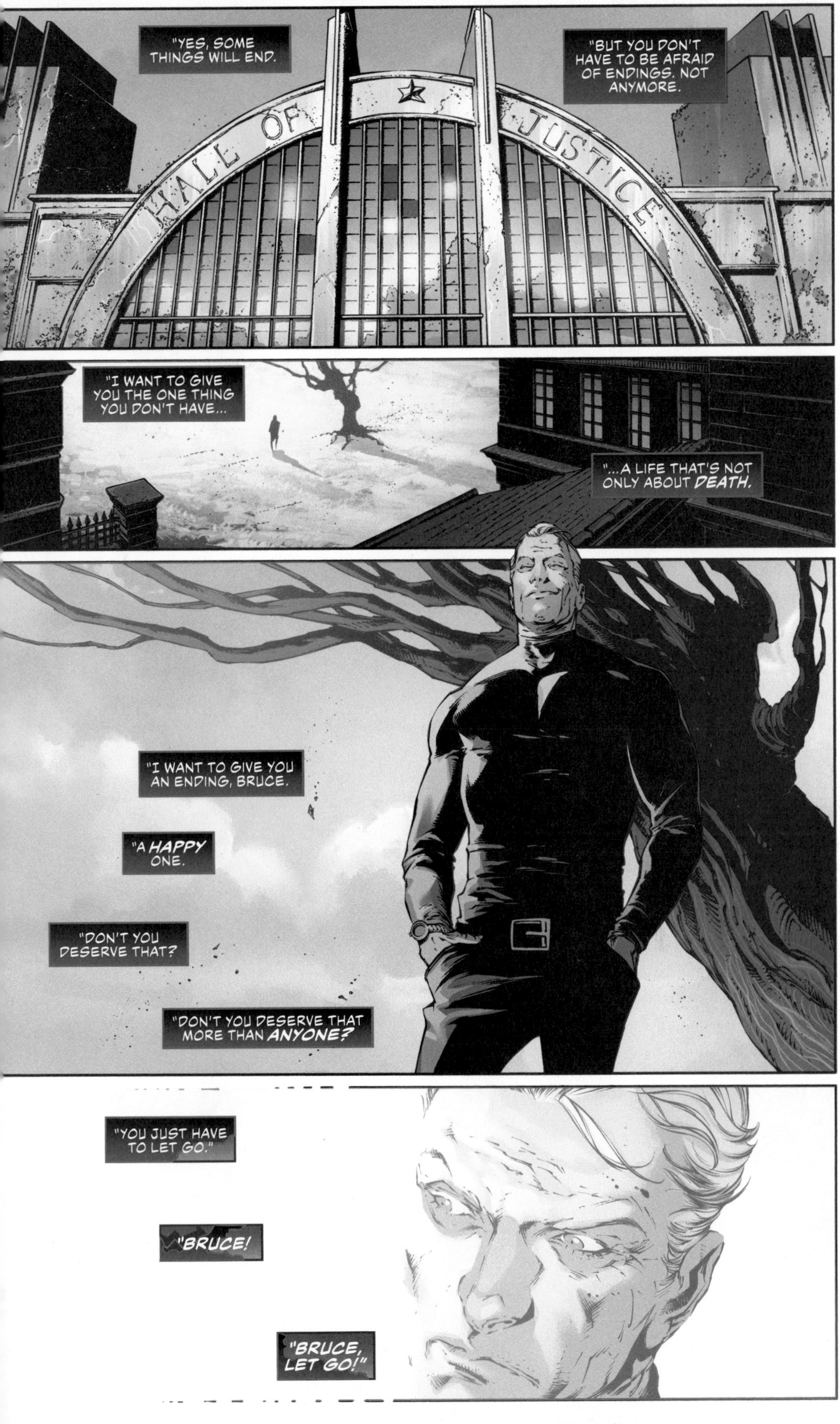
"YES, SOME THINGS WILL END.
"BUT YOU DON'T HAVE TO BE AFRAID OF ENDINGS. NOT ANYMORE.
"I WANT TO GIVE YOU THE ONE THING YOU DON'T HAVE...
"...A LIFE THAT'S NOT ONLY ABOUT DEATH.
"I WANT TO GIVE YOU AN ENDING, BRUCE.
"A HAPPY ONE.
"DON'T YOU DESERVE THAT?
"DON'T YOU DESERVE THAT MORE THAN ANYONE?
"YOU JUST HAVE TO LET GO."
"BRUCE!
"BRUCE, LET GO!"

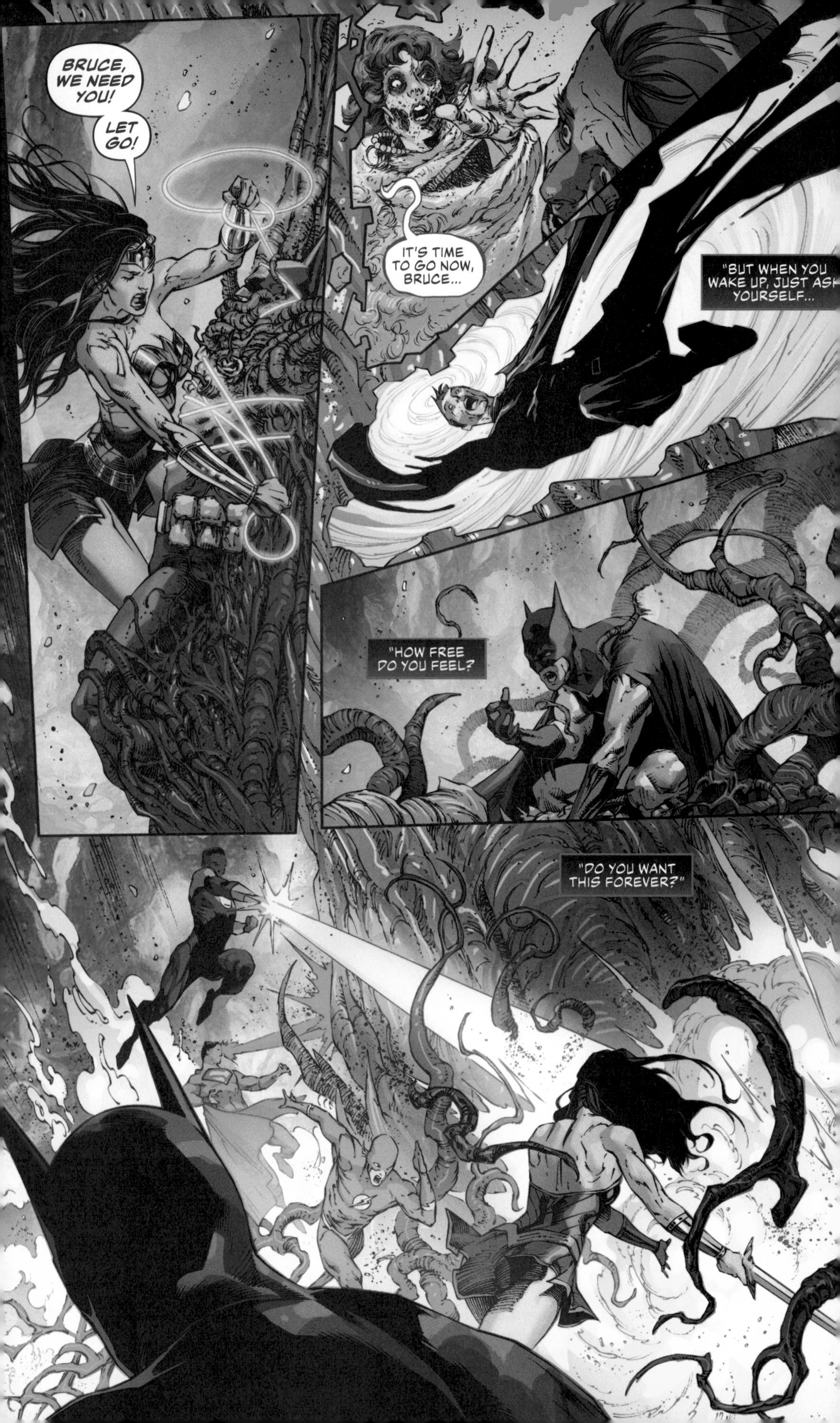
BRUCE, WE NEED YOU!
LET GO!
IT'S TIME TO GO NOW, BRUCE...
"BUT WHEN YOU WAKE UP, JUST ASK YOURSELF...
"HOW FREE DO YOU FEEL?
"DO YOU WANT THIS FOREVER?"

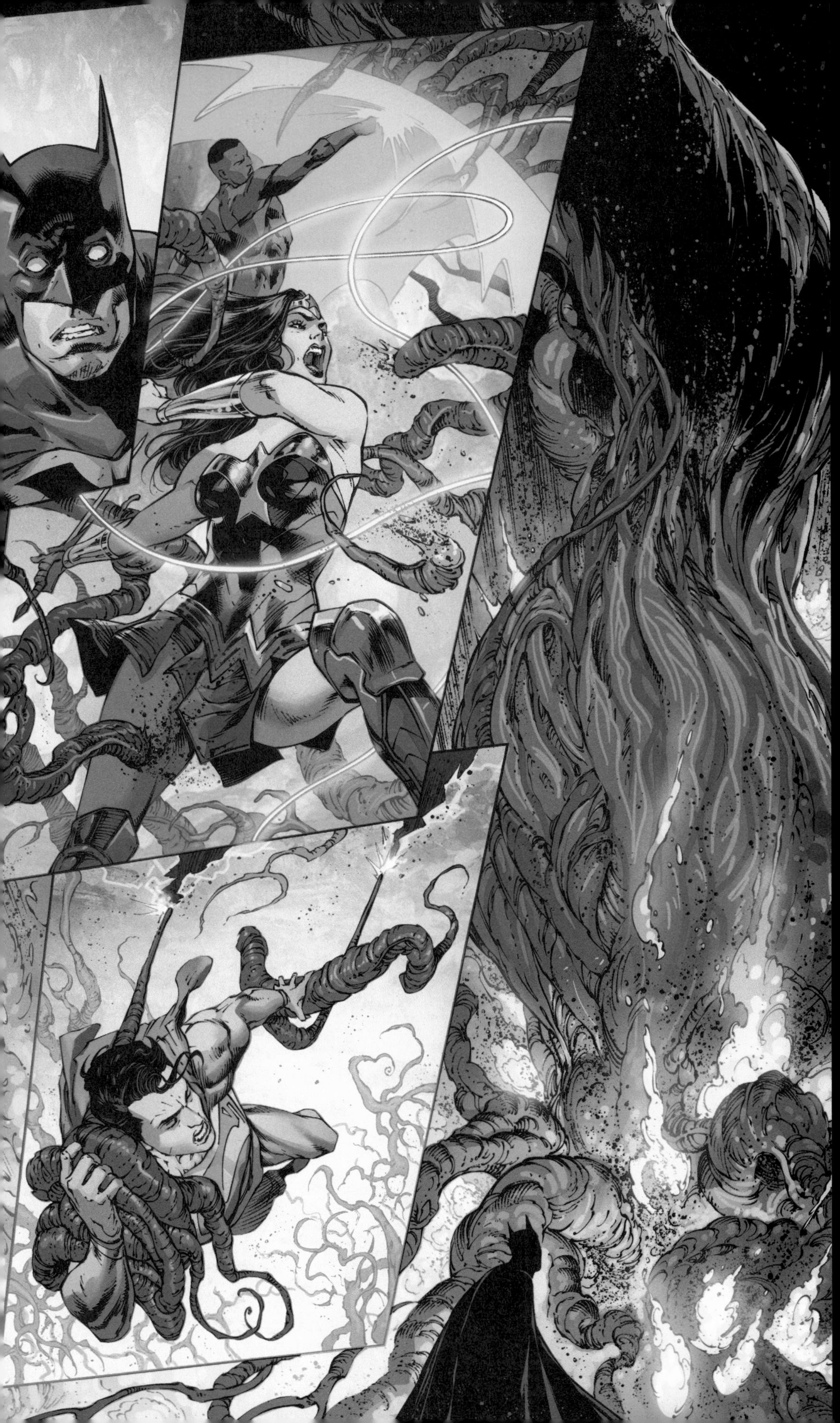

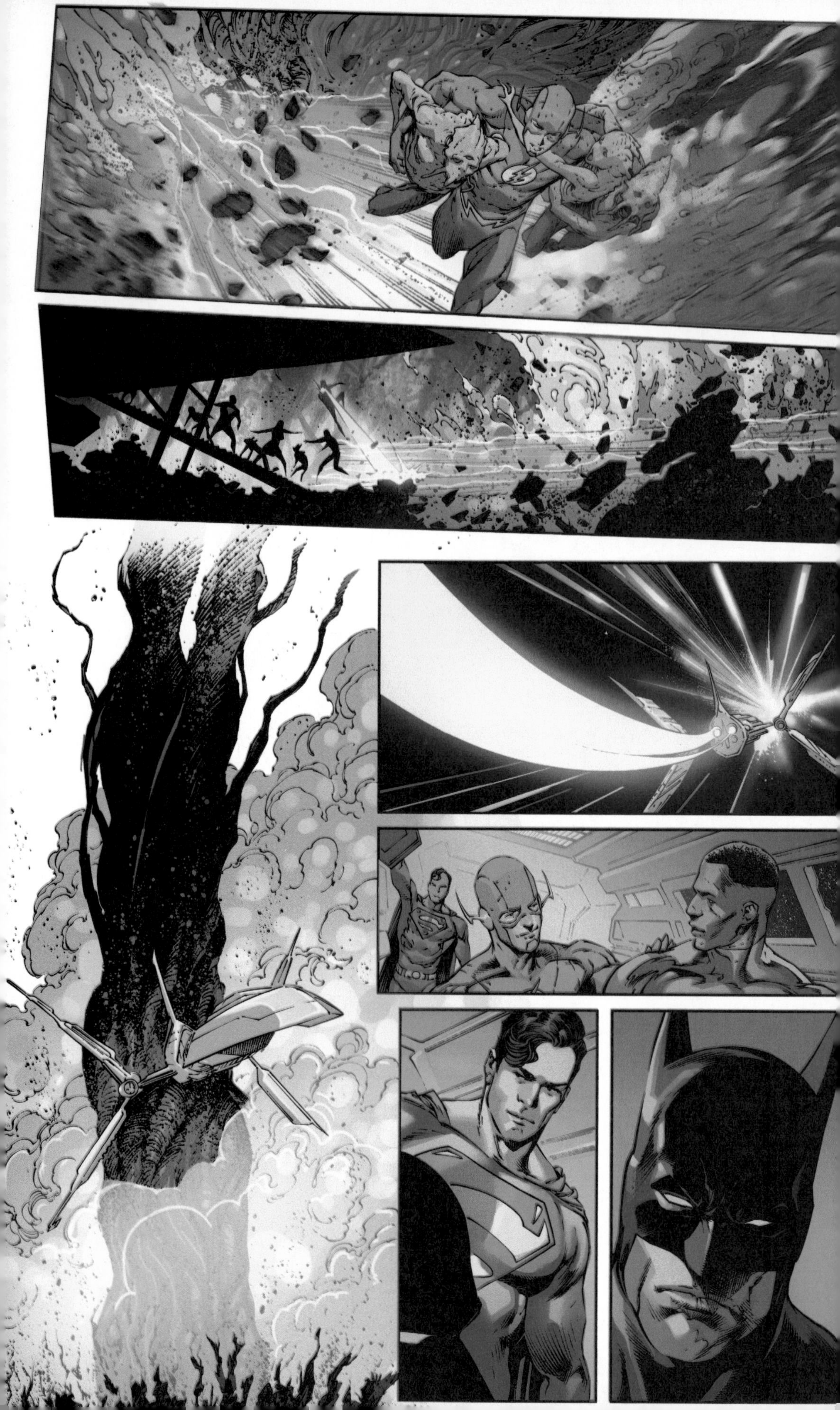

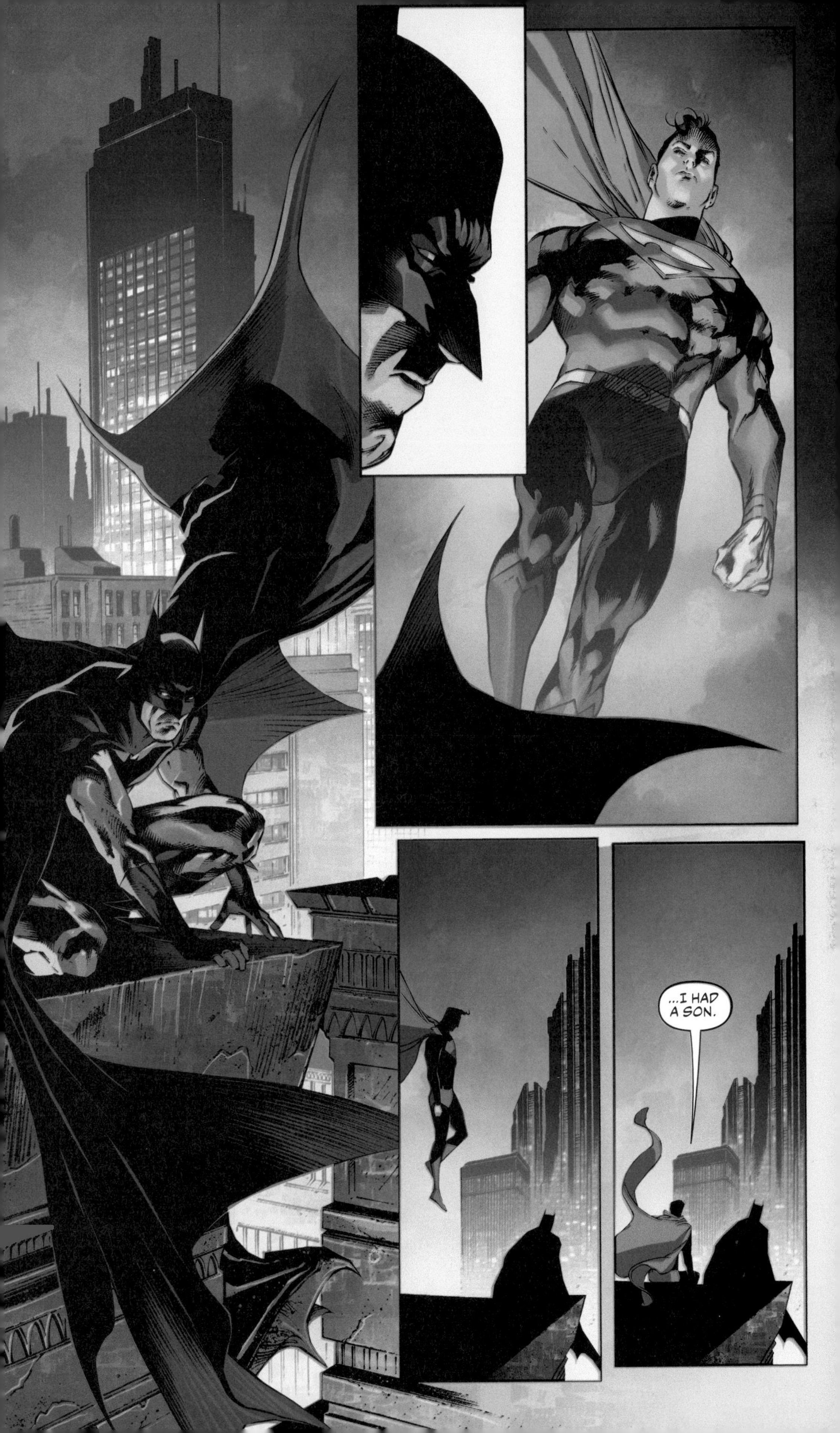
...I HAD A SON.

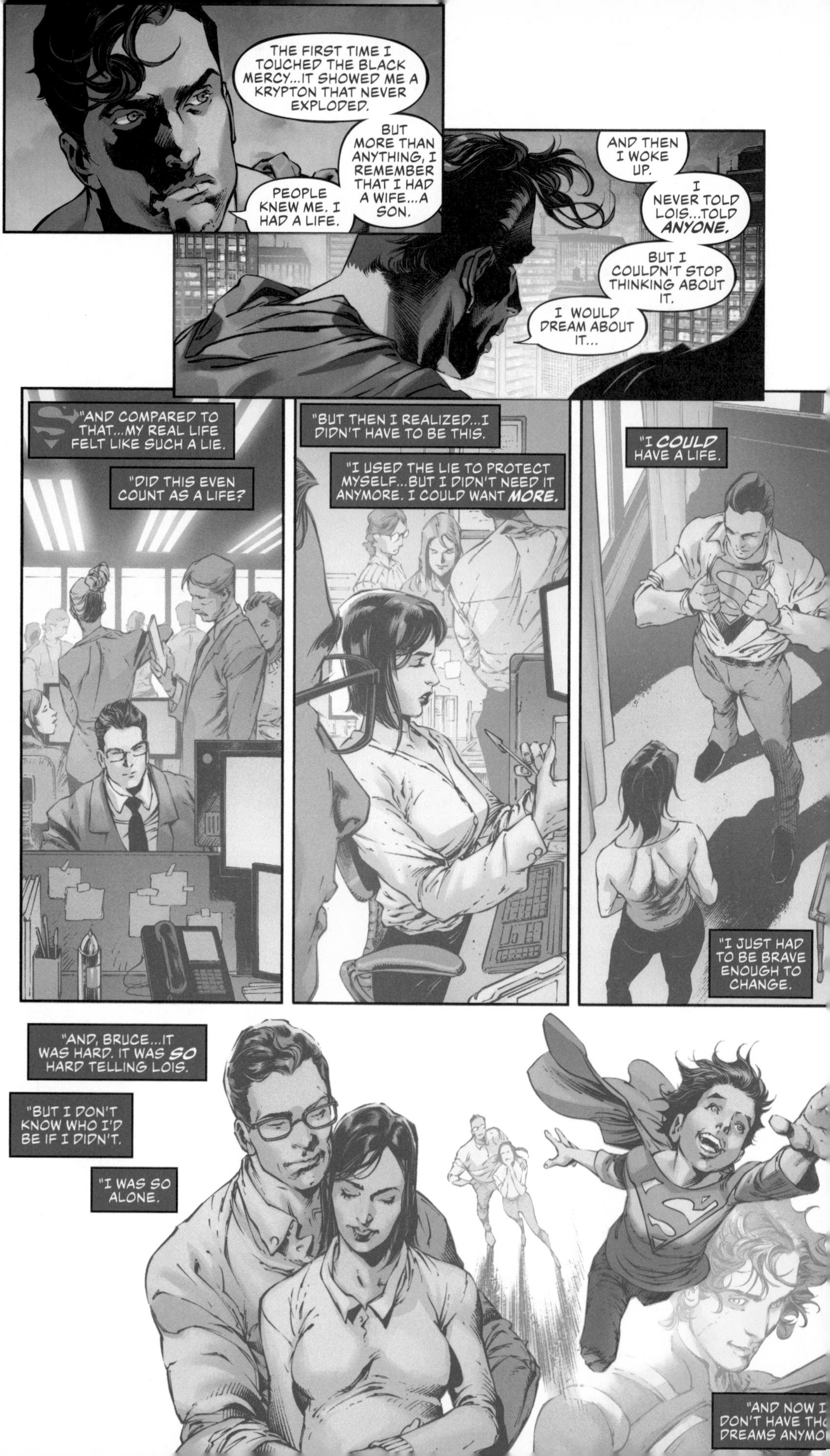
THE FIRST TIME I TOUCHED THE BLACK MERCY...IT SHOWED ME A KRYPTON THAT NEVER EXPLODED.
PEOPLE KNEW ME. I HAD A LIFE.
BUT MORE THAN ANYTHING, I REMEMBER THAT I HAD A WIFE...A SON.
AND THEN I WOKE UP.
I NEVER TOLD LOIS...TOLD *ANYONE.*
BUT I COULDN'T STOP THINKING ABOUT IT.
I WOULD DREAM ABOUT IT...
"AND COMPARED TO THAT...MY REAL LIFE FELT LIKE SUCH A LIE.
"DID THIS EVEN COUNT AS A LIFE?
"BUT THEN I REALIZED...I DIDN'T HAVE TO BE THIS.
"I USED THE LIE TO PROTECT MYSELF...BUT I DIDN'T NEED IT ANYMORE. I COULD WANT *MORE.*
"I *COULD* HAVE A LIFE.
"I JUST HAD TO BE BRAVE ENOUGH TO CHANGE.
"AND, BRUCE...IT WAS HARD. IT WAS *SO* HARD TELLING LOIS.
"BUT I DON'T KNOW WHO I'D BE IF I DIDN'T.
"I WAS SO ALONE.
"AND NOW I DON'T HAVE THO DREAMS ANYMO

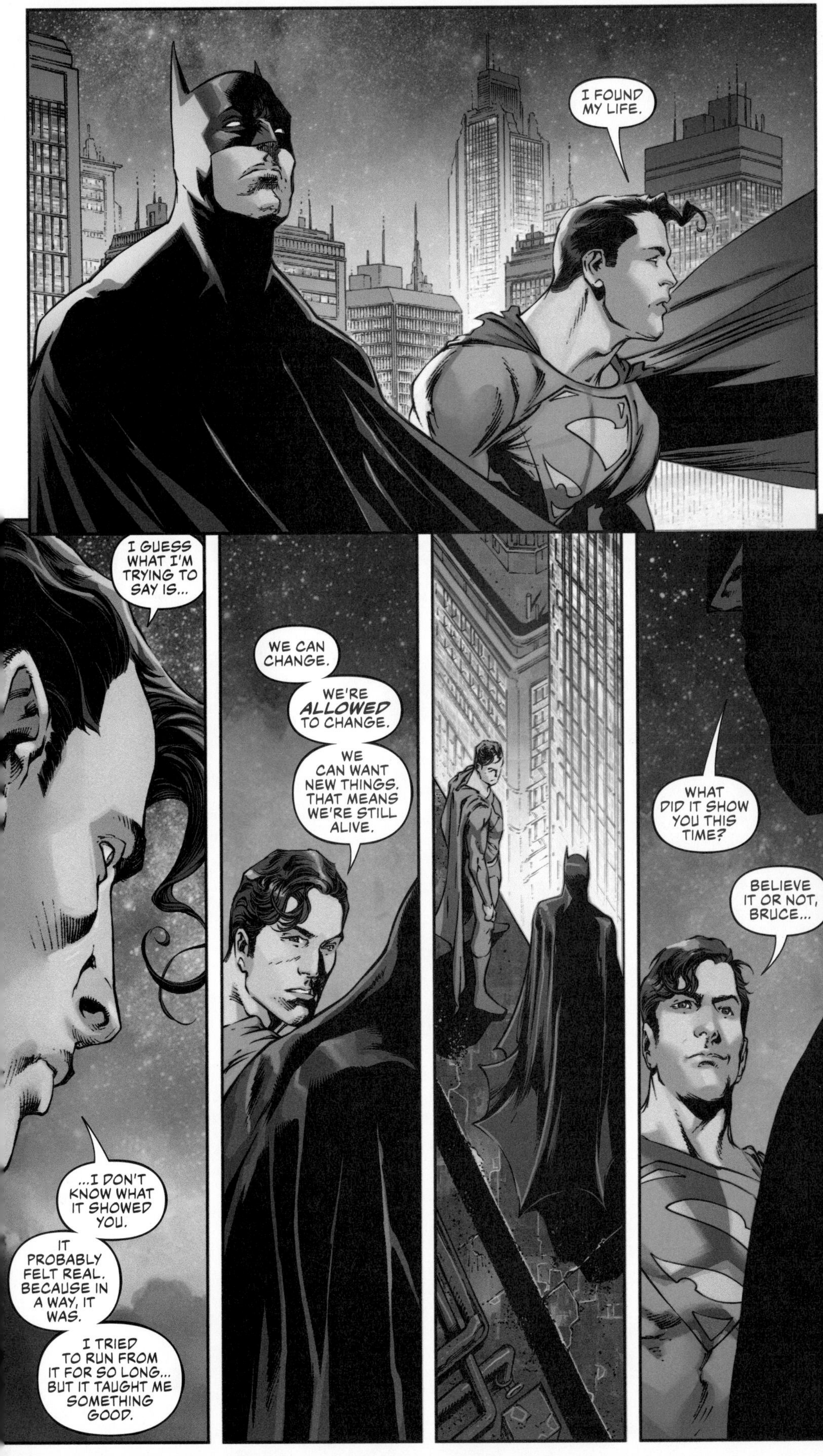
I FOUND MY LIFE.
I GUESS WHAT I'M TRYING TO SAY IS...
...I DON'T KNOW WHAT IT SHOWED YOU.
IT PROBABLY FELT REAL. BECAUSE IN A WAY, IT WAS.
I TRIED TO RUN FROM IT FOR SO LONG... BUT IT TAUGHT ME SOMETHING GOOD.
WE CAN CHANGE.
WE'RE ALLOWED TO CHANGE.
WE CAN WANT NEW THINGS. THAT MEANS WE'RE STILL ALIVE.
WHAT DID IT SHOW YOU THIS TIME?
BELIEVE IT OR NOT, BRUCE...

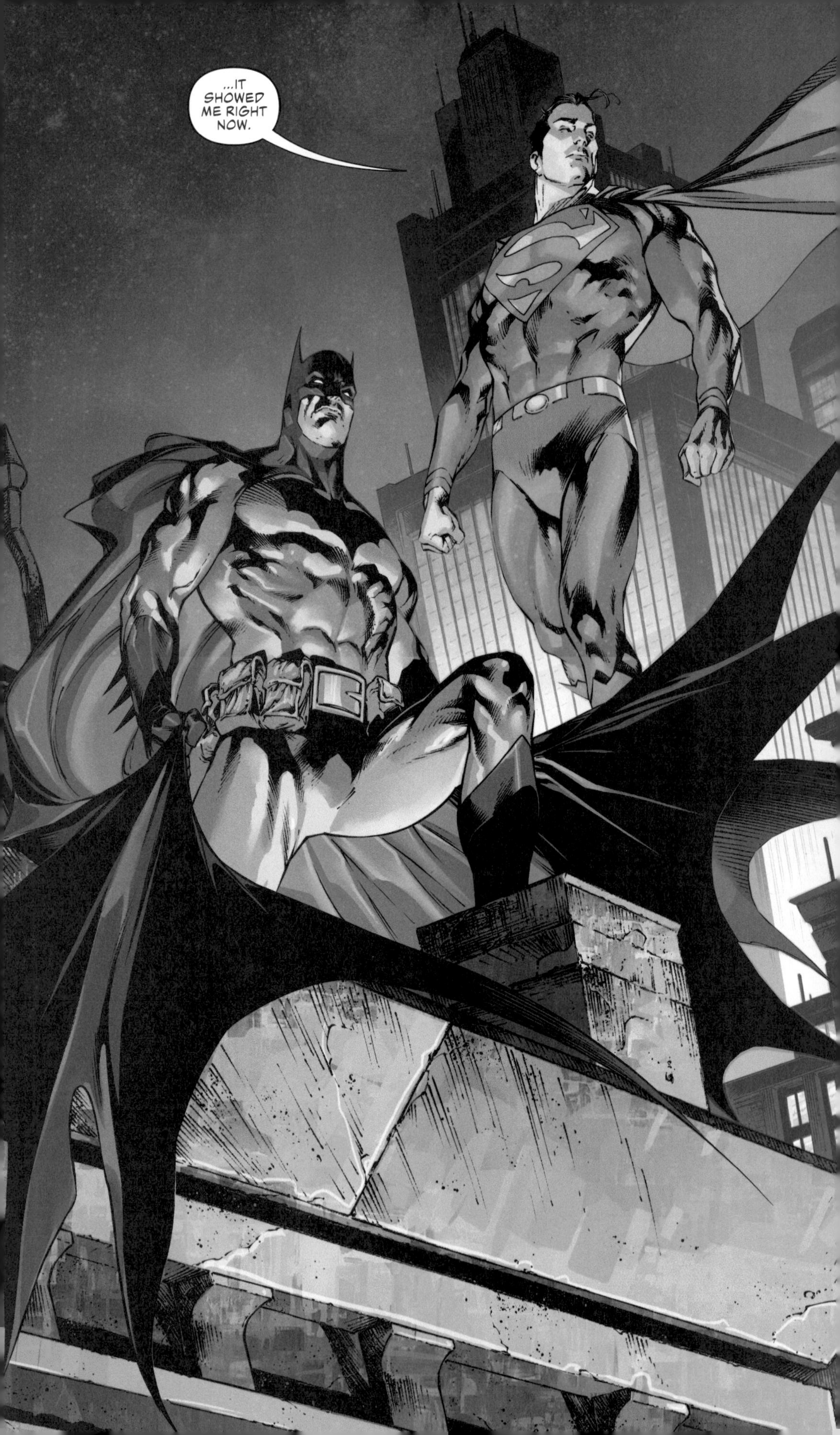
...IT SHOWED ME RIGHT NOW.

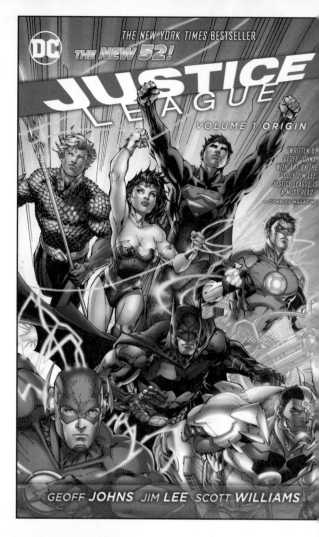

"Welcoming to new fans looking to get into superhero comics for the first time and old fans who gave up on the funny-books long ago."
– SCRIPPS HOWARD NEWS SERVICE

JUSTICE LEAGUE

VOL. 1: ORIGIN
GEOFF JOHNS and JIM LEE

**JUSTICE LEAGUE
VOL. 2: THE VILLAIN'S JOURNEY**

**JUSTICE LEAGUE
VOL. 3: THRONE OF ATLANTIS**

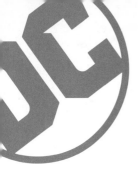

ead more adventures of the
'orld's Greatest Super Heroes
these graphic novels!

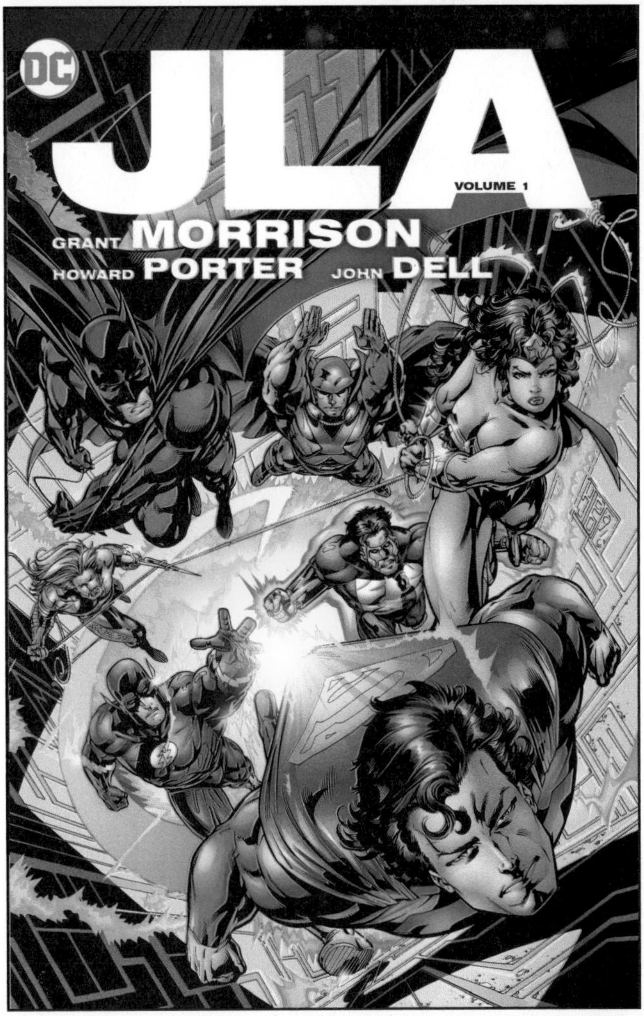

JLA
VOLUME 1
GRANT MORRISON
HOWARD PORTER JOHN DELL

JLA VOL. 1

RANT MORRISON
nd HOWARD PORTER

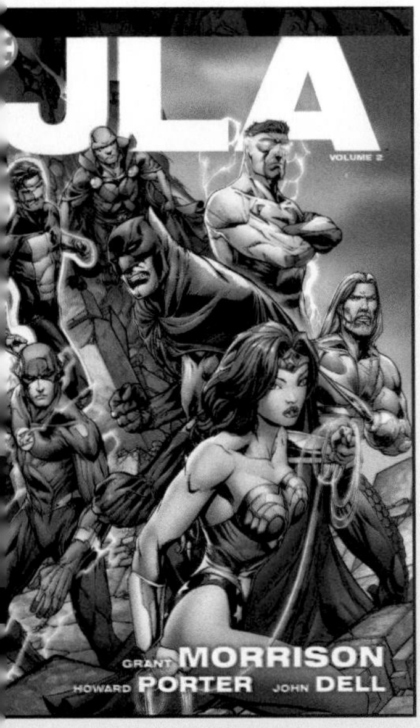

JLA
VOLUME 2
GRANT MORRISON
HOWARD PORTER JOHN DELL

JLA VOL. 2

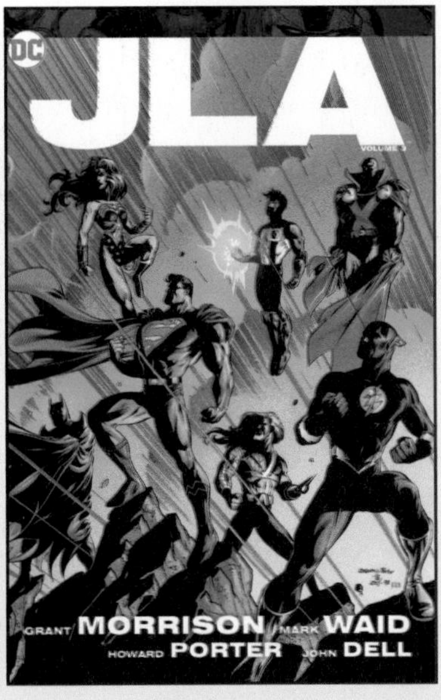

JLA
GRANT MORRISON MARK WAID
HOWARD PORTER JOHN DELL

JLA VOL. 3

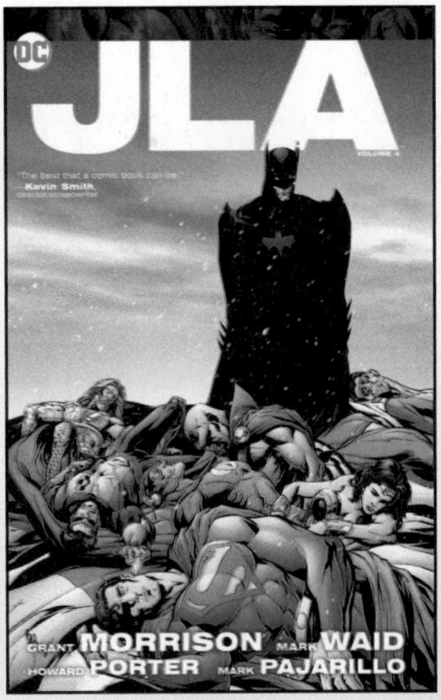

JLA
GRANT MORRISON MARK WAID
HOWARD PORTER MARK PAJARILLO

JLA VOL. 4

Get more DC graphic novels wherever comics and books are sold!

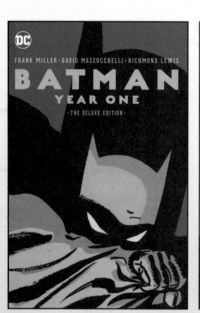